Draw Manga Villains

Draw Manga Villains
First Published in the United States of America in 2017 by
Impact Books, an imprint of F+W Media, Inc., 10151
Carver Road, Suite 200, Blue Ash, Ohio 45242. (800) 289-0963.
First Edition.

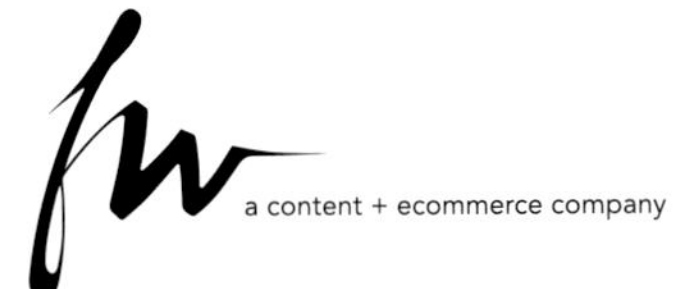

www.fwmedia.com

Original Japanese edition published in Japanese language by Genkosha Co., Ltd, Tokyo, Japan

English language rights, translation & production by
World Book Media, LLC
Email: info@worldbookmedia.com

DISTRIBUTED IN CANADA BY FRASER DIRECT
100 Armstrong Avenue
Georgetown, ON, Canada L7G 5S4
Tel: (905) 877-4411

DISTRIBUTED IN THE U.K. AND EUROPE BY
F&W Media International
Pynes Hill Court
Pynes Hill
Rydon Lane
Exeter
EX2 5AZ
United Kingdom Tel: (+44) 1392 797680
Email: enquiries@fwmedia.com

ISBN-13: 9781440351617
Manufactured in China.

Draw Manga Villains

Create 50 Sinister Characters

GENKOSHA

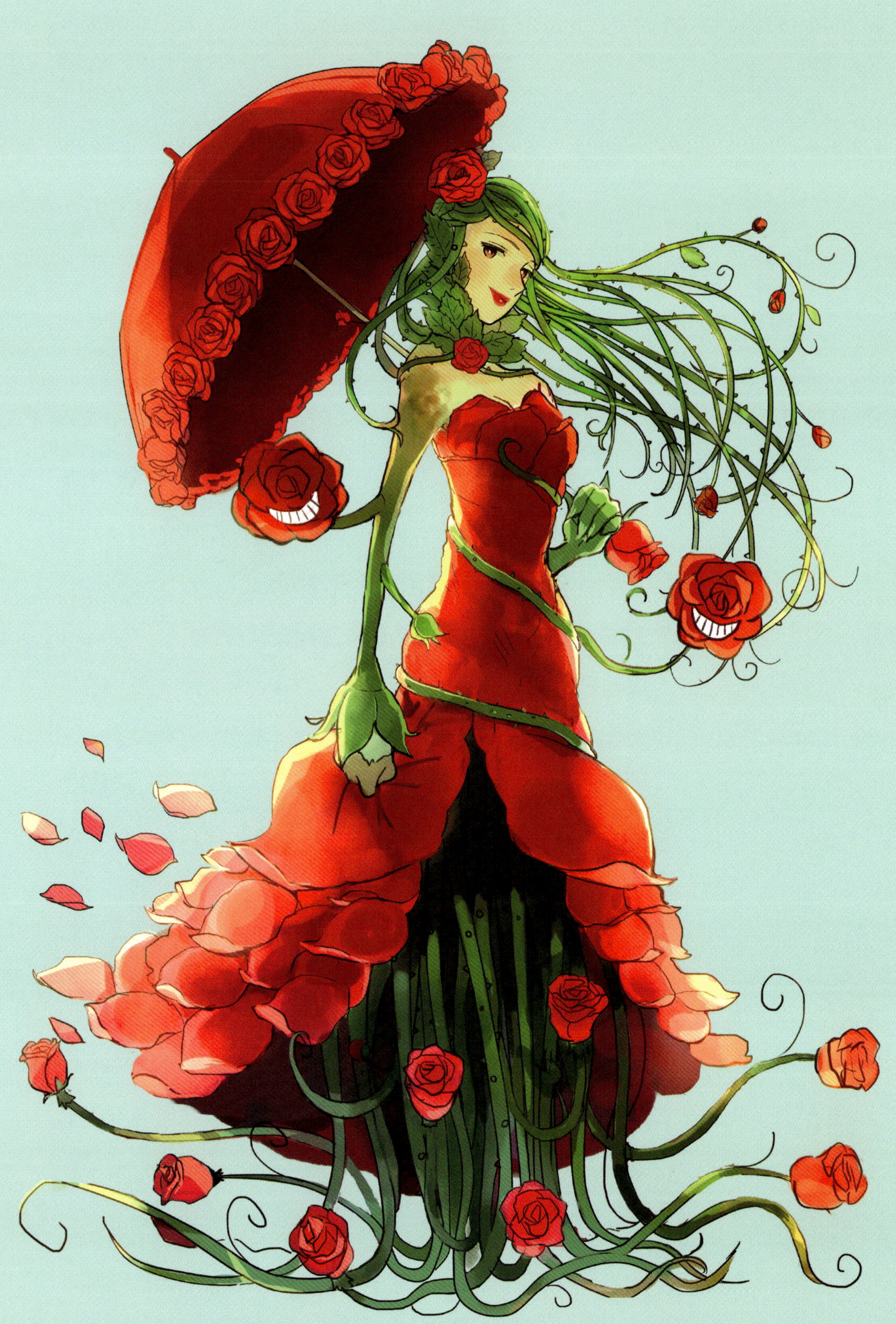

In recent years, there's been an explosion in the popularity of non-human characters within the world of manga. When you hear the phrase "non-human," you probably think of animal/human hybrids, like centaurs and mermaids, but that's just the beginning—from animals to vegetables to minerals, there are endless possibilities! And because they blur the line between reality and fantasy, these unique characters make excellent villains.

When you first attempt to draw these characters, you'll see how difficult it can be to attain a balance between the two influences. Which human elements should you keep? How do you prevent your character from looking like a human wearing a costume?

This book includes a variety of non-human villains inspired by animals, sea creatures, insects, plants and elements. Several illustrations are provided for each character, so you can imagine the villain in action. Throughout this book, you'll find tips and techniques for creating realistic, multidimensional characters, as well as some background information on manga villains. We hope you are inspired to use these characters as a guide for creating your own one-of-a-kind manga villains.

CONTENTS

THE ORIGIN OF NON-HUMAN CHARACTERS

Non-human characters have existed since mythological times.

The history of non-human characters dates back to the era of mythology. Ancient Greek culture is a famous source of mythological animal/human hybrids. For example, Harpy was a ferocious monster with a woman's face and a bird's wings and claws. She was the inspiration for the Shadow Huntress villain featured on page 28.

The centaur is another example of an animal/human hybrid originating from Greek mythology. Centaurs are half-human, half-horse creatures.

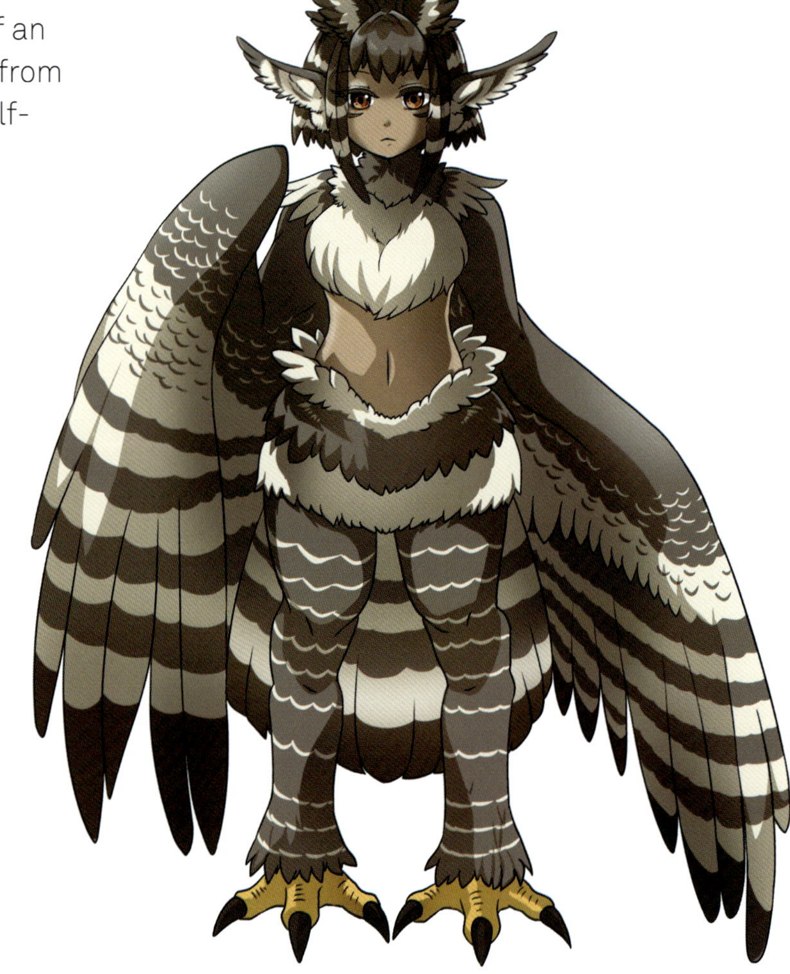

Non-human characters are also present throughout Japanese folklore. According to Japanese legend, (this one from the Edo period) a *jorōgumo* is a spider that can change its appearance into that of a seductive woman. She lures handsome young men into her home and distracts them by playing the lute. She then binds her victims in strong silk threads to prevent their escape and uses her powerful venom to inflict a long and painful death.

Although these creatures are sometimes frightening, we are often drawn to them because of their human elements. One thing is for sure: They stimulate our imaginations and provide an endless source of inspiration when developing manga characters.

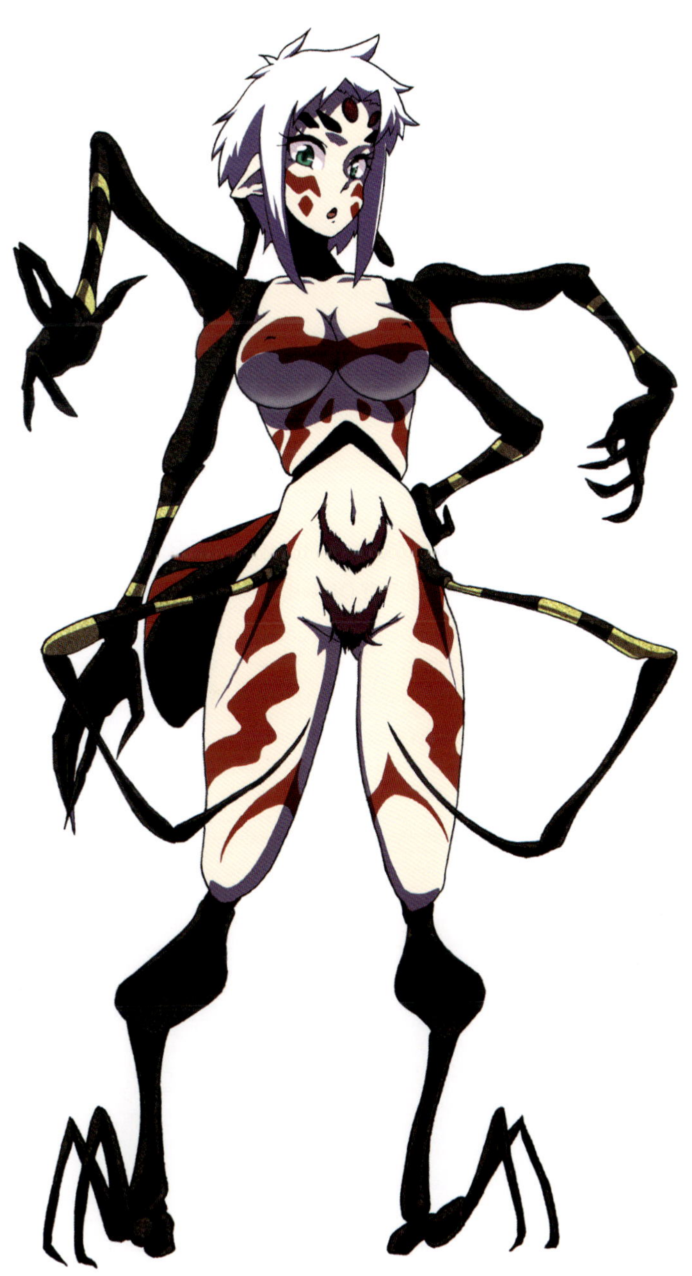

DEVELOPING CHARACTER TRAITS

Brainstorm personality traits to find the perfect villain

Before you start drawing, it's important to develop your character's personality since this will influence several elements within the illustration. It will also help you to select the right type of villain for your story.

For instance, if you're looking for an intelligent, sly villain, a snake-inspired character would be the perfect fit. But if you're looking for a strong, physically imposing villain, a robotic soldier made from metal would be a better choice.

Think about your story's setting, time period and plot, then jot down ideas for your villain.

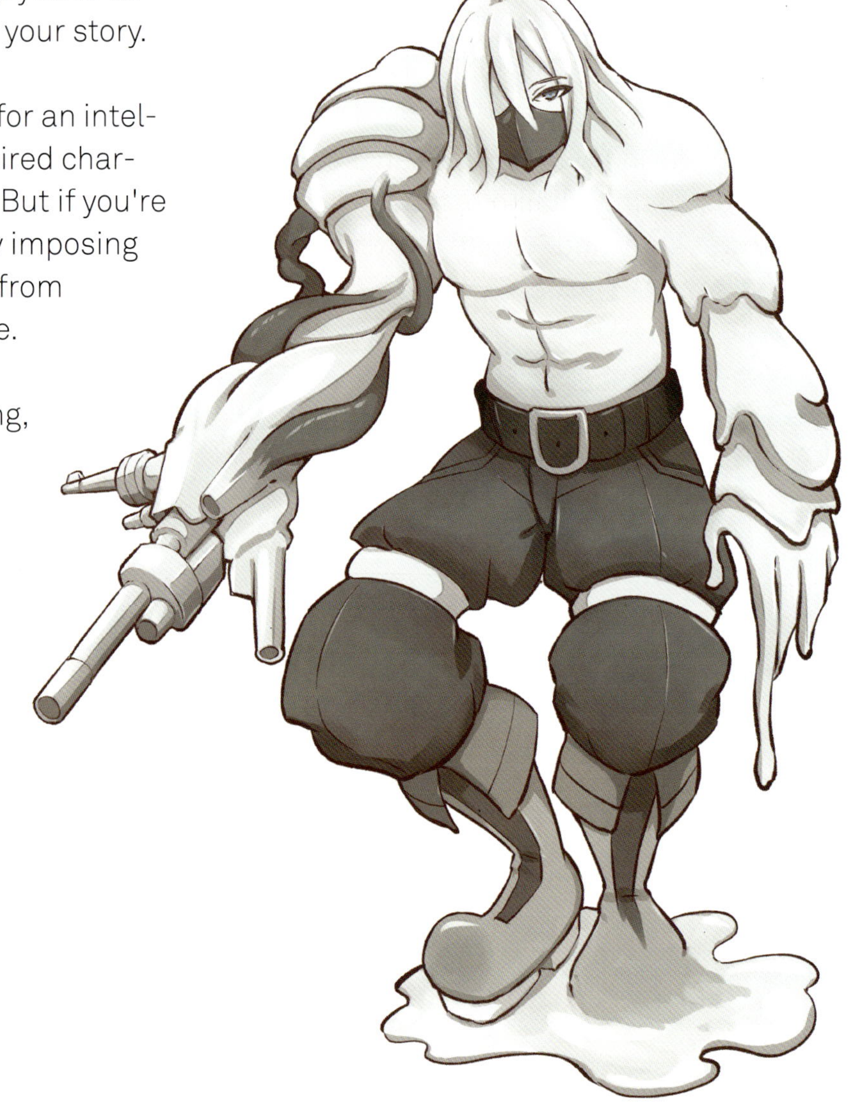

HOW TO CREATE A VILLAIN

Achieving the balance of good vs. evil

It's important to attain a balance between villain and human elements within a character, otherwise your character will be one-dimensional and not very interesting. This principle applies to both the physical appearance of the character, as well as to the more subtle nuances of personality.

When drawing villains, you can create a dramatic effect by using villainous features for just the head or lower body and human features for the rest of the character. If you want the human elements to be more dominant, use more understated features like animal ears, horns or a tail.

When creating your own characters, always strive to achieve balance, both in appearance and in action.

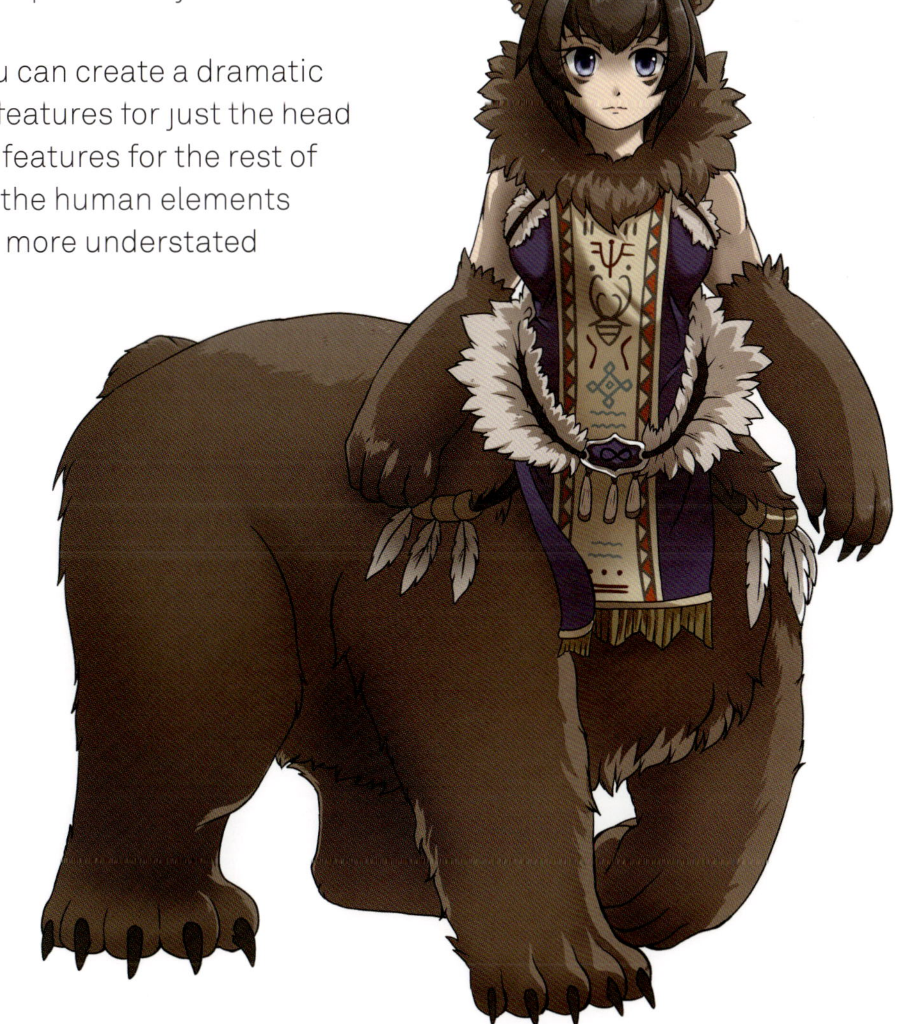

HOW TO USE THIS BOOK

This book is divided into five chapters: Animals, Sea Creatures, Insects, Plants and Elements. Within each chapter, you'll find various subcategories of villains. Each subcategory includes a child, male and female version.

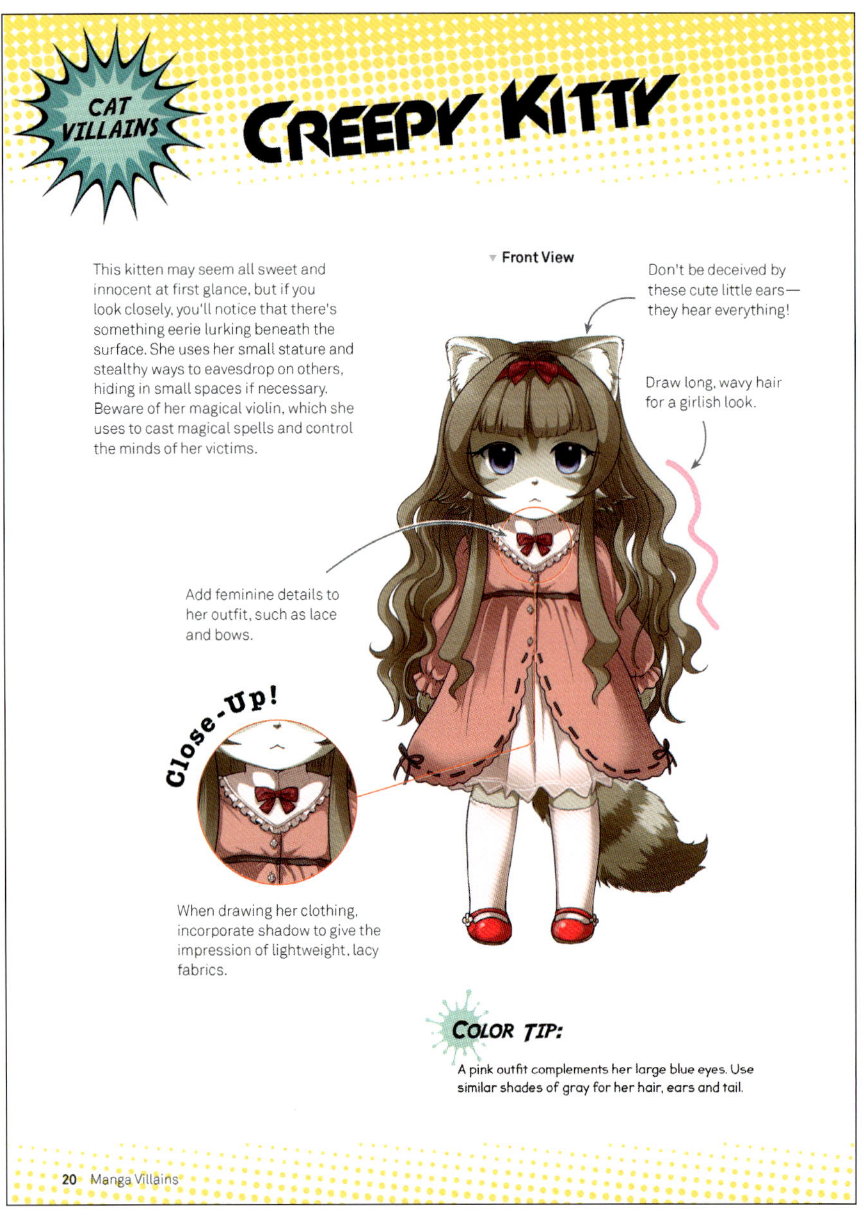

For each villain, you'll find a large, full color illustration on the first page. Key elements of the drawing are noted with captions. You'll also find some background information on the character which will help set the scene.

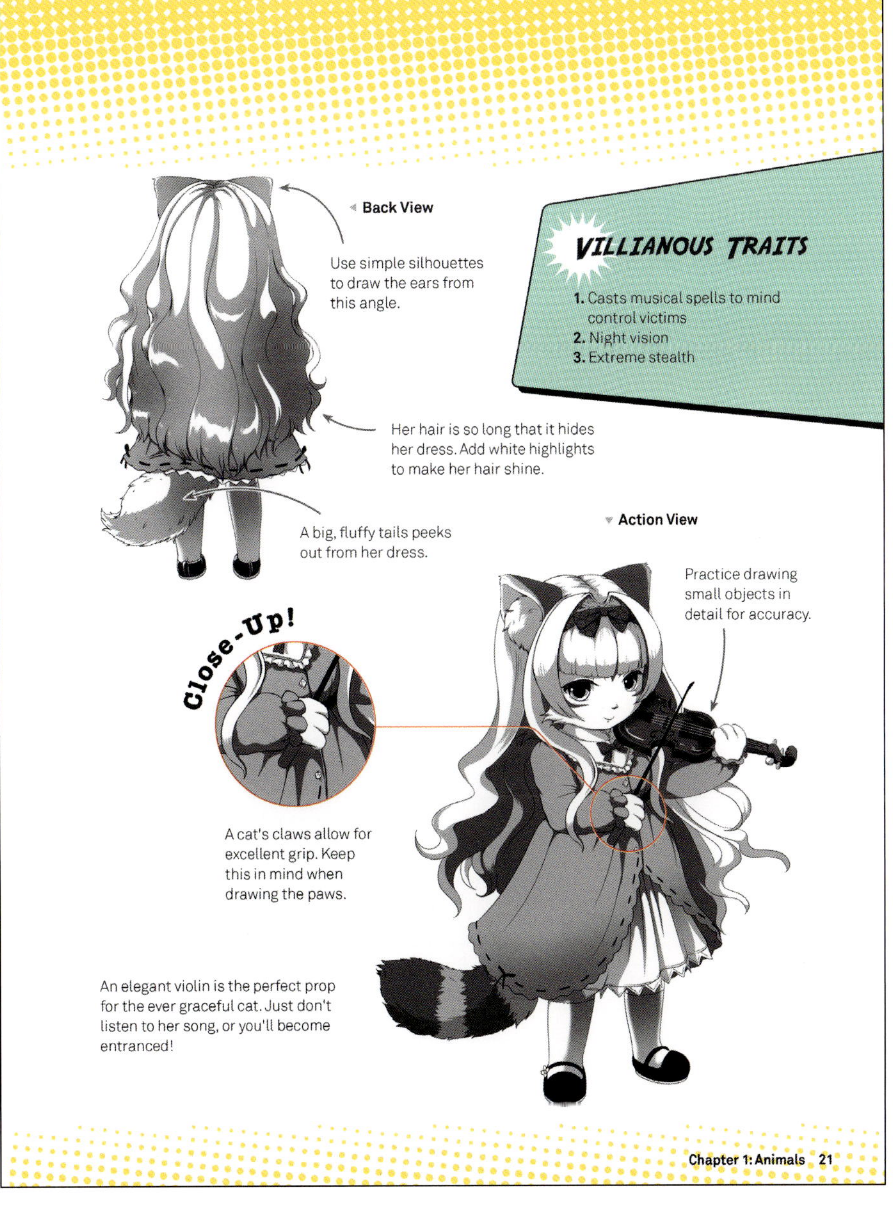

A back view and an action view are also included for each villain. These illustrations are presented in grayscale in order to help identify shape and movement. A list of villainous traits is also included for each character to help you focus on important elements of the drawing.

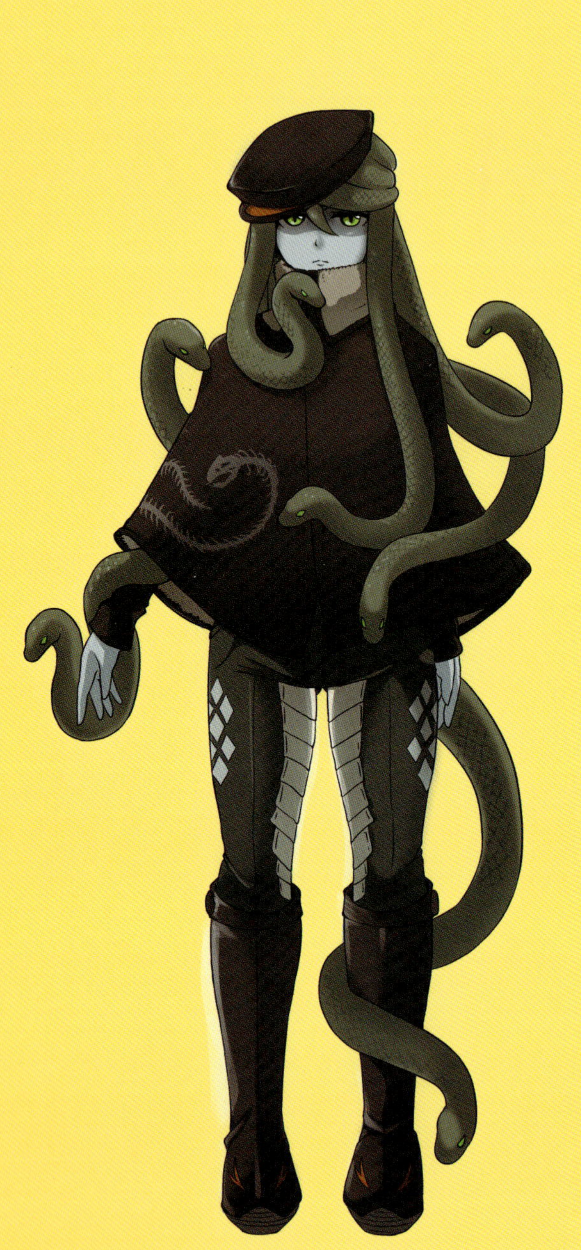

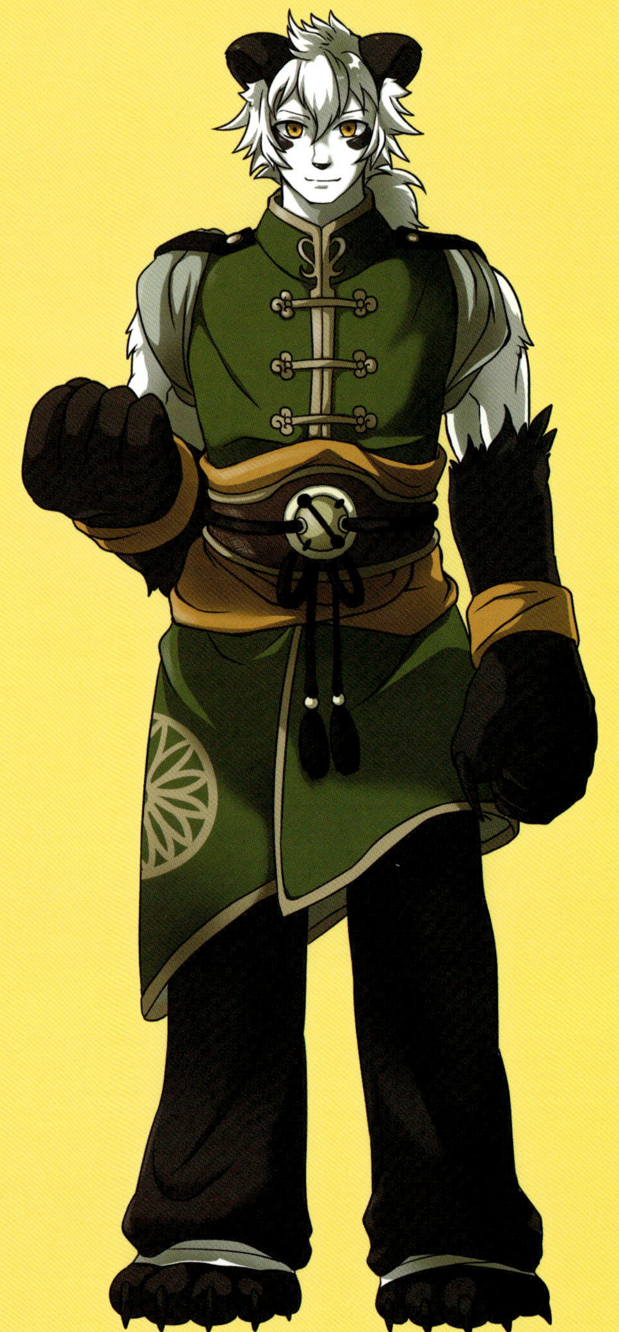

CHAPTER 1

ANIMALS

This collection of villains was inspired by common land animals. To create these villains, start out by drawing a human-inspired face, then add ears, fangs and other animal features. The more fluently you mix human and animal elements, the more interesting the resulting character.

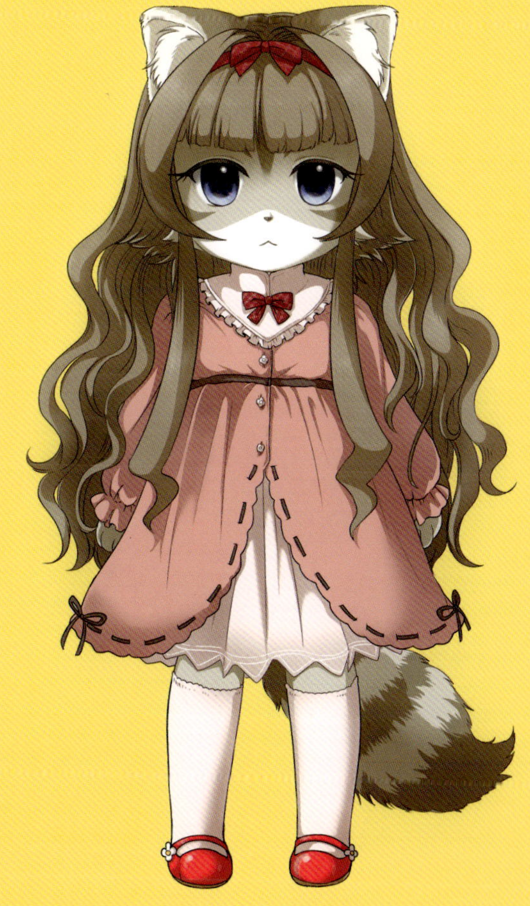

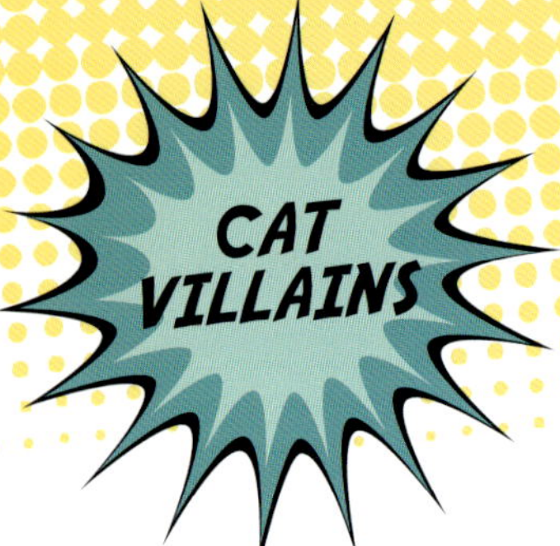

The Feline Fatale

This party girl has a magnetic personality that attracts followers wherever she goes. But once you get on her bad side, beware! She is notoriously unforgiving and has superhuman powers of scent, allowing her to hunt down anything or anyone she desires.

▼ **Front View**

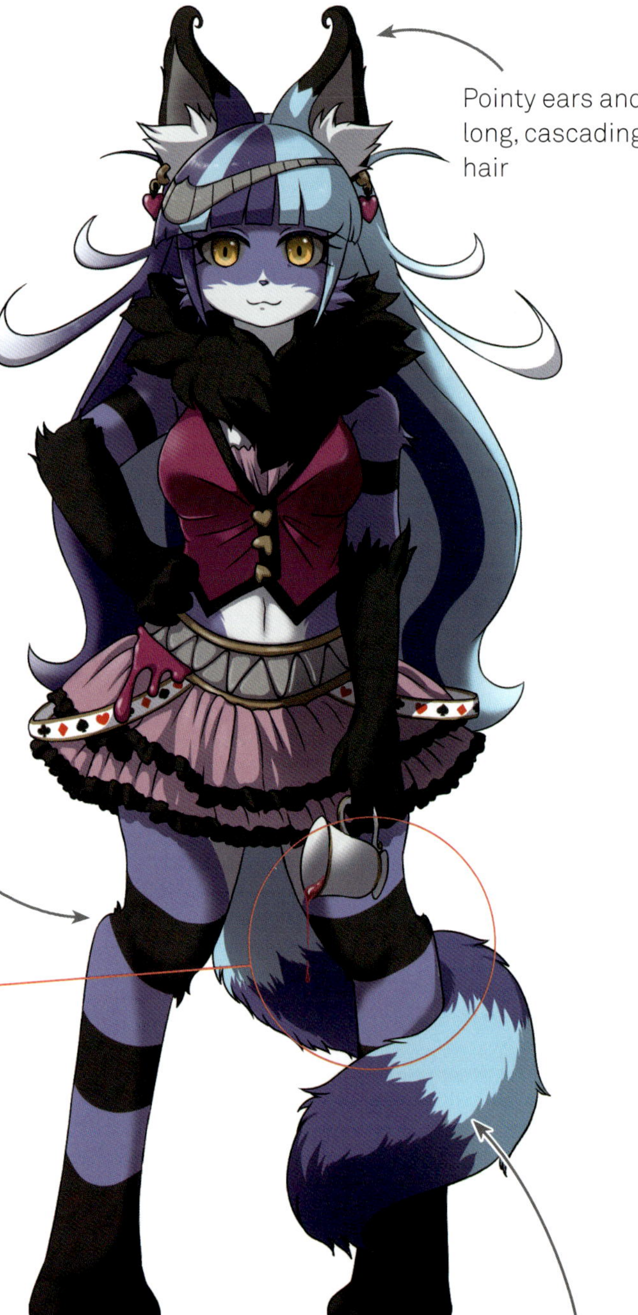

Pointy ears and long, cascading hair

Cats balance on their toes, allowing them to run faster. To capture this unique characteristic, draw this joint so it looks as if it's facing backward.

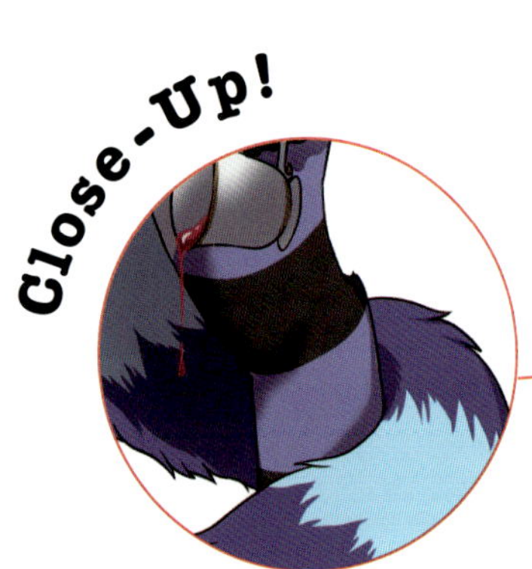

She uses her tail as both a method of attraction and a lethal weapon.

Coil the tail around the leg for a sexy come-hither look.

COLOR TIP:

The dominant use of cool tones suggests an icy and distant personality. Use purple as the main color, then add shades of blue and gray.

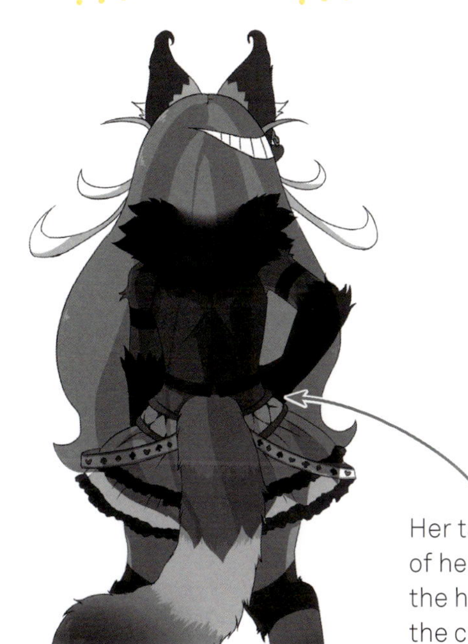

Back View

VILLAINOUS TRAITS

1. Manipulative
2. Has nine lives
3. Enhanced jumping skills

Her tail emerges from the waistline of her dress. Keep the silhouette of the hidden leg in mind when drawing the curving tail.

Action View

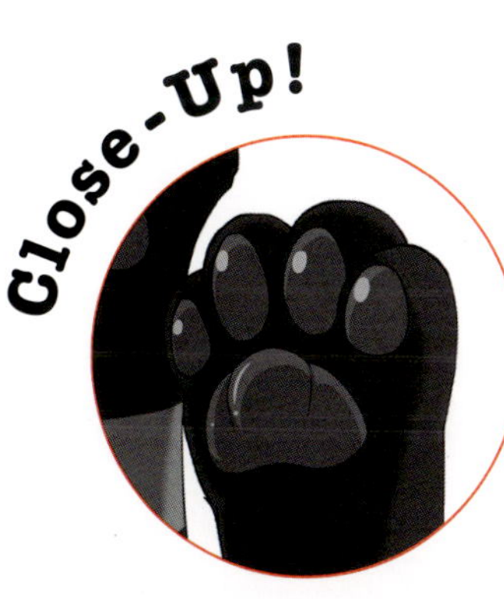

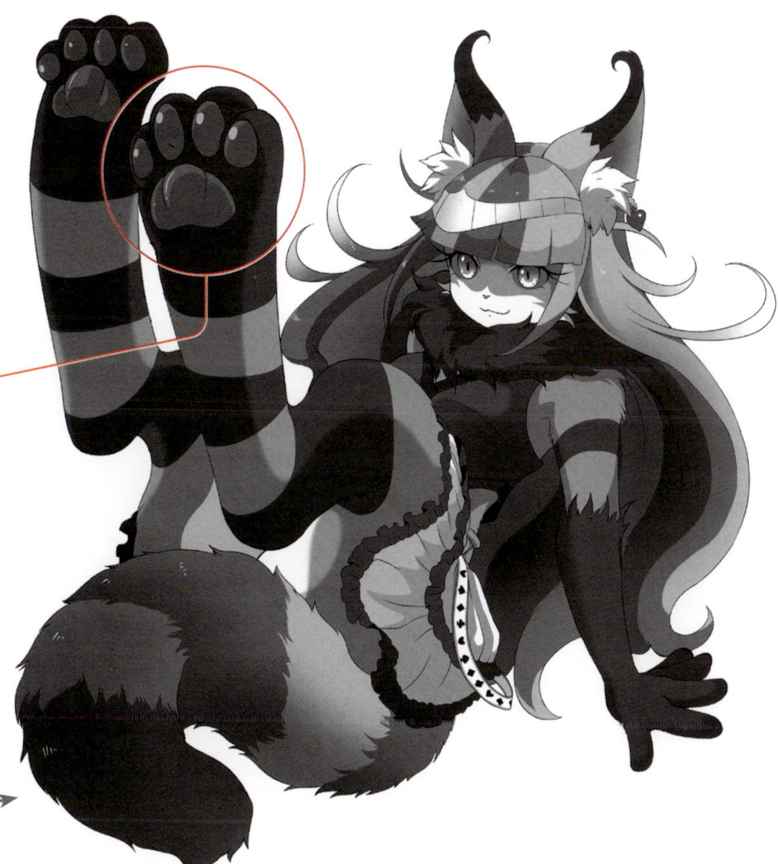

Elongated feet and large paw pads contribute to superior agility and explosive power. Use highlights to emphasize the roundness of the paw pads.

Powerful tail that can be used as an effective weapon

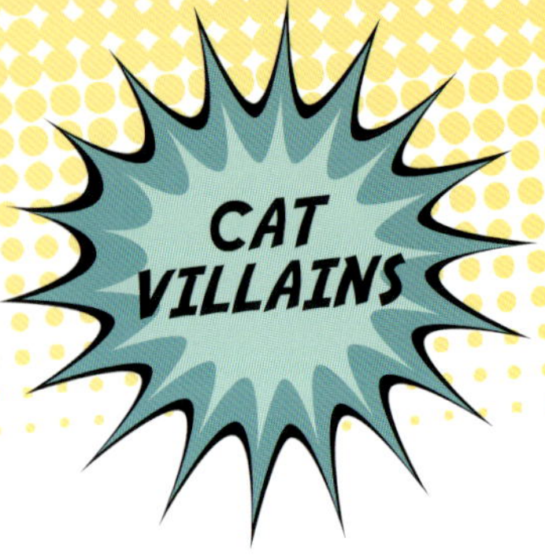

Emo Cat Boy

▼ **Front View**

Don't be fooled by his harmless appearance ... this angst-ridden teen has a dark side! This nerdy introvert is a dangerous computer hacker who can ruin your life with the push of a button.

Long, disheveled hair

Color Tip:

Green eyes suggest a sensitive nature and provide that classic cat look.

Position of joints alludes to uniquely feline flexibility

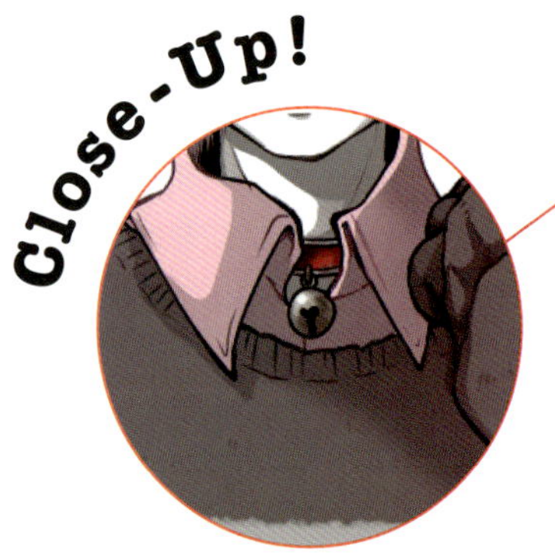

The tail does not coil around the leg; instead, it hangs loosely at the back.

Forced to wear a GPS tracker after being busted for computer hacking.

Color Tip:

Use unassuming neutrals such as gray and brown to suggest his shy, reserved personality.

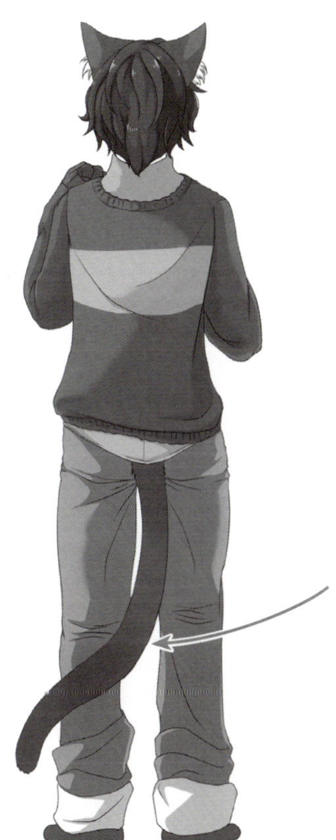

Back View

Draw a simple, curved tail.

VILLAINOUS TRAITS

1. Master computer hacker
2. Highly intelligent
3. Enhanced hearing

Action View

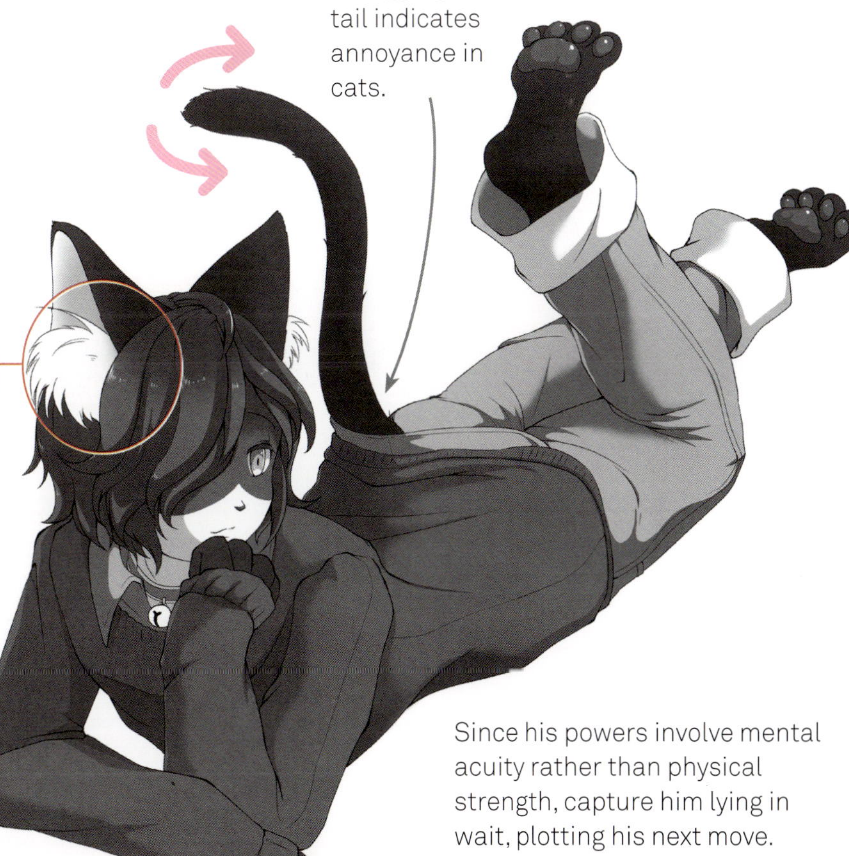

A wagging tail indicates annoyance in cats.

Close-Up!

Large, pointy ears portend his excellent hearing abilities.

Since his powers involve mental acuity rather than physical strength, capture him lying in wait, plotting his next move.

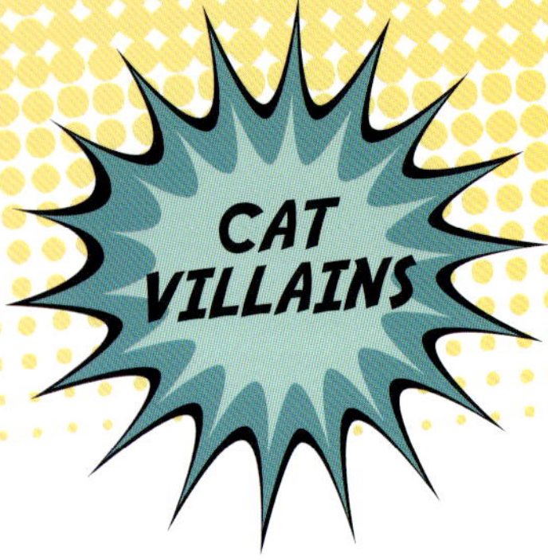

Creepy Kitty

This kitten may seem all sweet and innocent at first glance, but if you look closely, you'll notice that there's something eerie lurking beneath the surface. She uses her small stature and stealthy ways to eavesdrop on others, hiding in small spaces if necessary. Beware of her violin, which she uses to cast magical spells and control the minds of her victims.

▼ **Front View**

Don't be deceived by these cute little ears—they hear everything!

Draw long, wavy hair for a girlish look.

Add feminine details to her outfit, such as lace and bows.

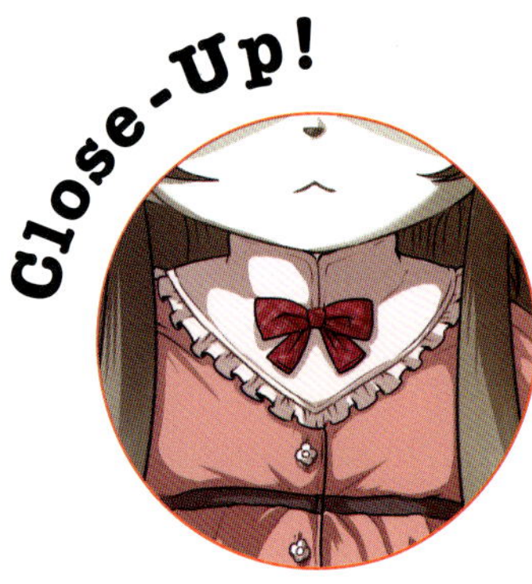

When drawing her clothing, incorporate shadow to give the impression of lightweight, lacy fabrics.

Color Tip:

A pink outfit complements her large blue eyes. Use similar shades of gray for her hair, ears and tail.

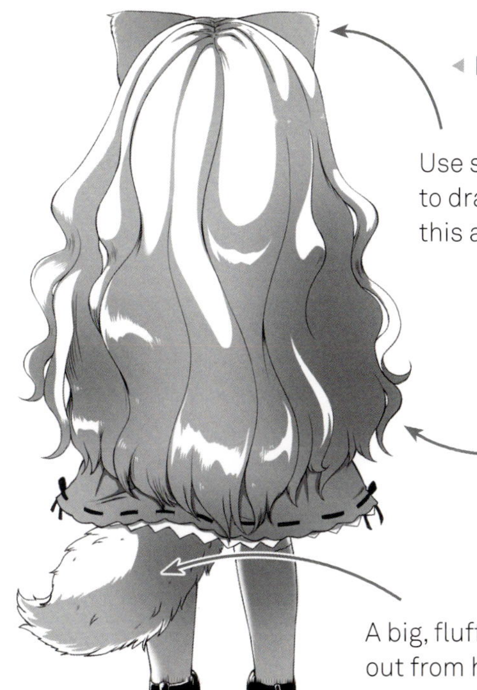

Back View

Use simple silhouettes to draw the ears from this angle.

Her hair is so long that it hides her dress. Add white highlights to make her hair shine.

A big, fluffy tails peeks out from her dress.

VILLAINOUS TRAITS

1. Casts musical spells to mind control victims
2. Night vision
3. Extreme stealth

Action View

Practice drawing small objects in detail for accuracy.

Close-Up!

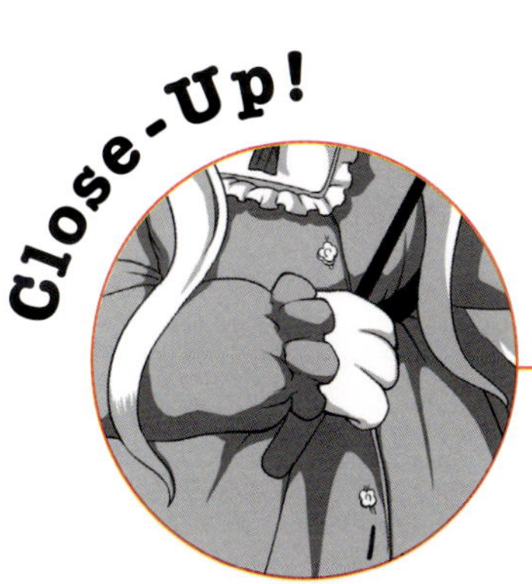

A cat's claws allow for excellent grip. Keep this in mind when drawing the paws.

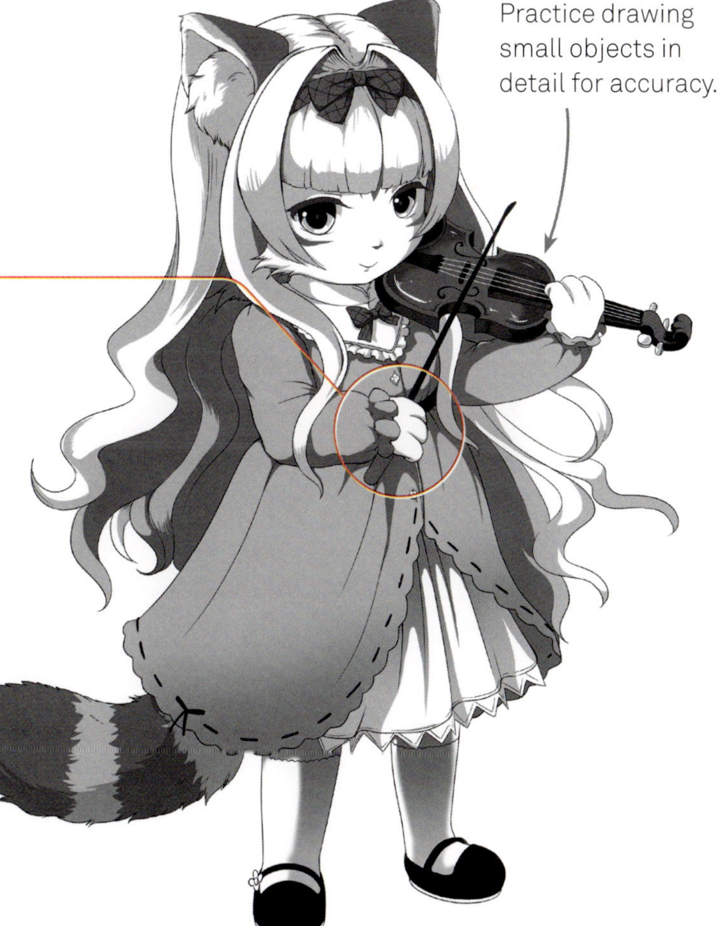

An elegant violin is the perfect prop for the ever graceful cat. Just don't listen to her song, or you'll become entranced!

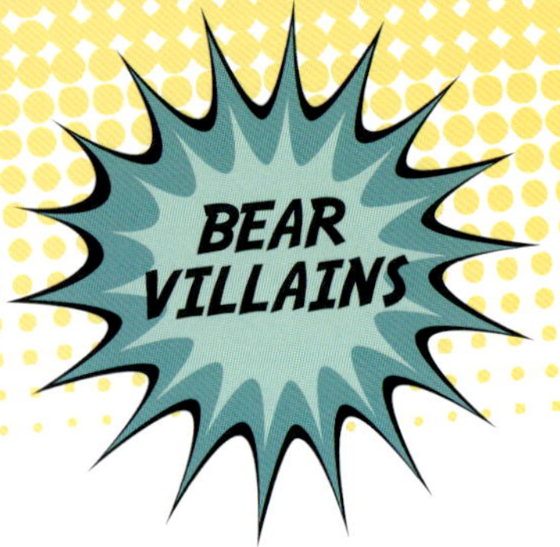

The Den Mother

This powerful half-human, half-bear is a fierce matriarch. As chief, she is a strong leader who is extremely protective of her tribe.

▼ **Front View**

She possesses the upper body of a woman and the lower body of a brown bear.

Uses her immense forearms to swipe at prey and destroy her enemies

COLOR TIP:

The rich jewel tones of this traditional Native American dress work well with her dark brown fur.

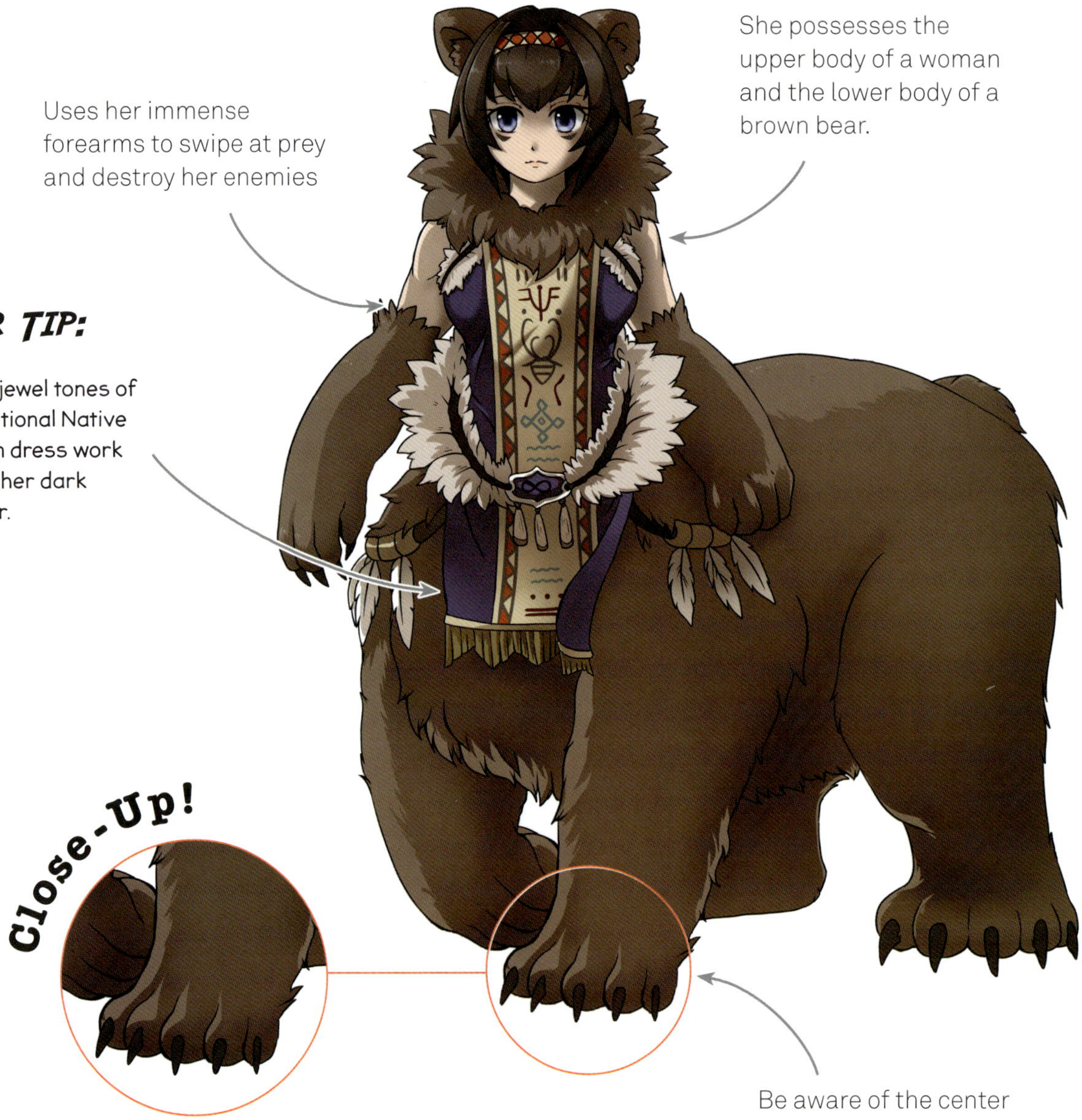

Close-Up!

Razor-sharp claws

Be aware of the center of gravity between the four legs.

VILLAINOUS TRAITS

1. Extremely protective
2. Acute sense of smell
3. Superstitious

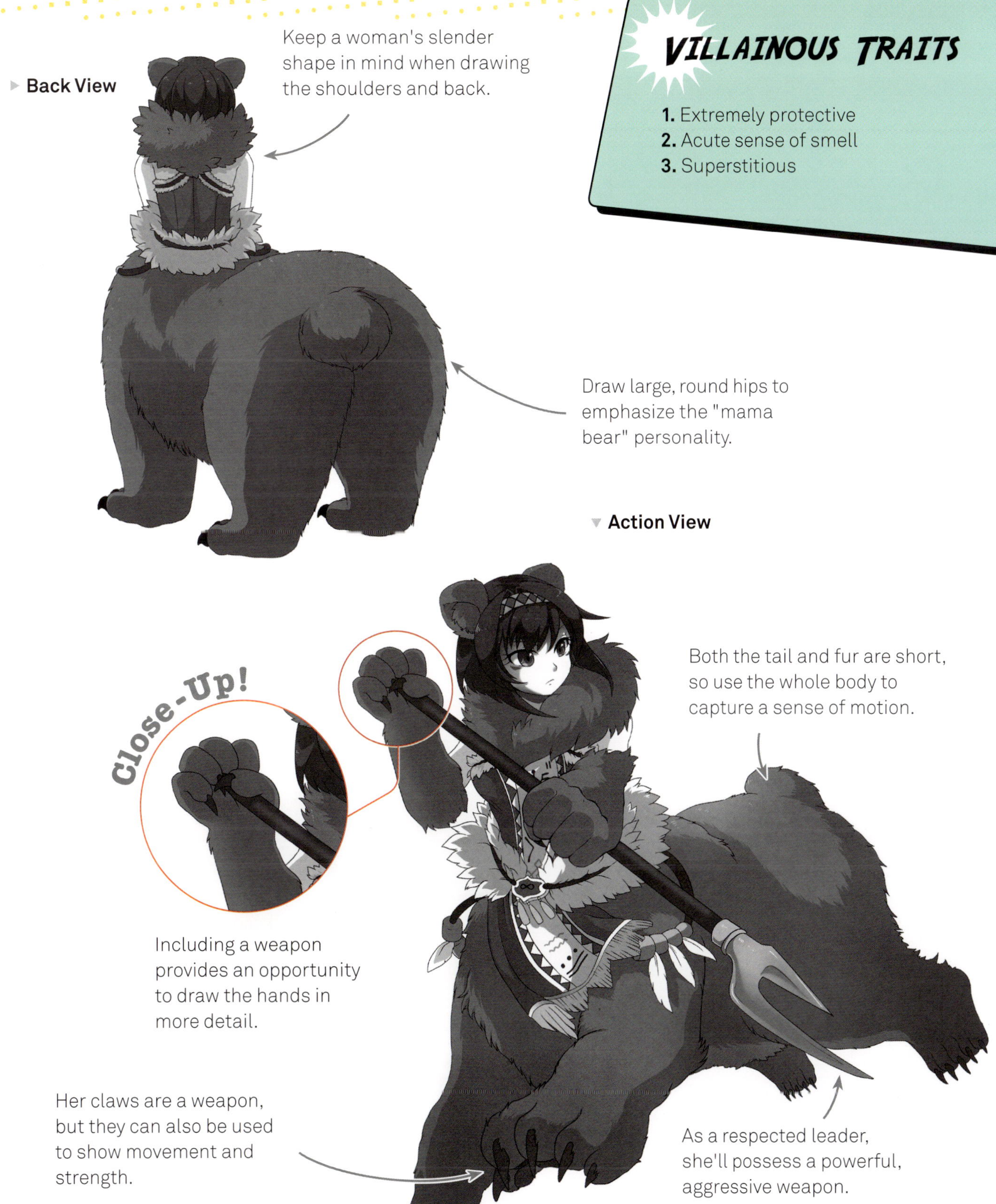

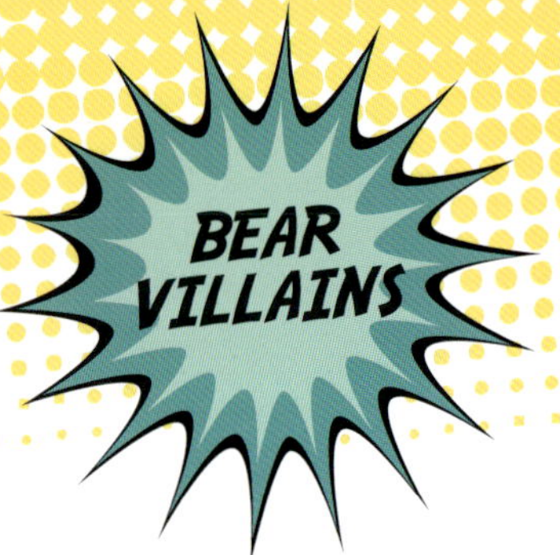

THE KUNG FU MASTER

This strong, handsome panda/man hybrid is a natural-born leader. His well-developed body and disciplined attitude are the result of years of kung fu training. He is always in control, but can unleash massive power whenever necessary.

▼ **Front View**

Draw black ears for the classic panda look.

COLOR TIP:

Use yellow to create a supernatural expression in the eyes.

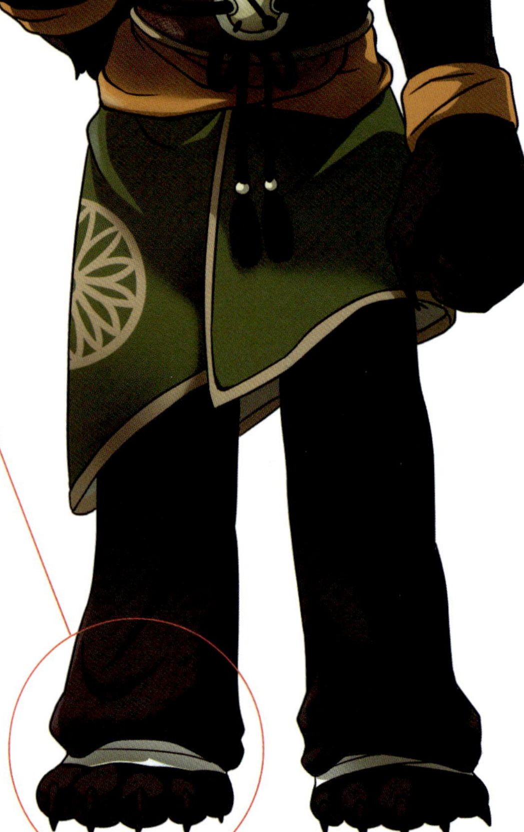

Large, powerful hands suggest his masterful kung fu abilities.

Close-Up!

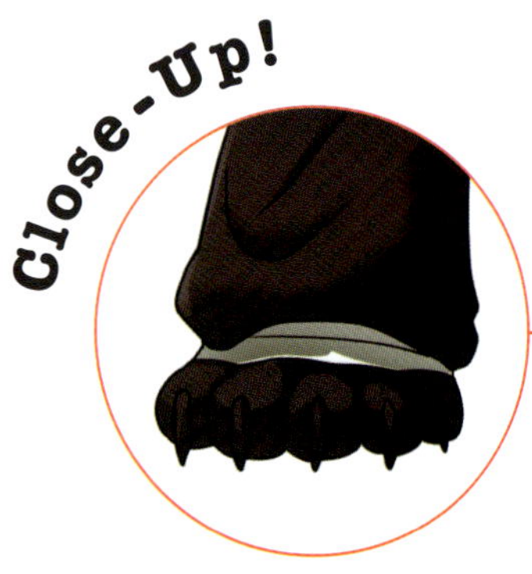

Just like other bears, giant pandas possess large, sharp claws.

COLOR TIP:

Use a combination of black and white for the body, locating the black fur on the ears, eye patches, muzzle and limbs. Incorporate color into the uniform—green and brown evoke a traditional Chinese military uniform.

VILLAINOUS TRAITS

1. Massive strength
2. Expert combat skills
3. Razor-sharp claws

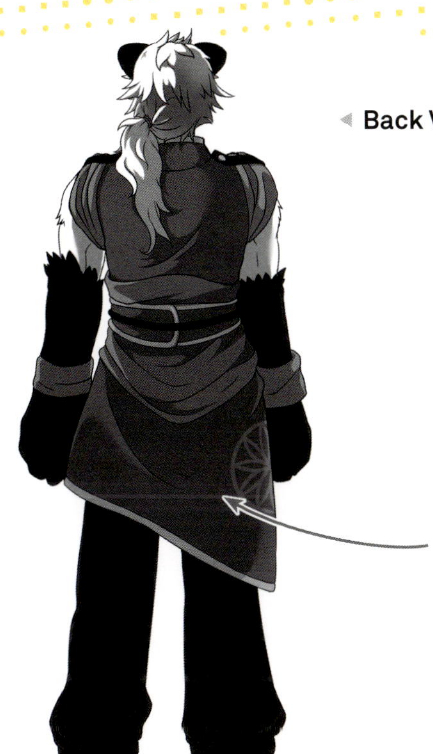

Back View

As a kung fu master, he has lightning fast reflexes and is always on alert, even when his back is turned.

Action View

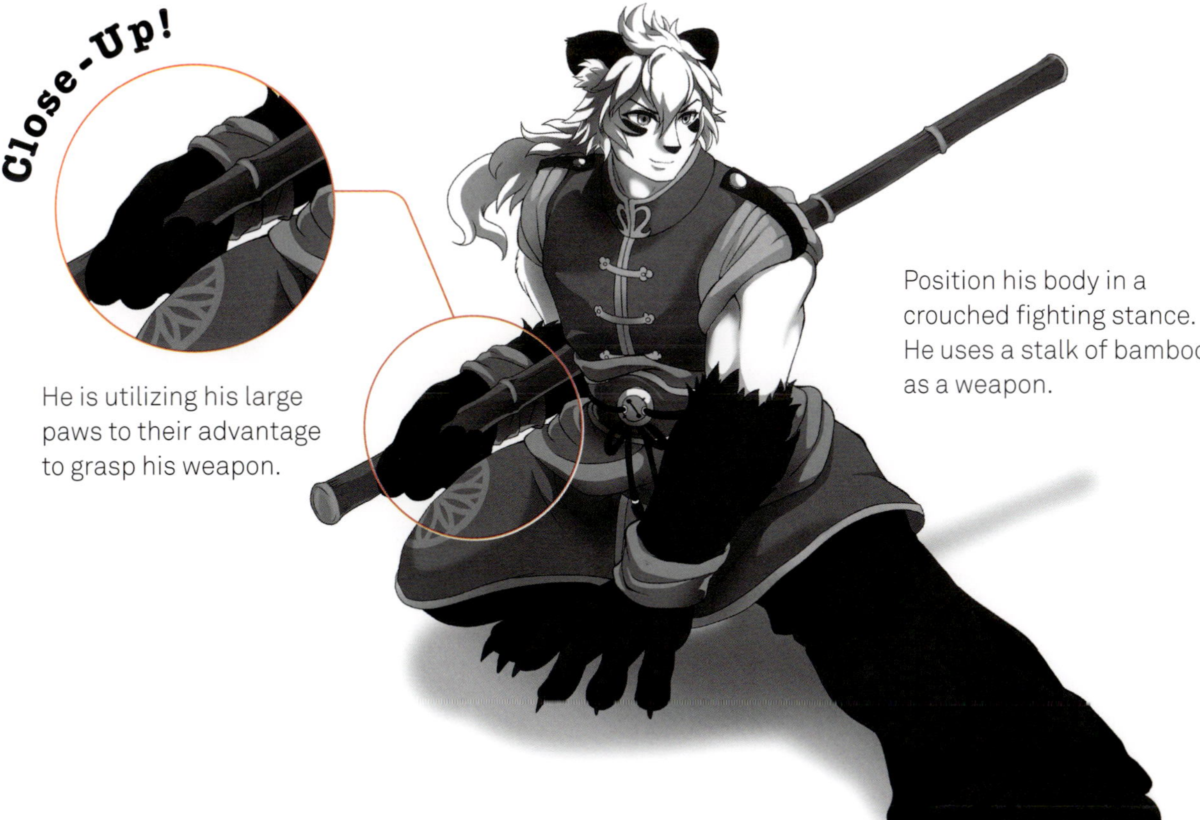

He is utilizing his large paws to their advantage to grasp his weapon.

Position his body in a crouched fighting stance. He uses a stalk of bamboo as a weapon.

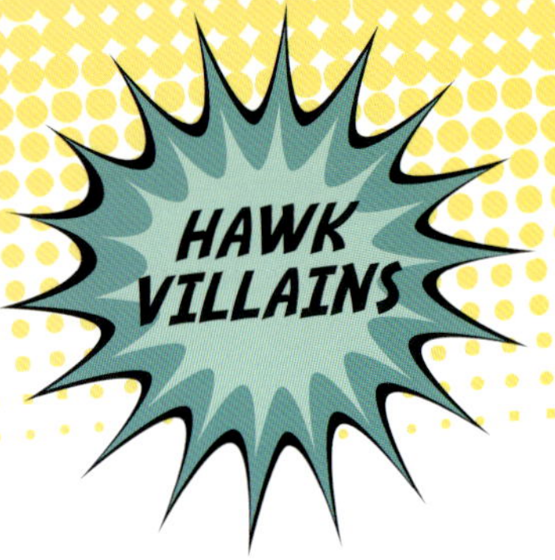

THE WARRIOR CHIEF

This menacing warrior figure is extremely observant and intelligent—nothing escapes his notice! As leader of his tribe, he is revered and feared by all and is universally acknowledged to be in control of the airspace.

Front View

Incorporate Native American design elements into his dress.

Use small triangles to represent the ears.

His body language suggests a no-nonsense personality.

Strong, slim legs accentuate the size of the talons.

COLOR TIP:

Use bold yellow and white accents as focal points among the mass of brown feathers.

VILLAINOUS TRAITS

1. Razor-sharp talons
2. Superior vision
3. Ruthlessness

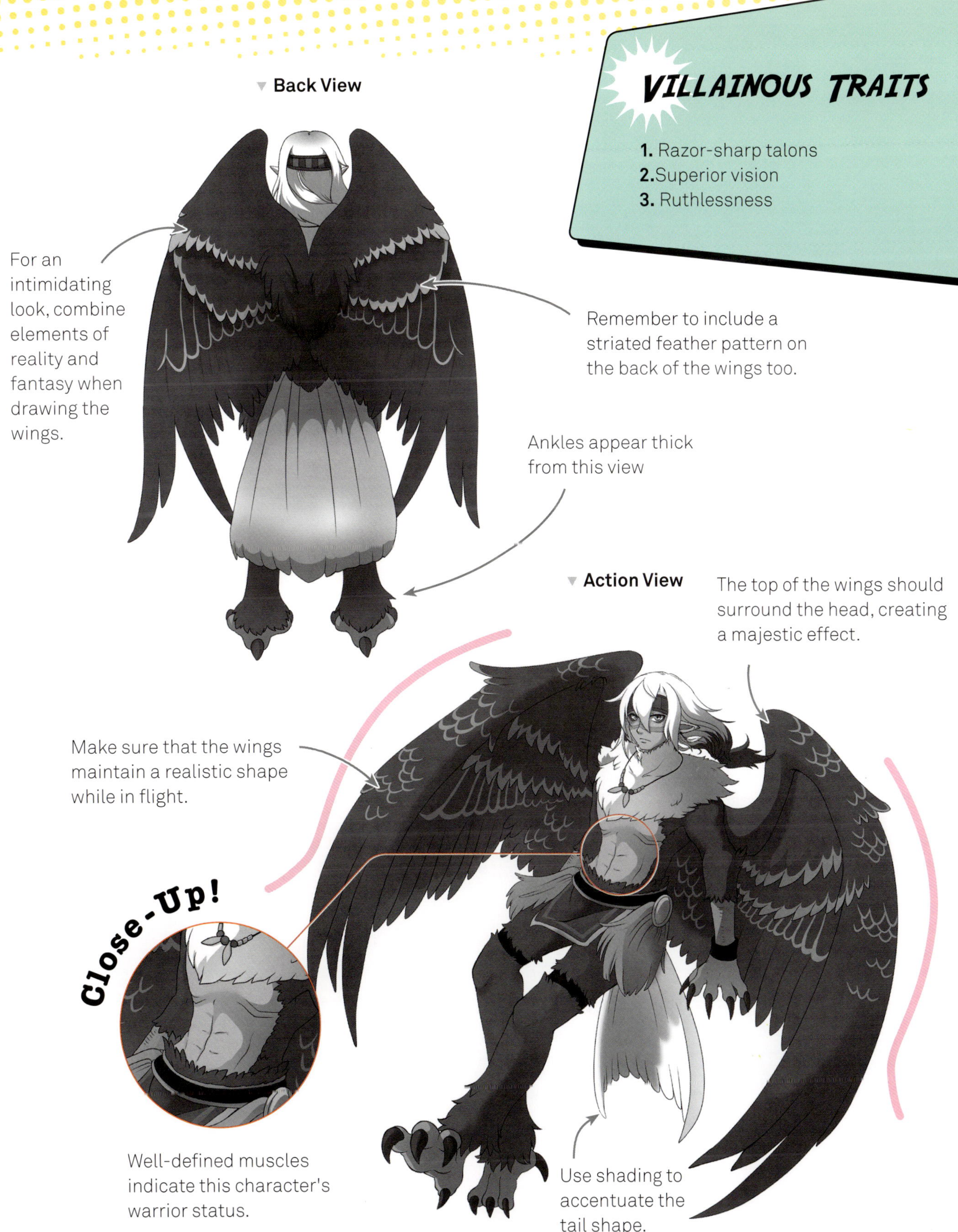

HAWK VILLAINS The Shadow Huntress

Mysterious and elusive, this exotic avian is the dark angel of the forest. She is extremely territorial and becomes very aggressive when challenged.

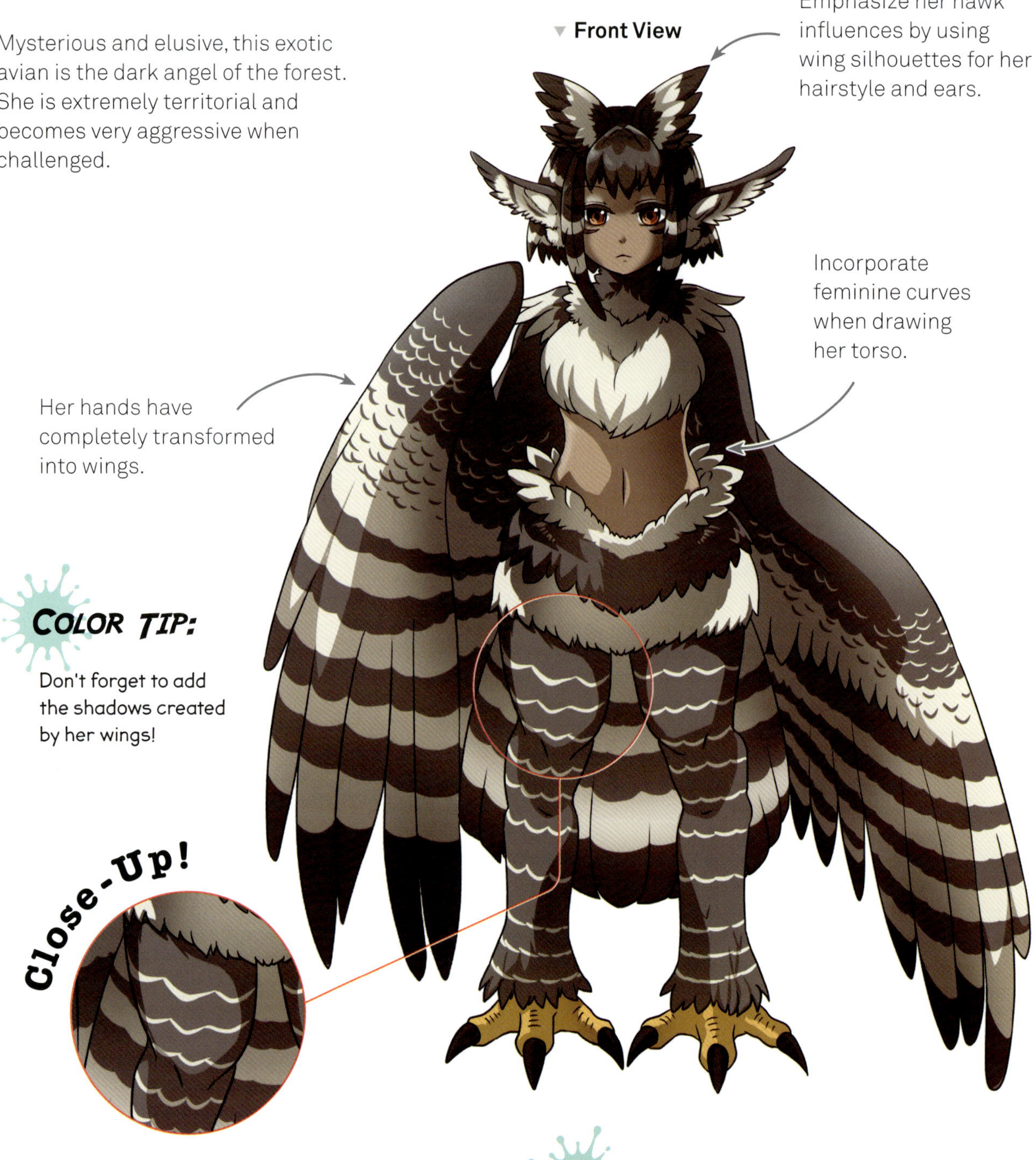

Emphasize her hawk influences by using wing silhouettes for her hairstyle and ears.

Incorporate feminine curves when drawing her torso.

Her hands have completely transformed into wings.

COLOR TIP:

Don't forget to add the shadows created by her wings!

Her powerful, muscular legs symbolize her strength.

COLOR TIP:

Use the classic gray and white striped pattern characteristic of hawks.

VILLAINOUS TRAITS

1. Aggressive
2. Territorial
3. Unmatched flight capabilities

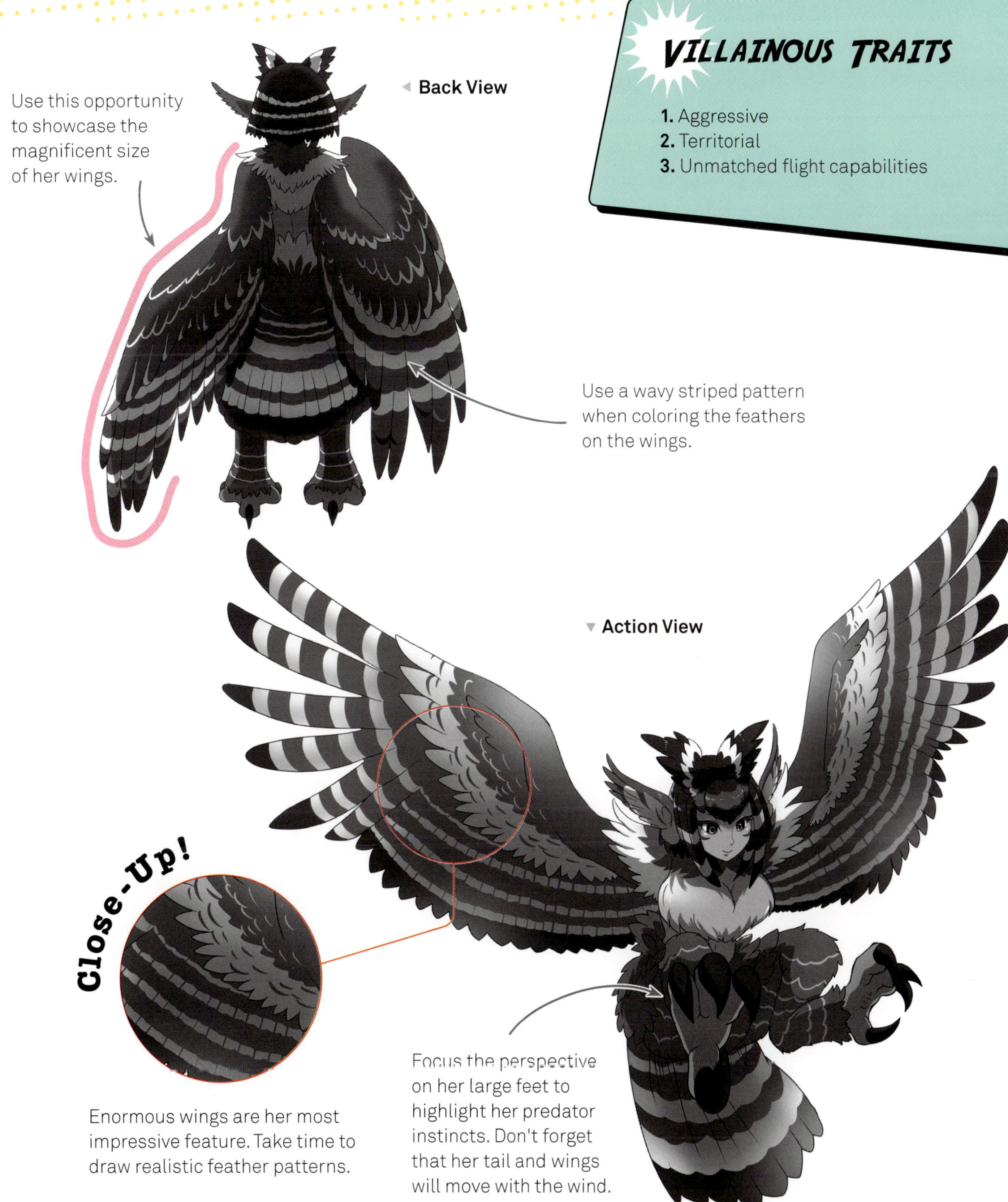

Enormous wings are her most impressive feature. Take time to draw realistic feather patterns.

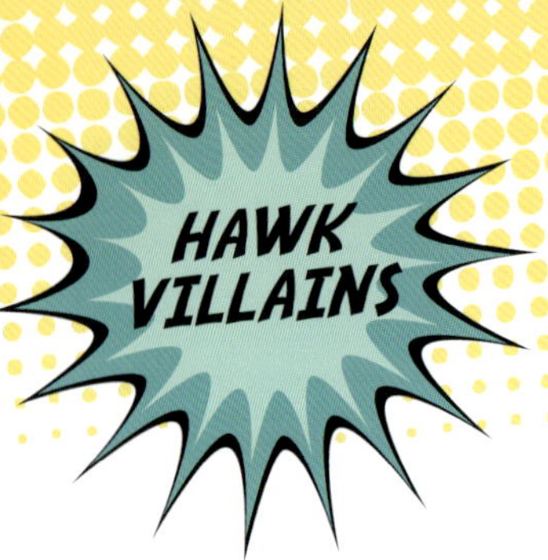

The Future Samurai

This young hawk is an apprentice samurai who aspires to become future leader of his tribe. His life is dedicated to training, but once in a while, he's overcome by curiosity and soars off to explore the forest.

Front View

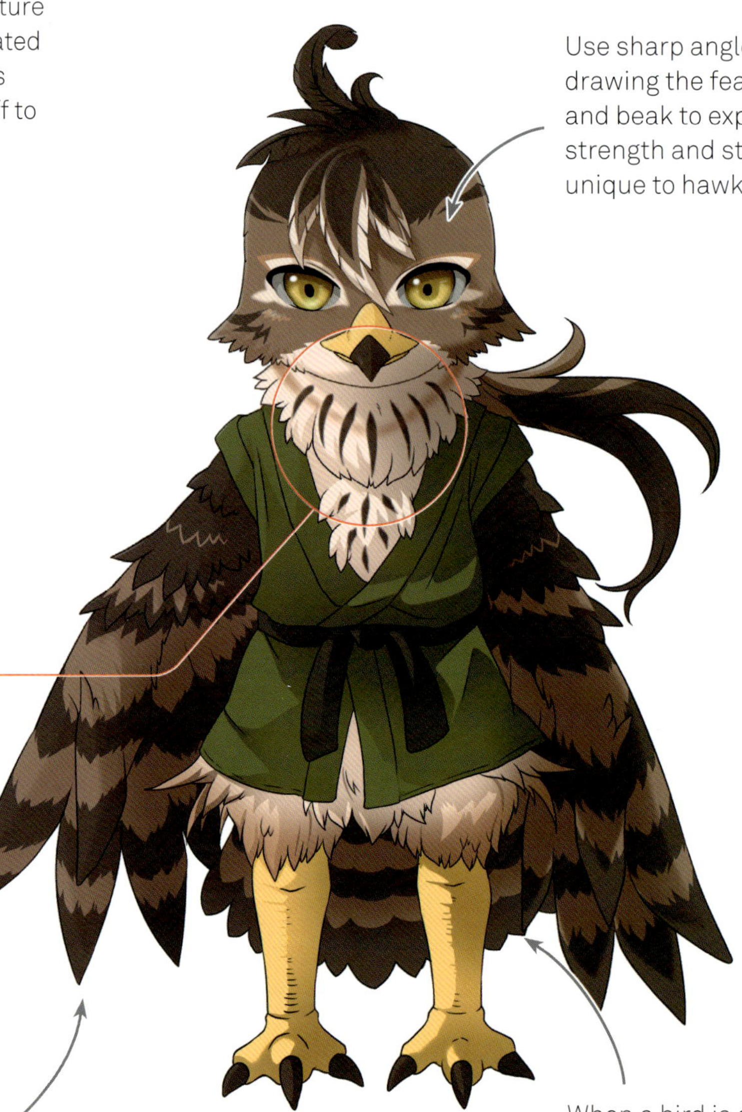

Use sharp angles when drawing the feathers, eyes and beak to express the strength and stoicism unique to hawks.

Close-Up!

The soft feathers poking out of his uniform suggest immaturity. He is wearing a *dōgi*, a Japanese martial arts uniform.

Divide each wing tip into five different sections to give the impression of long fingers. Since this hawk is young, the wings should be small in proportion to the body.

When a bird is at rest, a gap is created between the wings and body. Incorporate shadow to create a three-dimensional drawing.

Color Tip:

Soft, fluffy feathers indicate youth. Use gradated shades of brown for realistic looking wings.

VILLAINOUS TRAITS

1. Reckless curiosity
2. Sharp beak
3. Immature

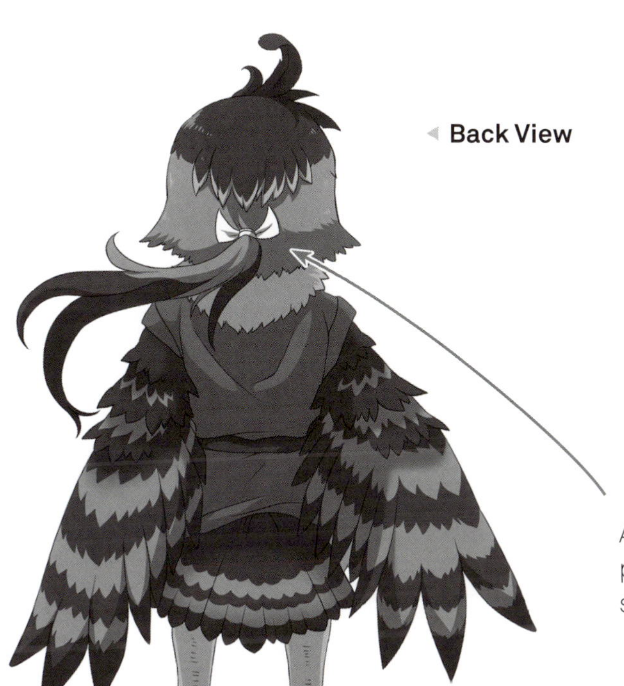

◂ **Back View**

A long ponytail provides the classic samurai look.

▾ **Action View**

His ponytail moves with the wind.

Close-Up!

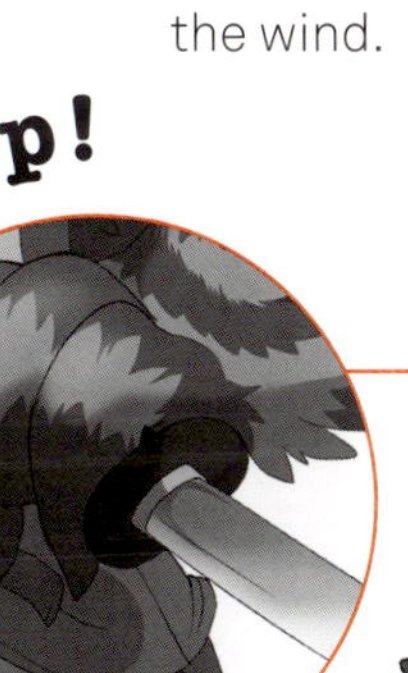

Express movement and perspective as he lunges forward, dagger in hand.

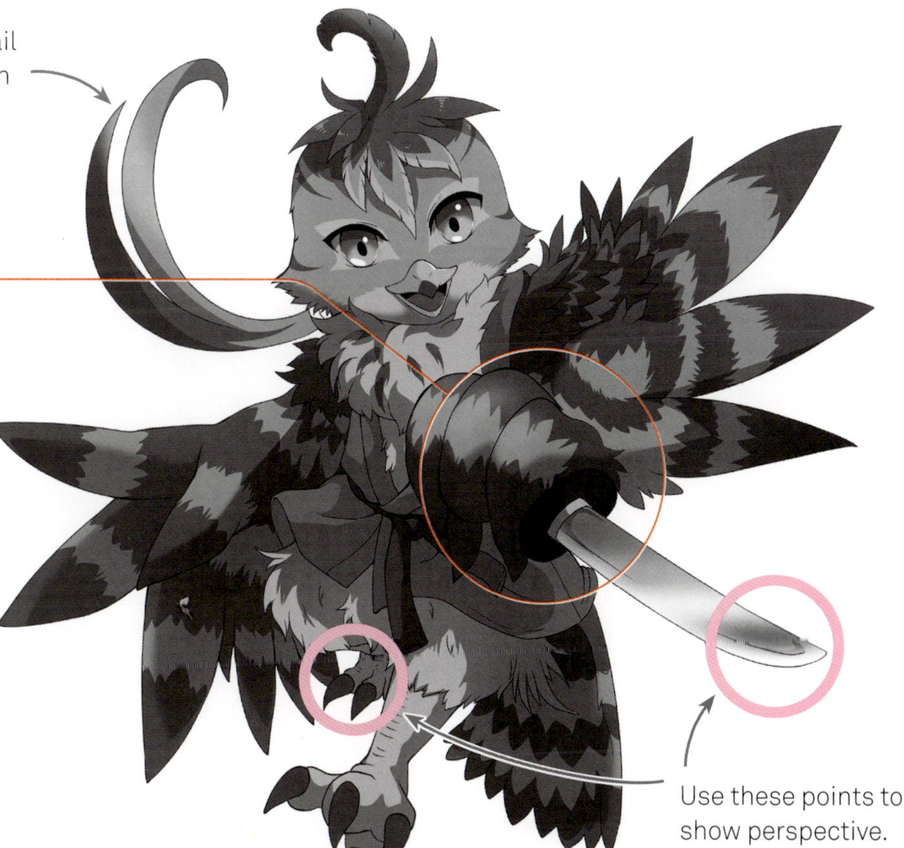

Use these points to show perspective.

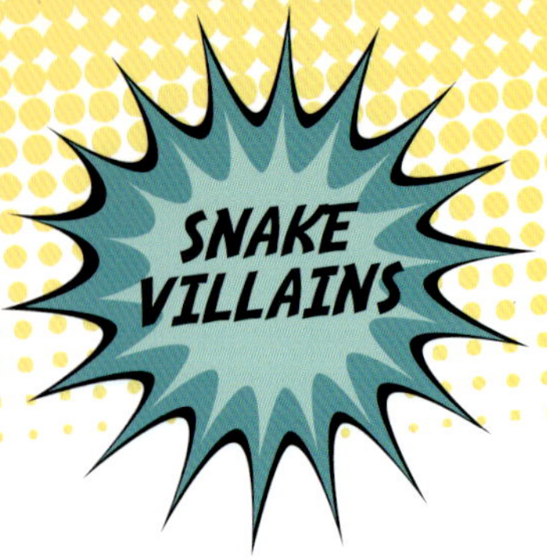

The Serpentine Seductress

▼ Front View

Dark and mysterious, this stylish seductress is a highly dangerous assassin. Her hair is composed of coiling, venomous snakes that possess the power to hypnotize and kill prey.

The snake bodies are camouflaged by her cap.

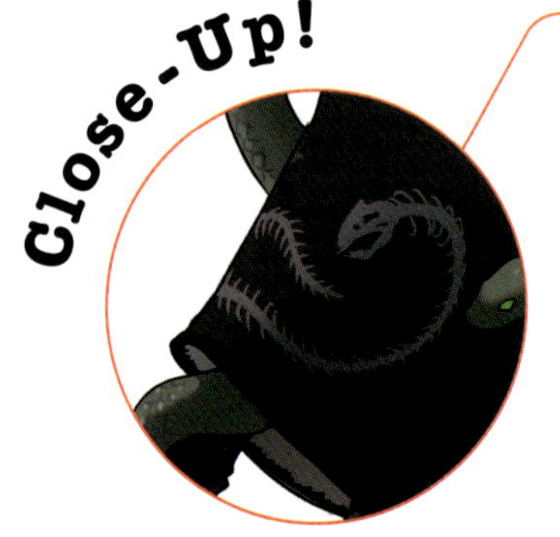

For a hypnotizing effect, use the same shade for both her eyes and the snake eyes.

Her stylish poncho features a snake skeleton. Incorporate this level of detail into a drawing to create a well-developed character.

Her leggings are made of snakeskin, while her boots evoke a snake's slit-like eyes.

Color Tip:

Use a dark green color scheme for the entire drawing since the snakes are actually an extension of the character's body. Dark gray clothing complements the green color scheme and draws attention to the most interesting aspect of the drawing: the snakes.

VILLAINOUS TRAITS

1. Poison generation
2. Brainwashing
3. Cold-blooded

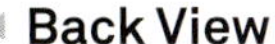

◂ **Back View**

Position her bottom high to create the appearance of long legs. Keep her overall hairstyle in mind when drawing the snakes.

▾ **Action View**

Close-Up!

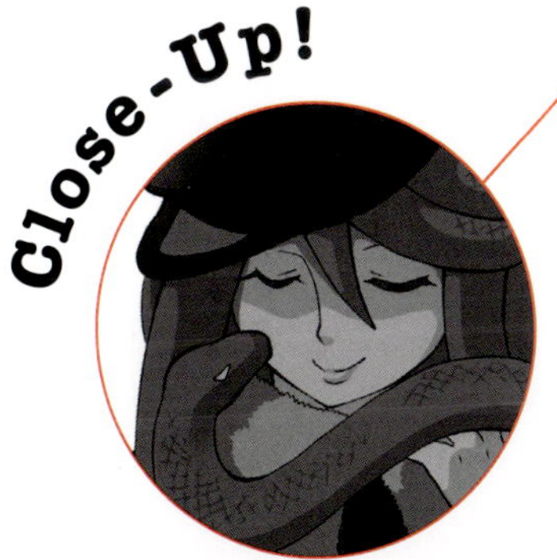

Draw closed eyes to capture the seductive, feminine look she uses to fool her victims.

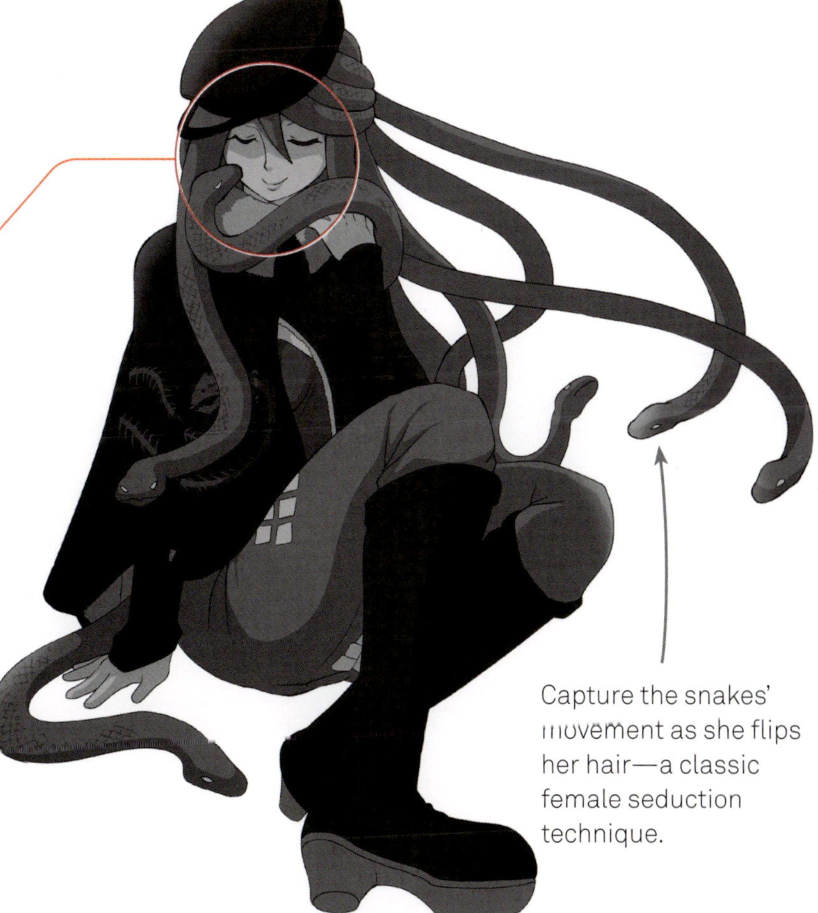

Capture the snakes' movement as she flips her hair—a classic female seduction technique.

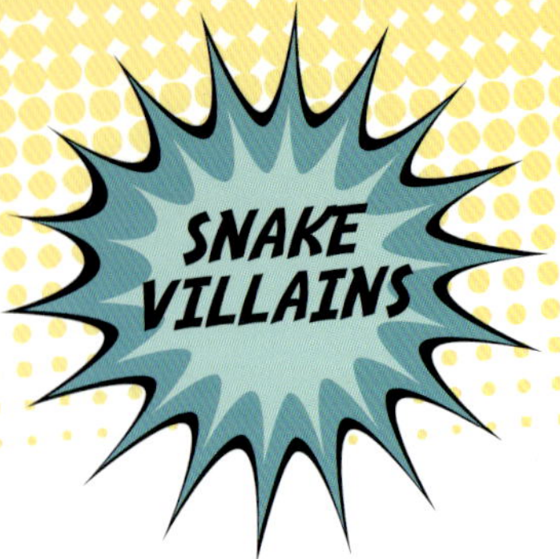

The Cobra King

This strong-willed warrior is considered to be the "King of the Cobras." He possesses unmatched offensive power and is never afraid to face his enemies. He is respected as a lone warrior figure.

▼ **Front View**

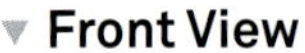

Long, elegant hair mimics the silhouette of a snake's body.

Body armor is essential because he is a leader who fights on the front lines.

Lizard-like hands

Color Tip:

Use varying shades of gray to capture the hard, metallic surface of the armor.

Close-Up!

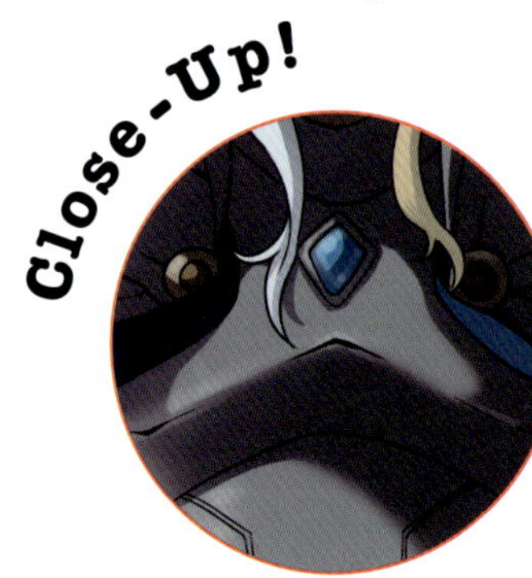

This large jewel distinguishes him as royalty.

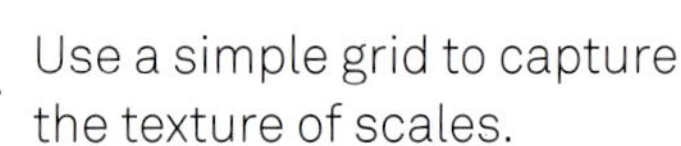

Use a simple grid to capture the texture of scales.

Naturally taper the body into a tail. He is very strong, so take care not to draw the torso too thin.

Color Tip:

The predominant use of gray makes it difficult for opponents to determine where his armor ends and his body begins. The use of dark blue as an accent color suggests strength.

VILLAINOUS TRAITS

1. Poison generation
2. Camouflage
3. Excessive pride

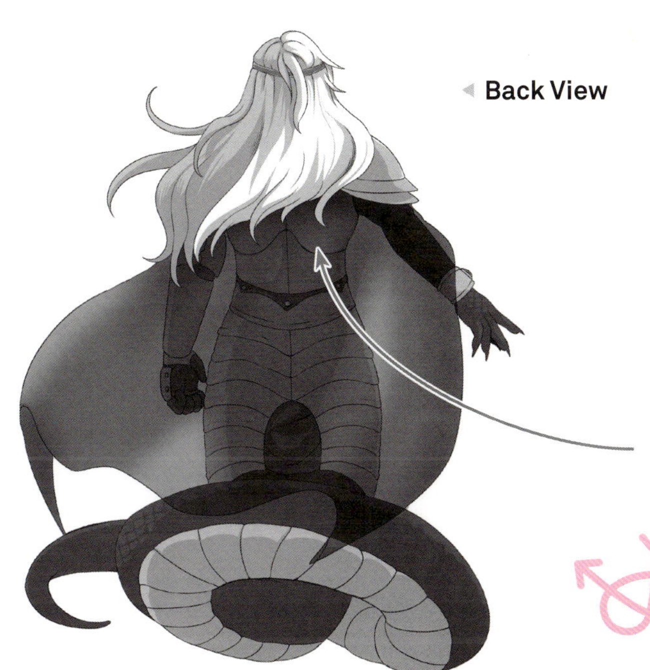

Back View

A fluttering cloak and long hair emphasize the sinuous shape of his body.

Practice this shape to master the coiled body.

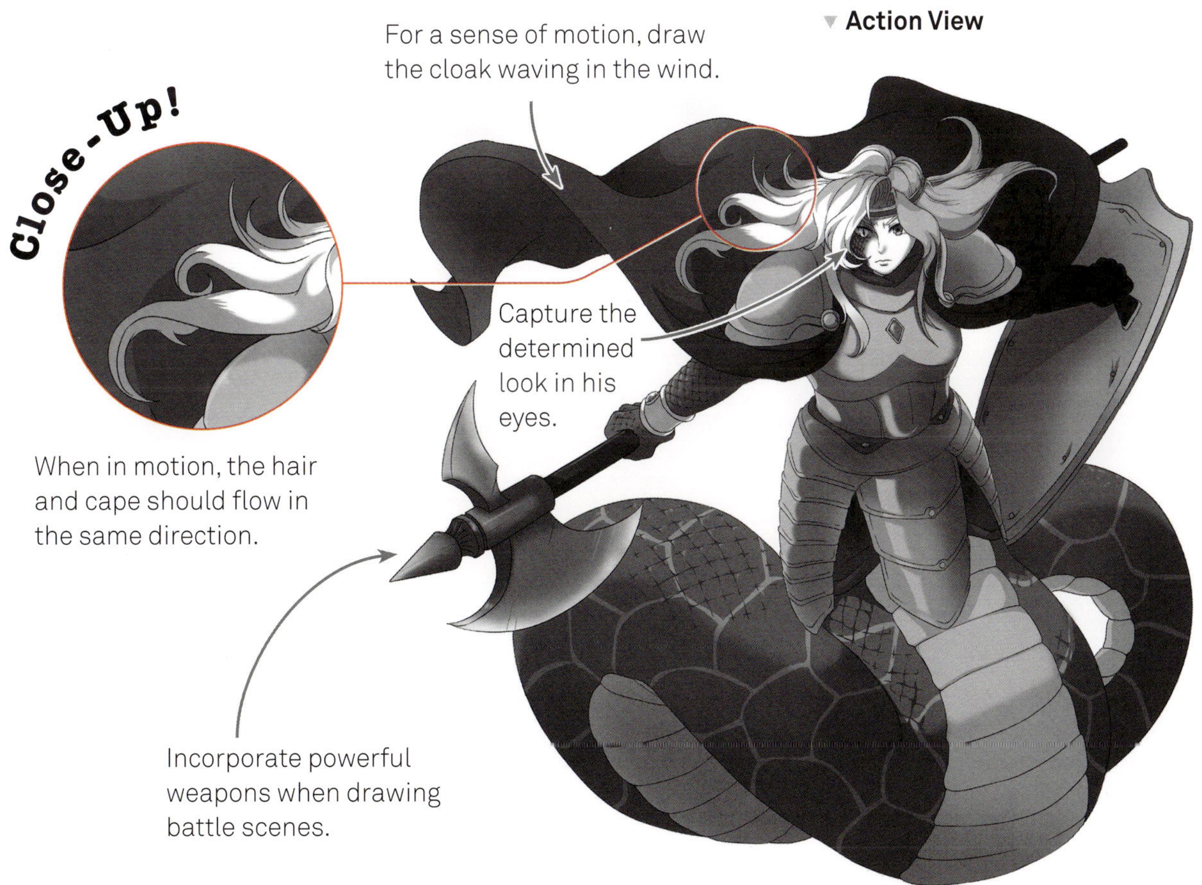

Action View

For a sense of motion, draw the cloak waving in the wind.

Capture the determined look in his eyes.

When in motion, the hair and cape should flow in the same direction.

Incorporate powerful weapons when drawing battle scenes.

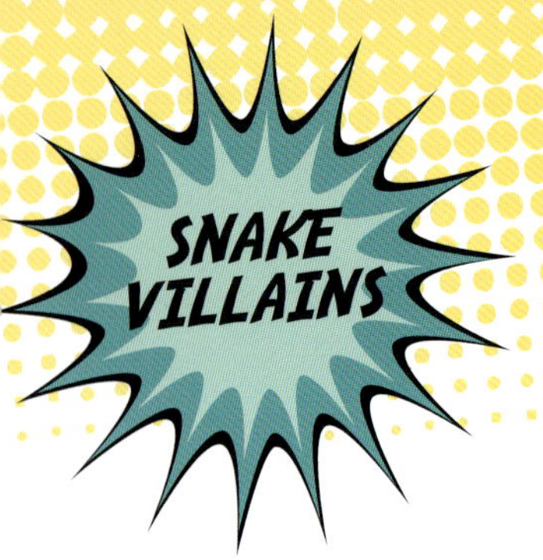

The Conniving Cutie

This creepy/cute snake girl is modeled after a *miko*, a traditional Japanese shrine attendant. She might look sweet, but she can be quite a mischievous little imp!

▼ **Front View**

Incorporate elements of traditional Japanese culture, including Heian era painted eyebrows and hair decorations.

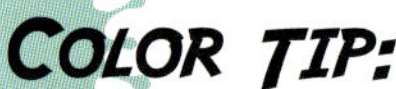

Use yellow to create eyes reminiscent of a snake.

Tiny fangs visible at the corners of the mouth

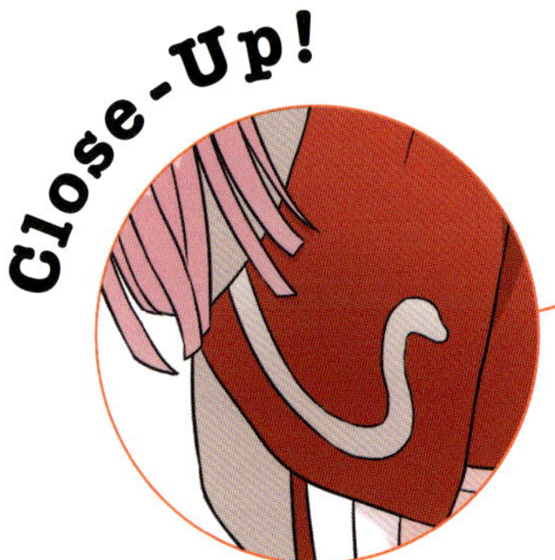

Incorporate a serpentine design into her dress.

Her body is coiled, indicating that she's ready to strike at any time.

COLOR TIP:

The pink and white color scheme creates a sweet and innocent first impression, while the red accents hint at her wild side.

VILLAINOUS TRAITS

1. Greedy
2. Immature
3. Sharp fangs

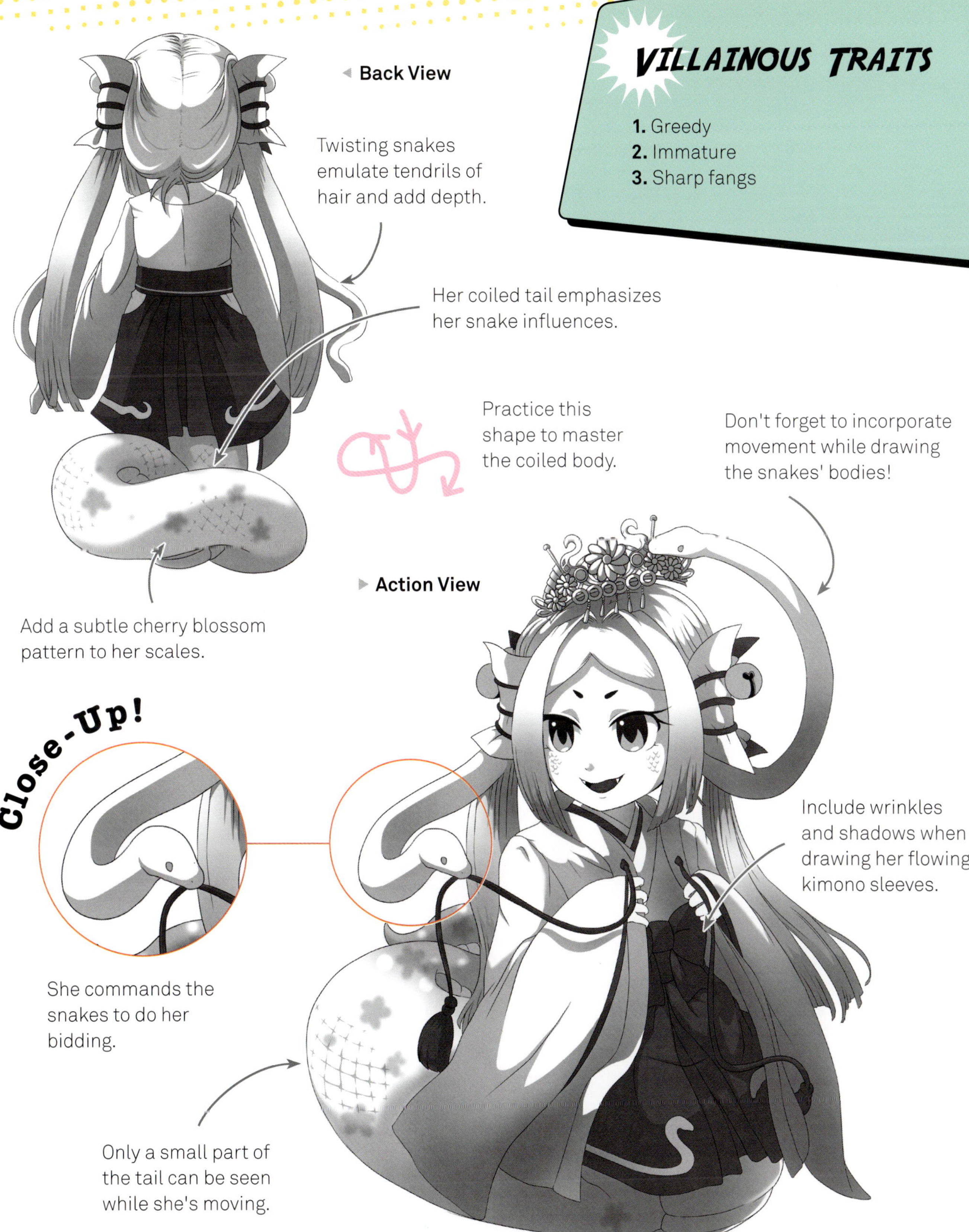

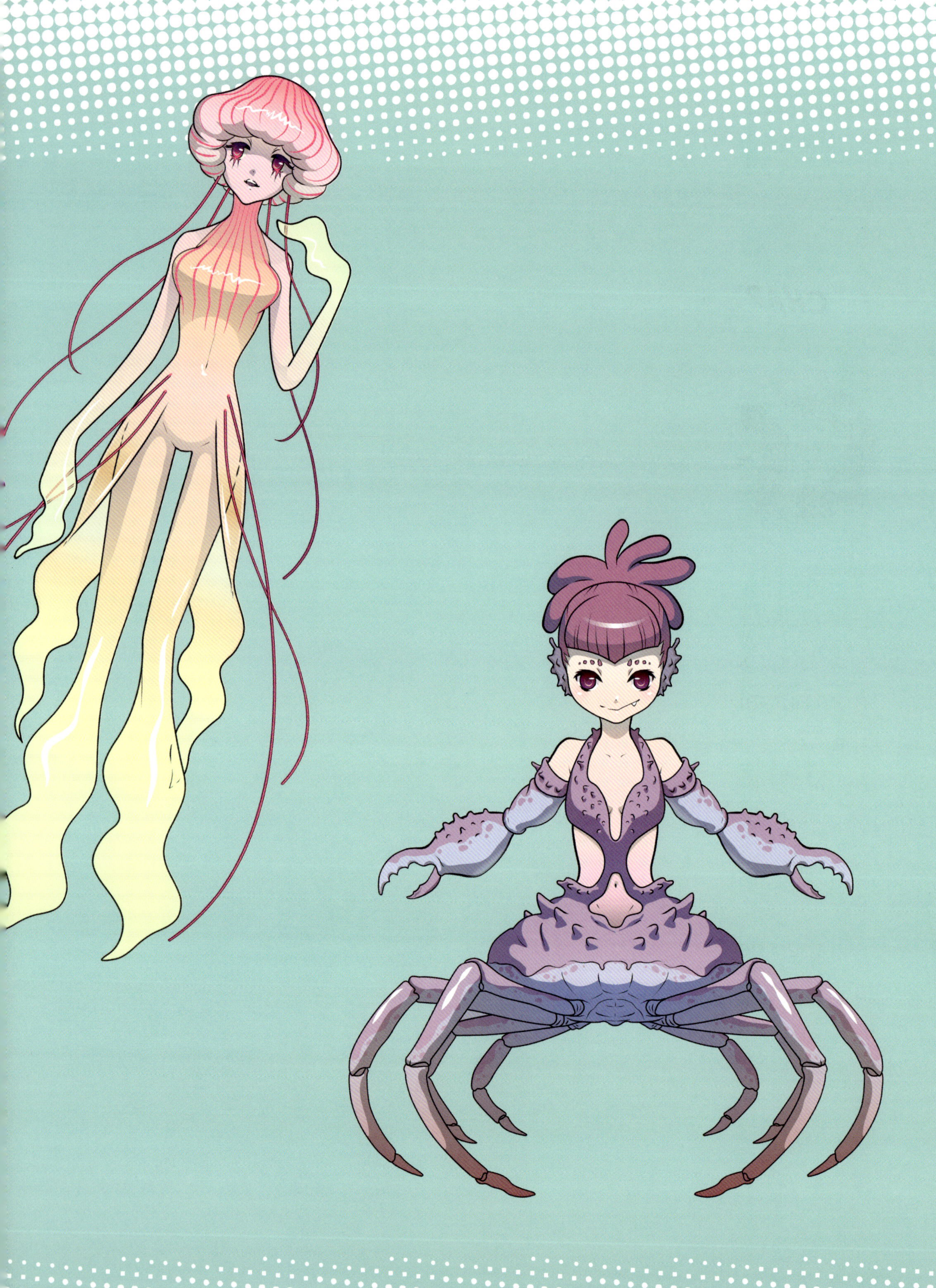

CHAPTER 2

Sea Creatures

Sea creatures possess such a distinct body structure from humans, making them a wonderful source of inspiration for non-human villains. When drawing these characters, it's important to consider the setting. How will their bodies navigate the underwater world?

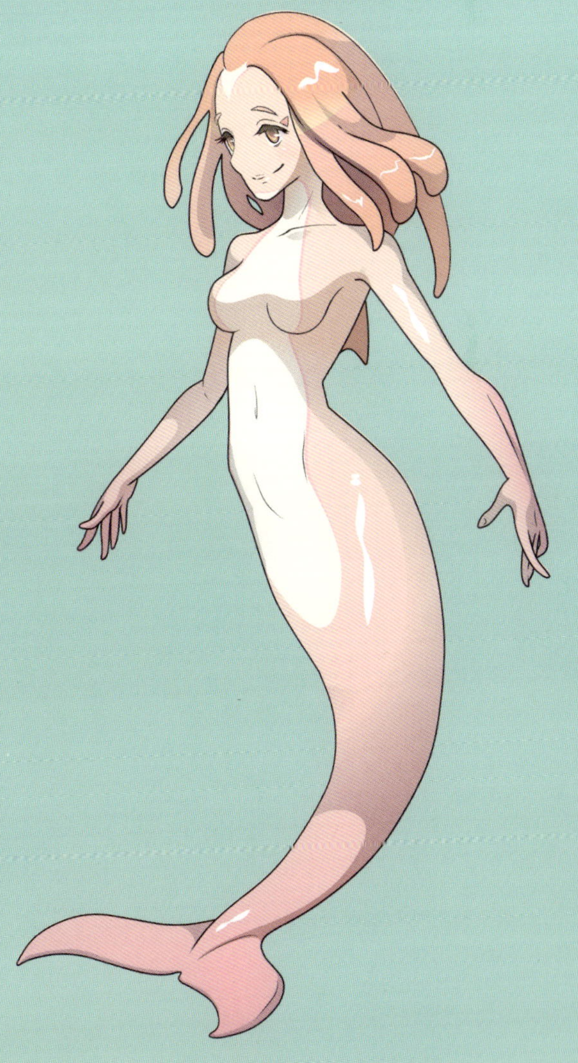

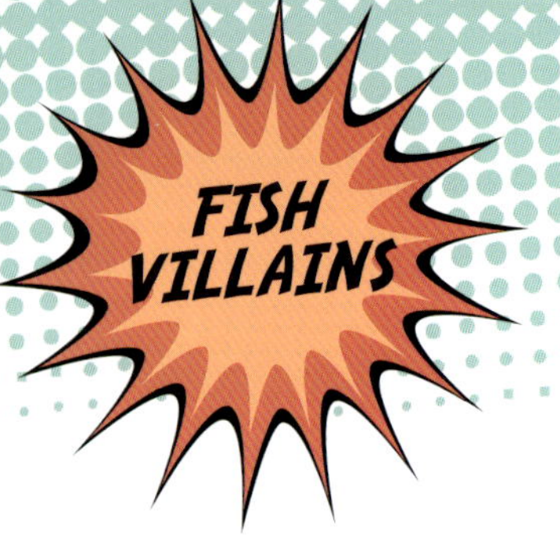

The Scorpion Fish

This dominant predator has very few rivals in his underwater habitat. He relies on his expert camouflage abilities to ambush unsuspecting prey, then uses his sharp, venomous spines to stun and paralyze his enemies.

Front View

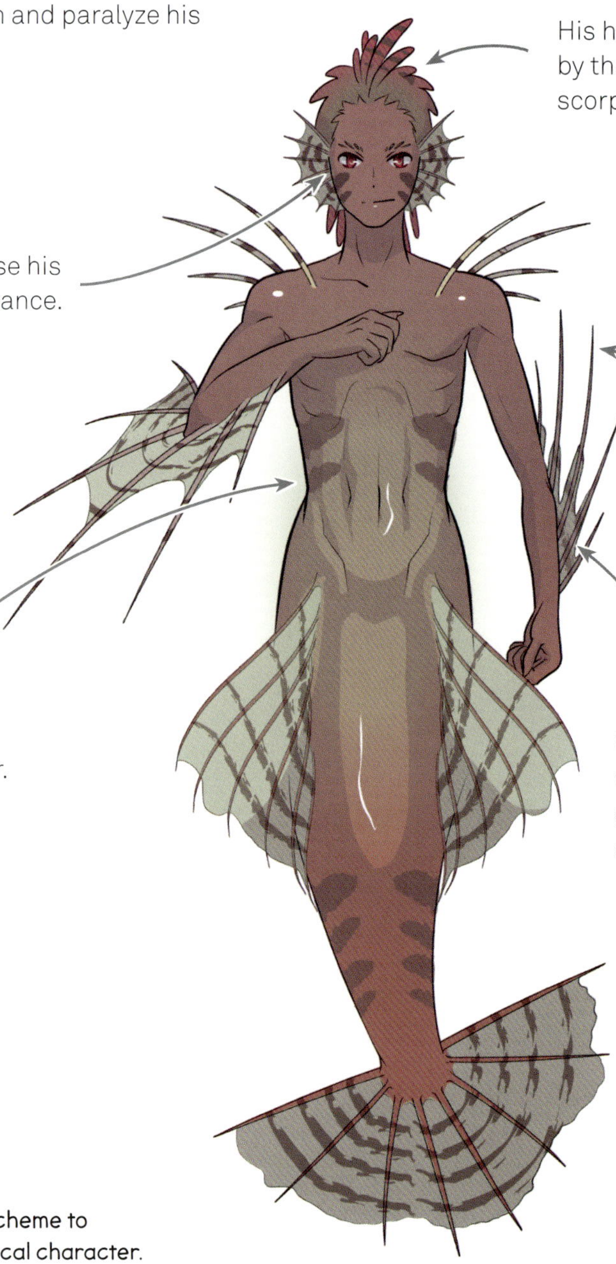

His hairstyle is inspired by the characteristic scorpion fish fins.

Red eyes increase his demonic appearance.

Sharp, poisonous fins

Athletic, muscular body indicates a powerful character.

When drawing the webbing, include sharp, boney spines.

COLOR TIP:

Use a reddish brown color scheme to suggest a dangerous, diabolical character.

VILLAINOUS TRAITS

1. Master of camouflage
2. Sharp, venomous spines
3. Conceited

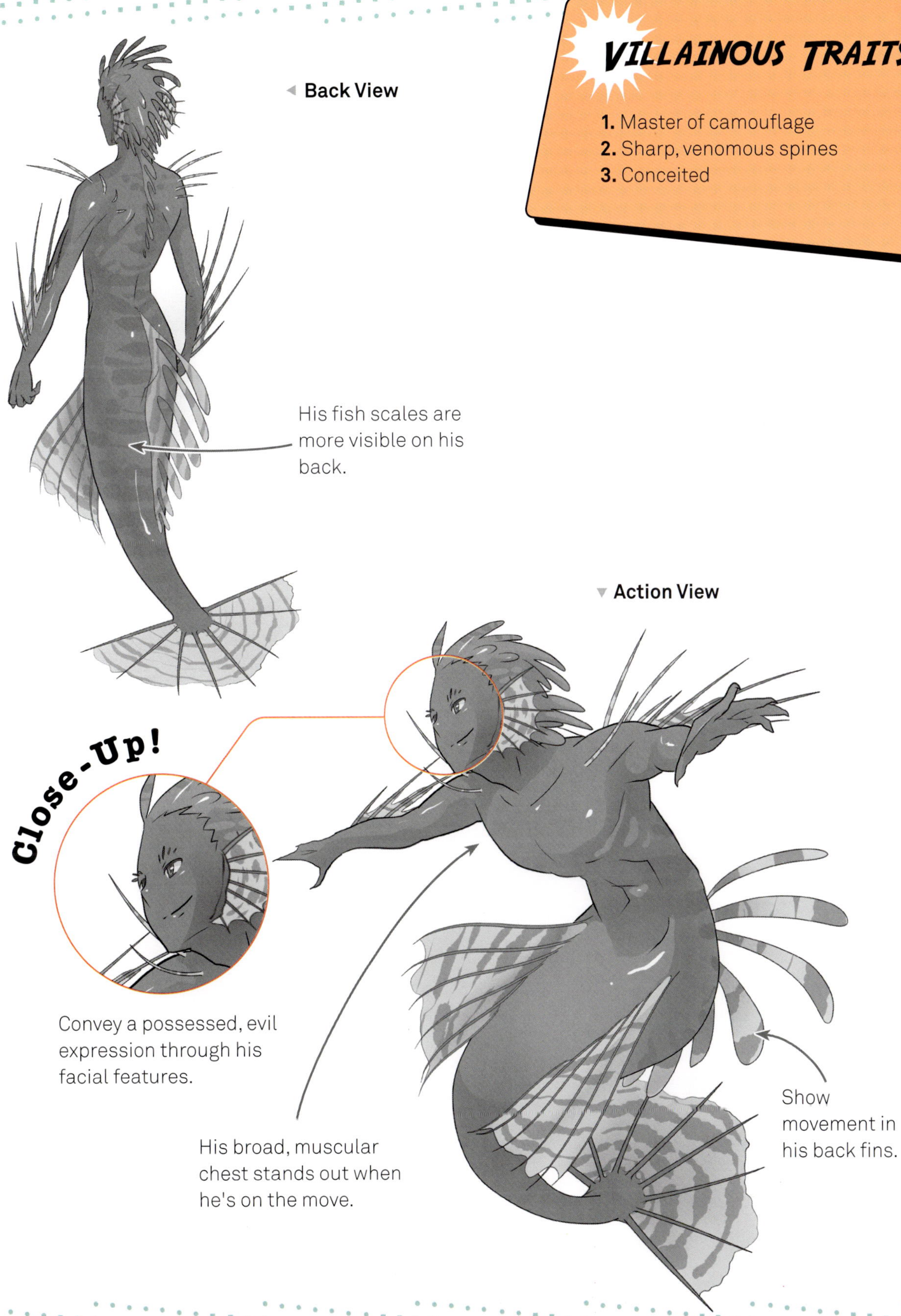

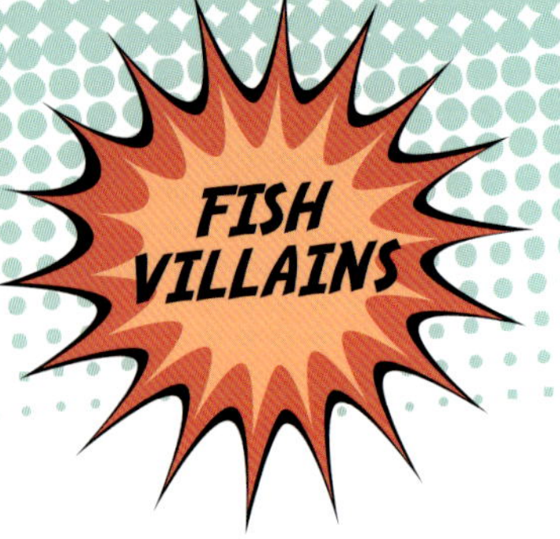

The Sea Sorceress

This bewitching beauty is a cross between an alluring mermaid and a dangerous scorpion fish. She possesses powerful abilities, including water manipulation and clairvoyance, which allow her to exert great control over her enemies.

▼ **Front View**

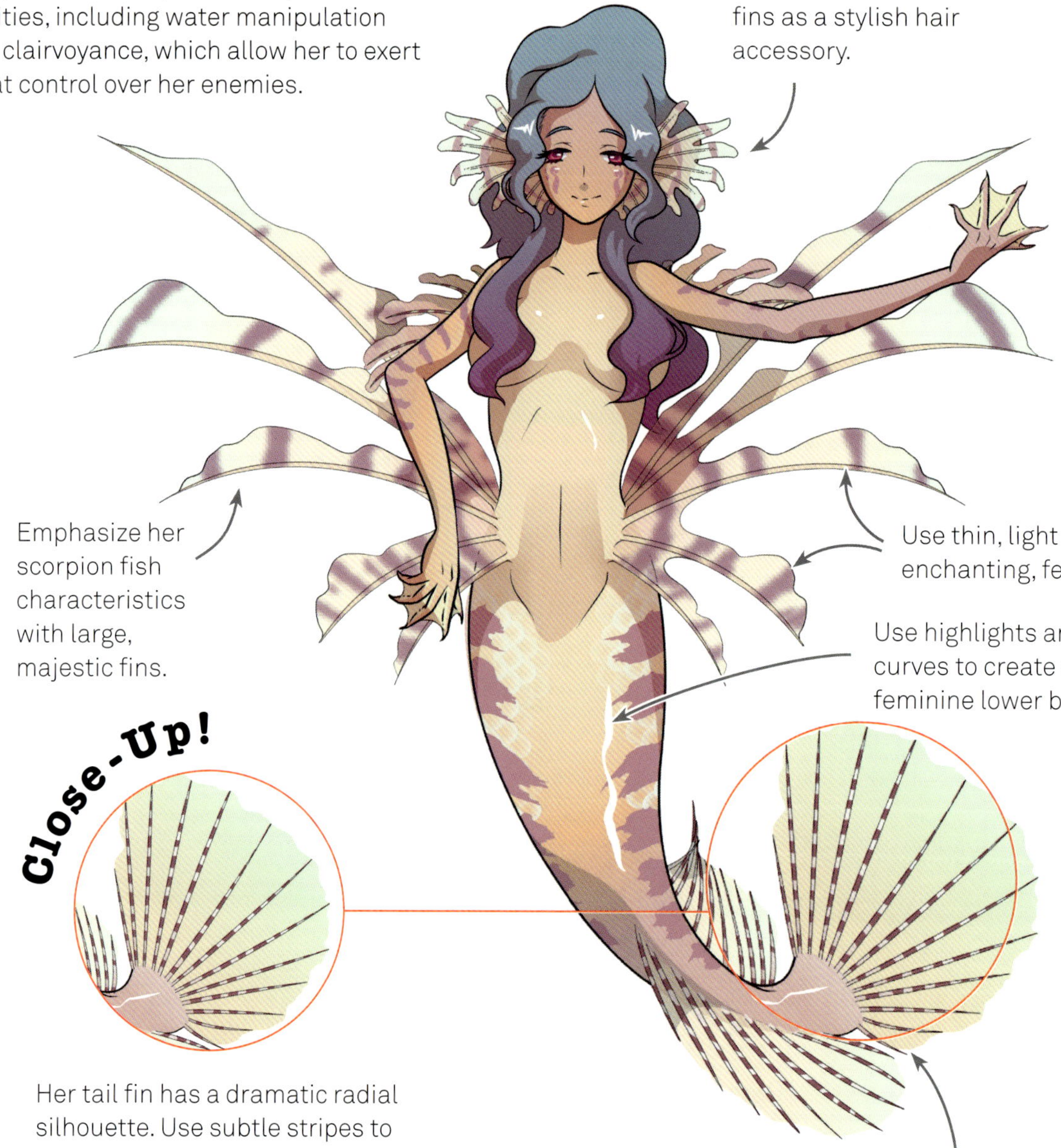

She wears her facial fins as a stylish hair accessory.

Emphasize her scorpion fish characteristics with large, majestic fins.

Use thin, light lines for an enchanting, feminine effect.

Use highlights and curves to create a feminine lower body.

Close-Up!

Her tail fin has a dramatic radial silhouette. Use subtle stripes to add interest to the bones.

Large, round tail fin

Color Tip:

Pastel hues create a feminine aura, while mysterious purple accents intimate her poisonous scorpion fish influences.

VILLAINOUS TRAITS

1. Water manipulation
2. Clairvoyance
3. Toxic poison reserves

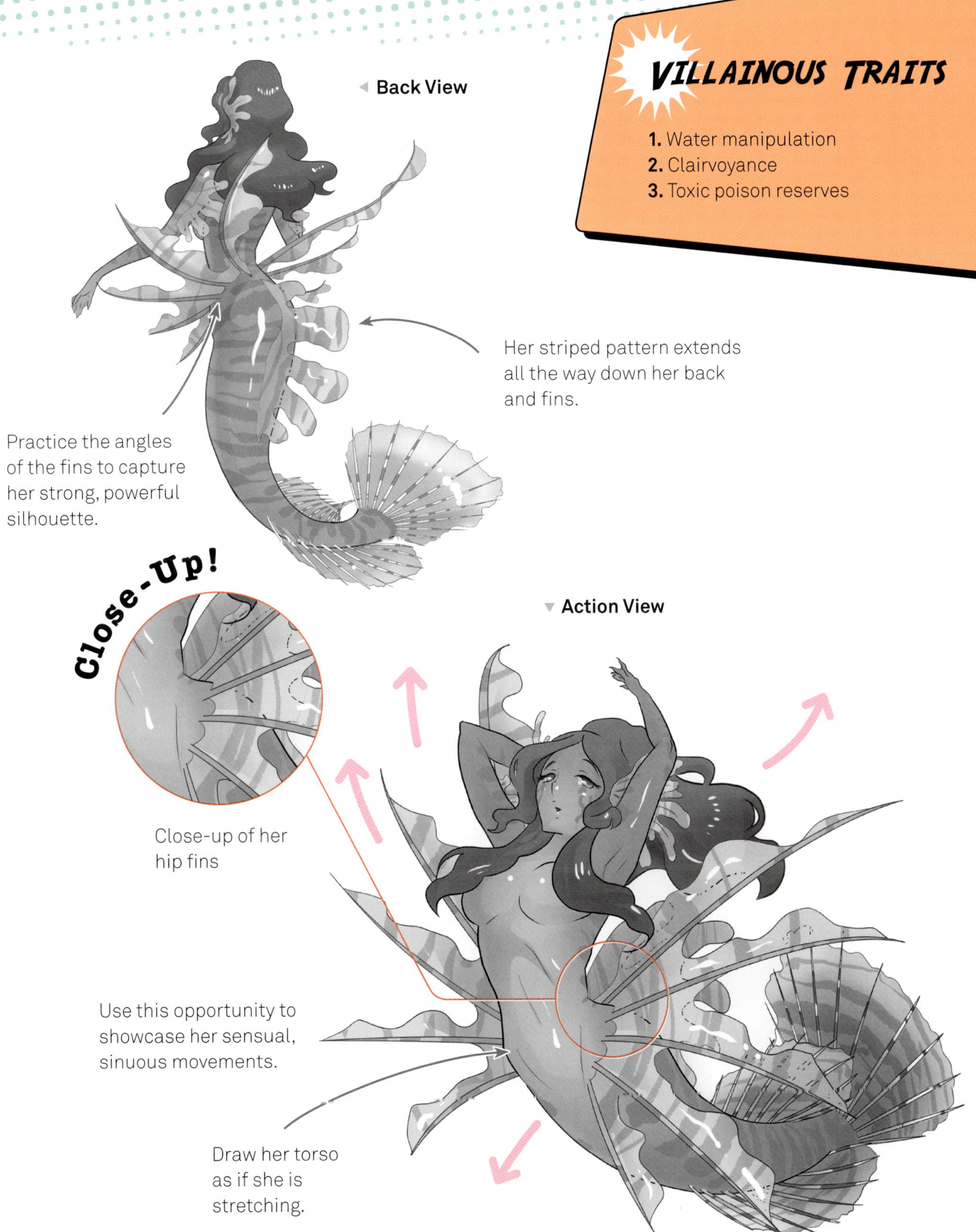

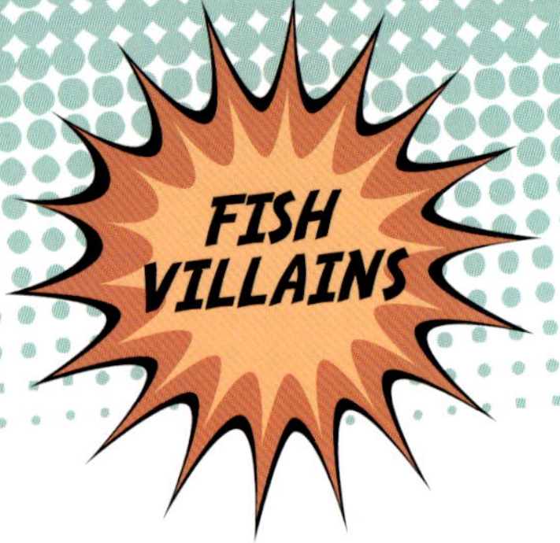

The Little Devil

Careful, this imp can be quite a little pest! Depending on his mood, he can range from a mere annoyance to the bane of your existence. He has an unsatiable appetite, short attention span, and a high-pitched obnoxious voice.

▼ **Front View**

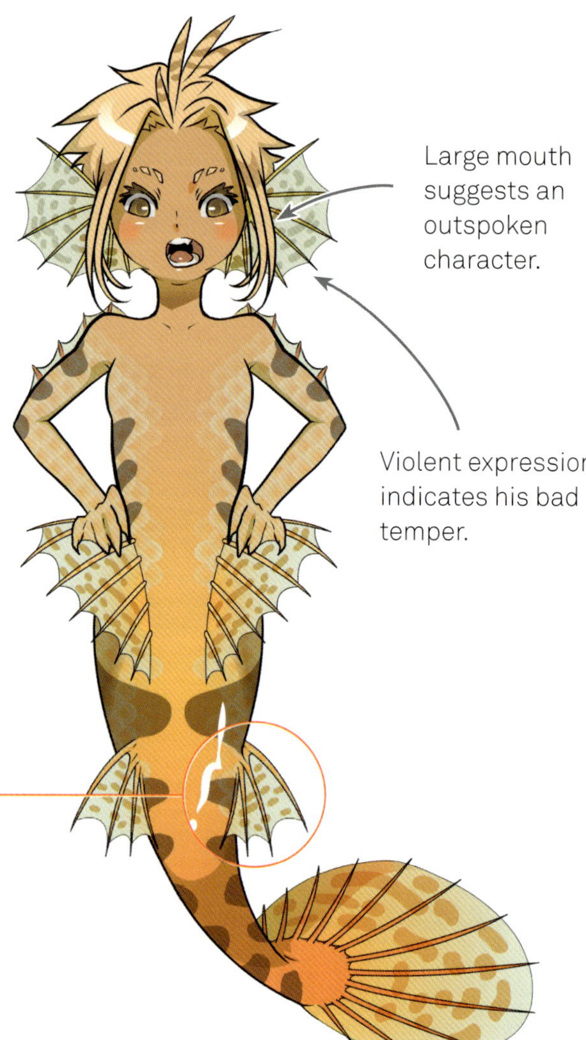

Large mouth suggests an outspoken character.

Violent expression indicates his bad temper.

Draw realistic scales for a creepy, primordial effect.

Close-Up!

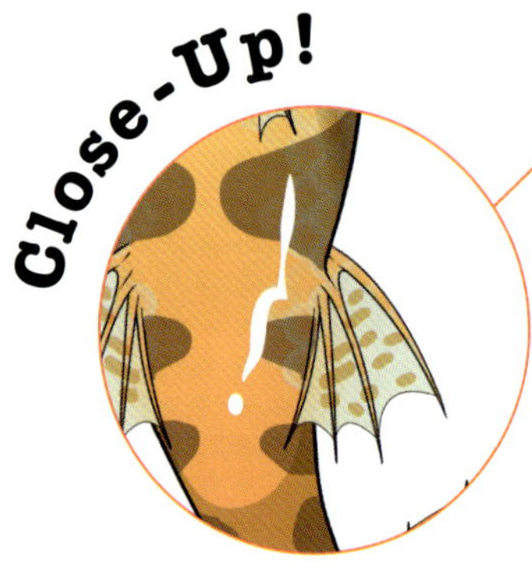

Draw sharp, angular fins for a menacing, intimidating look.

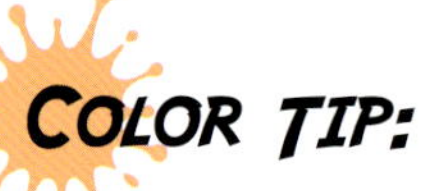

Use a warm color palette to emphasize his explosive temper.

VILLAINOUS TRAITS

1. Volatile
2. Unforgiving
3. Overconfident

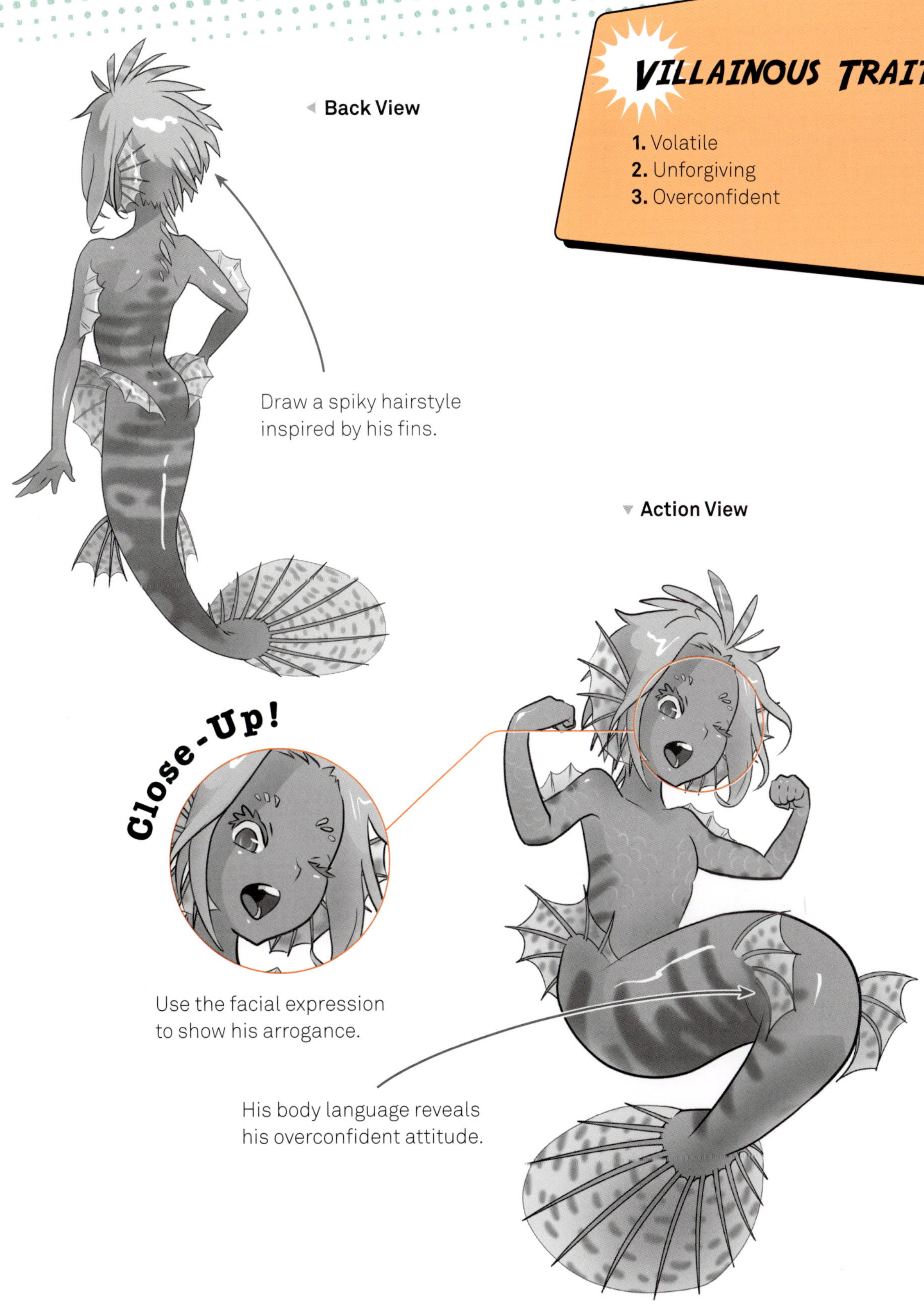

Jellyfish Villains
The Underwater Alien

This eerie deep sea being possesses mystical healing powers. In addition to being immortal, he has the capability to clone himself. He uses his massive gelatinous umbrella to trap his victims.

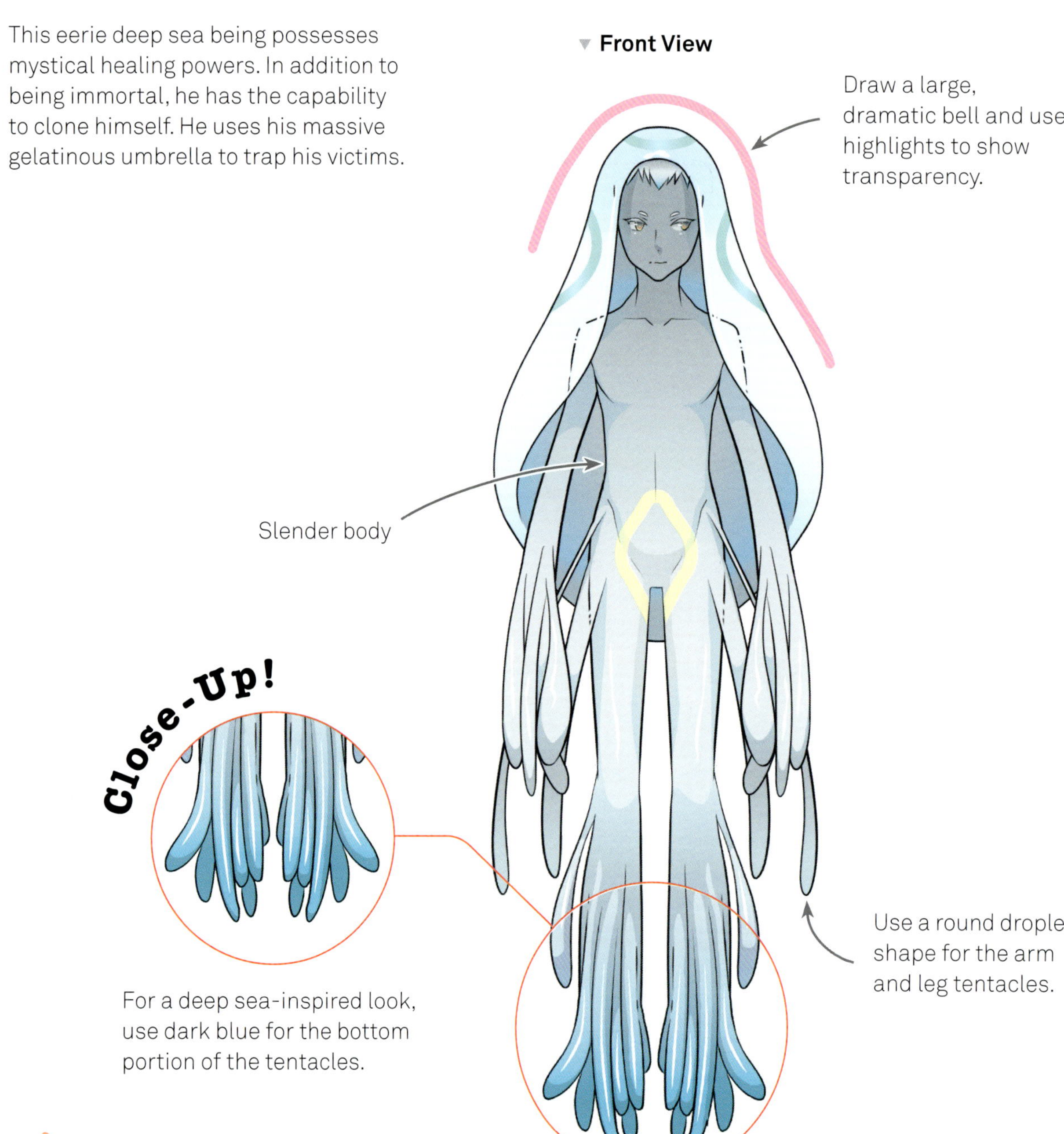

Color Tip:

Use a gradated gray/blue color scheme, starting from the center and working outward. The striking yellow accent, which is the source of his immortality, serves as a focal point.

VILLAINOUS TRAITS

1. Immortality
2. Cloning capabilities
3. Healing powers

◄ Back View

Draw a transparent, gelatinous umbrella so large that it covers half of the body.

▼ Action View

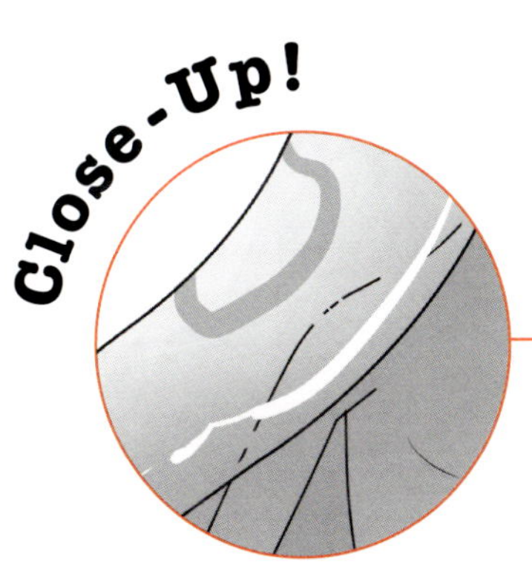

Use highlights to emphasize the transparent, mucilaginous texture.

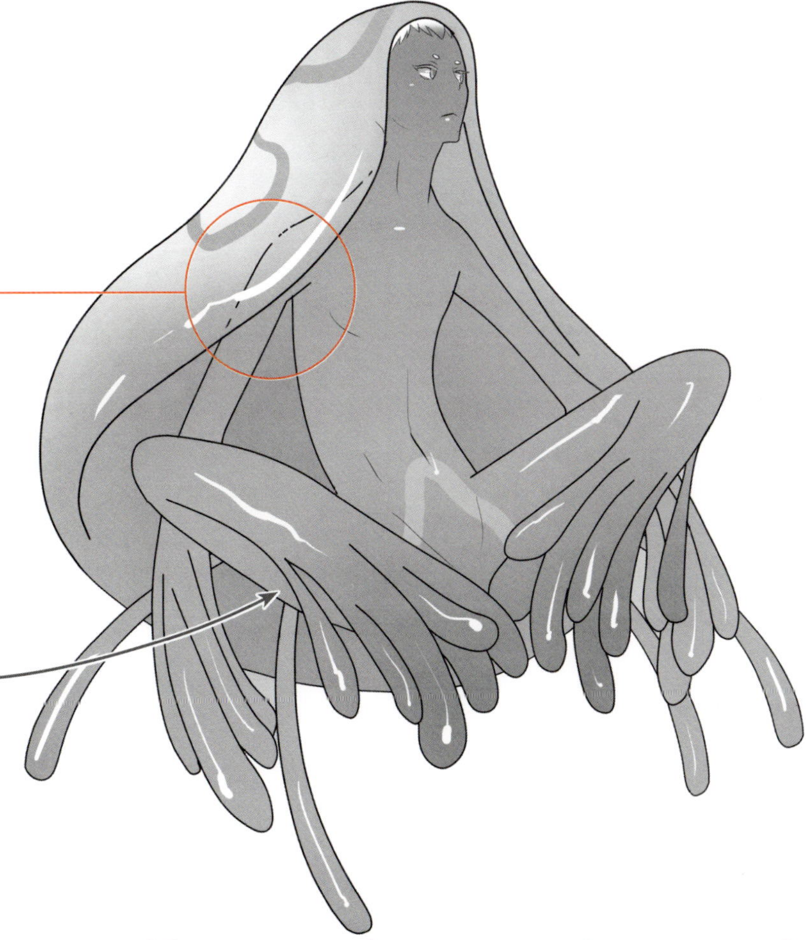

His viscous body composition allows for great flexibility.

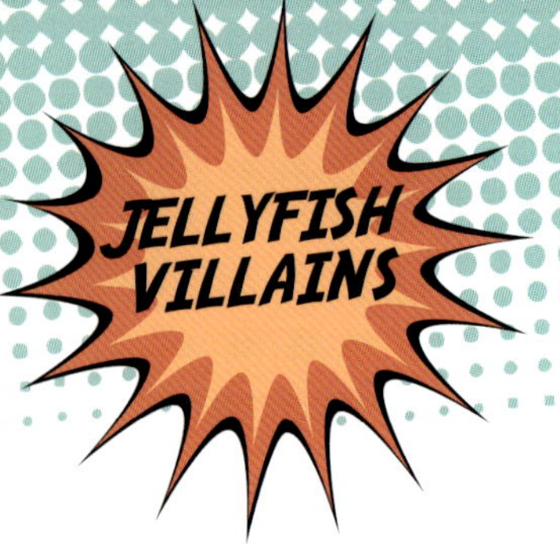

The Tentacled Telepathist

This otherworldly creature possesses extraordinary mental and physical powers. She uses telepathy to anticipate her enemies' next moves, then employs her toxic tentacles to sting them into submission. She can also change colors to blend in with her surroundings.

▼ **Front View**

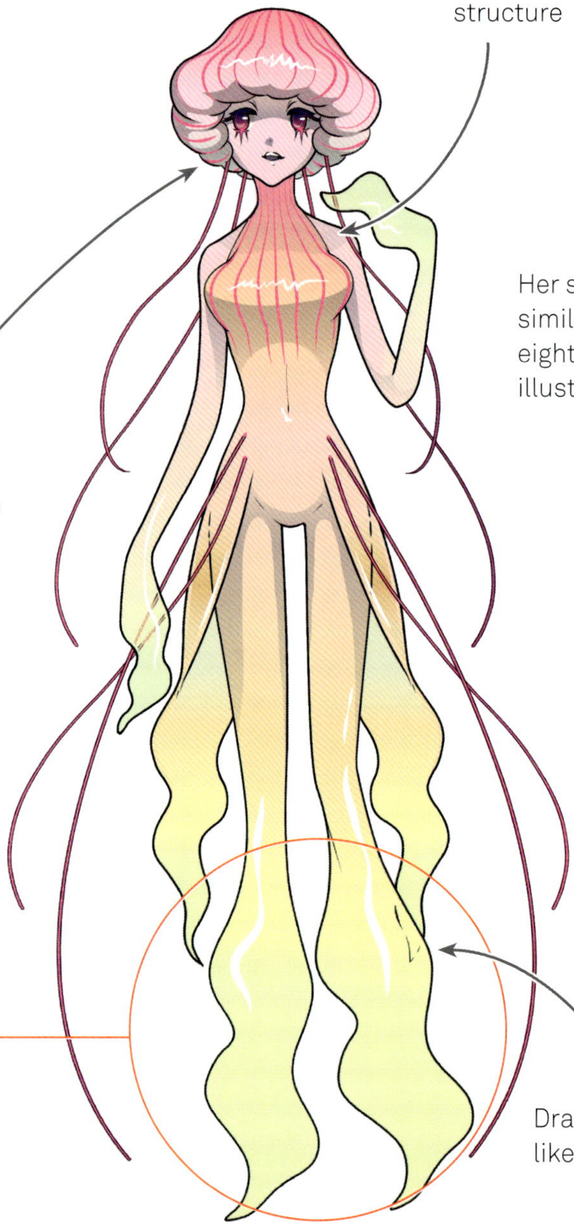

Vein-like internal structure

Her slender body is similar to a traditional eight head fashion illustration figure.

For the classic jellyfish look, include an umbrella-shaped "bell" and long, trailing tentacles.

Draw large feet-like tentacles.

Close-Up!

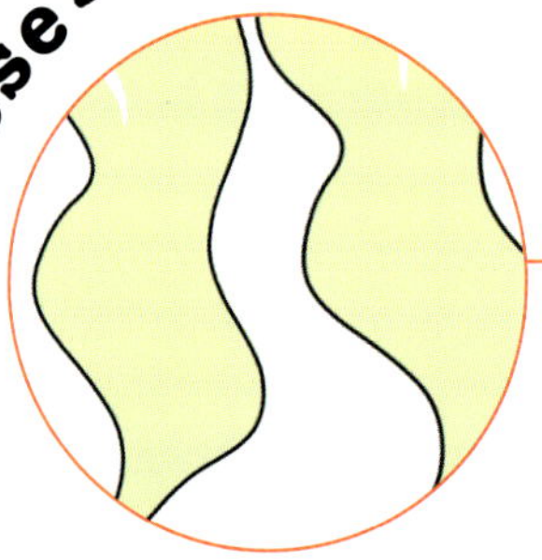

Use a wavy shape for the feet, which allow her to float through the ocean.

COLOR TIP:

Use an ombré effect to capture the transparent, yet colorful nature of jellyfish.

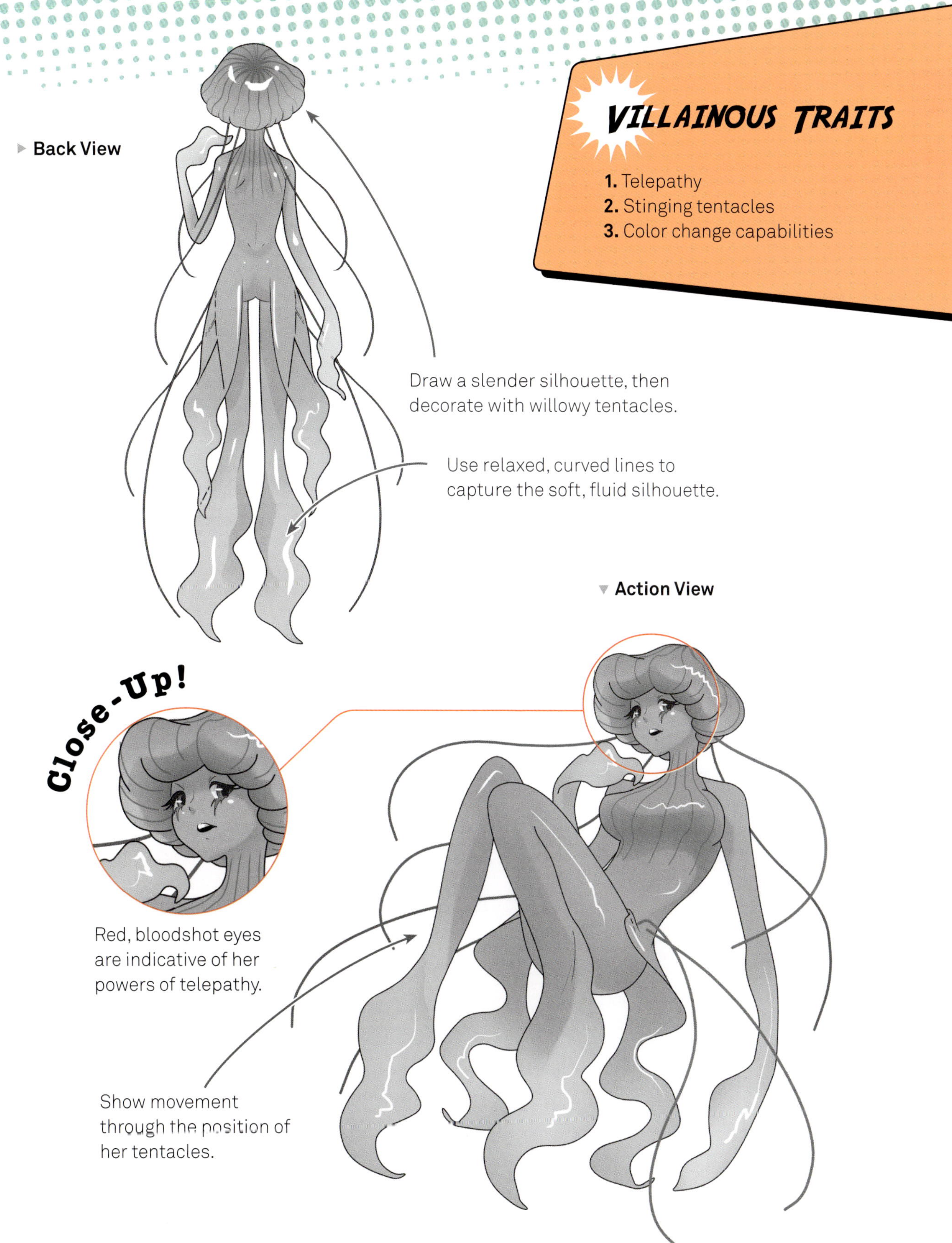

VILLAINOUS TRAITS

1. Telepathy
2. Stinging tentacles
3. Color change capabilities

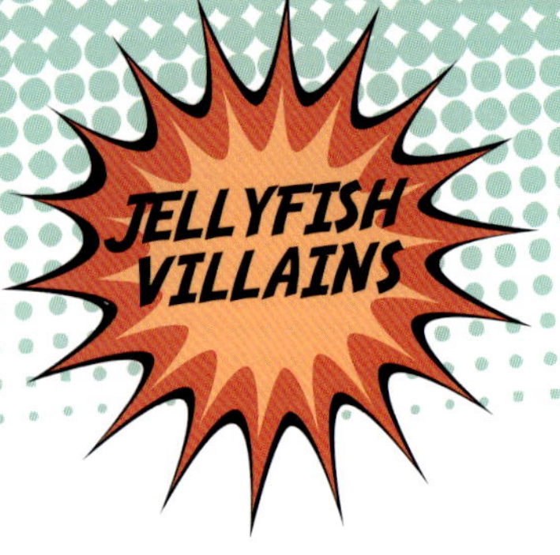

The Chosen One

This child prodigy possesses incomparable supernatural abilities. As a result, others travel the world to receive readings and advice from her. Because she is able to communicate with the dead, she's occasionally pulled over to the dark side and forced to carry out their wishes.

▼ **Front View**

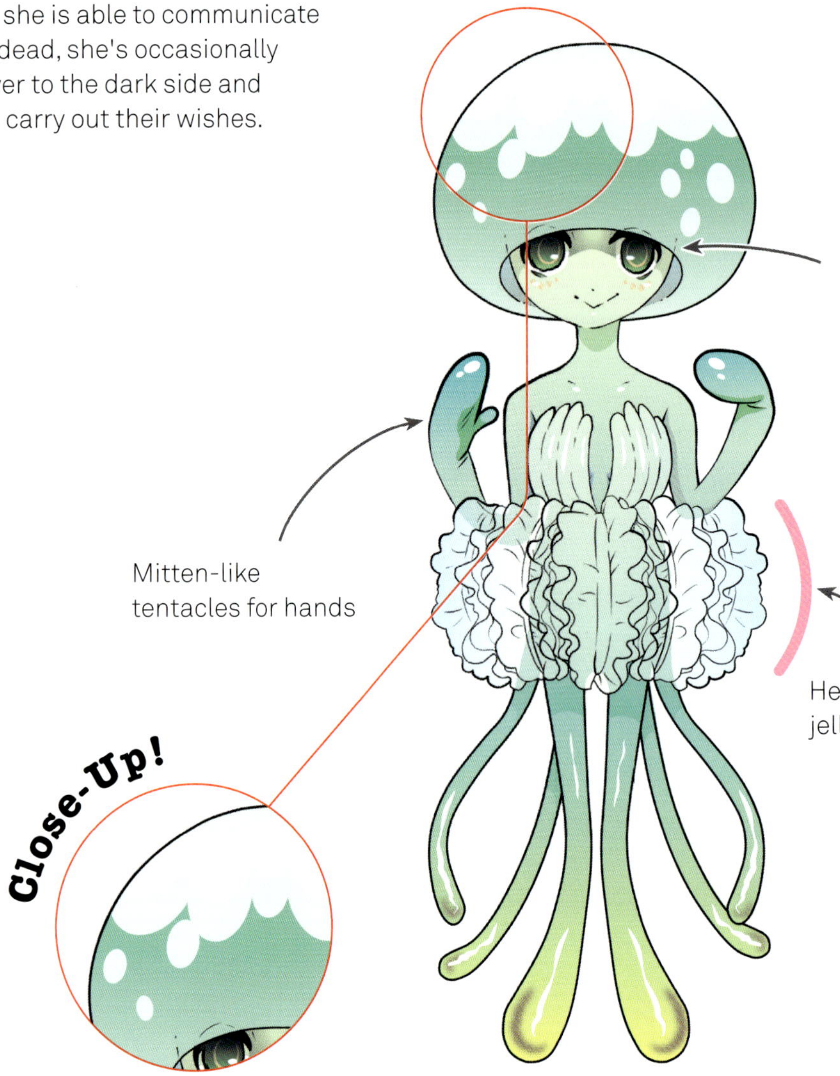

Her large, haunted eyes are a physical manifestation of her powerful psychic abilities.

Mitten-like tentacles for hands

Her skirt features jellyfish-style folds.

Close-Up!

Her large, glowing head serves as the receptor for her psychic visions.

Color Tip:

The ombré yellow, green and blue color scheme casts a mystical impression.

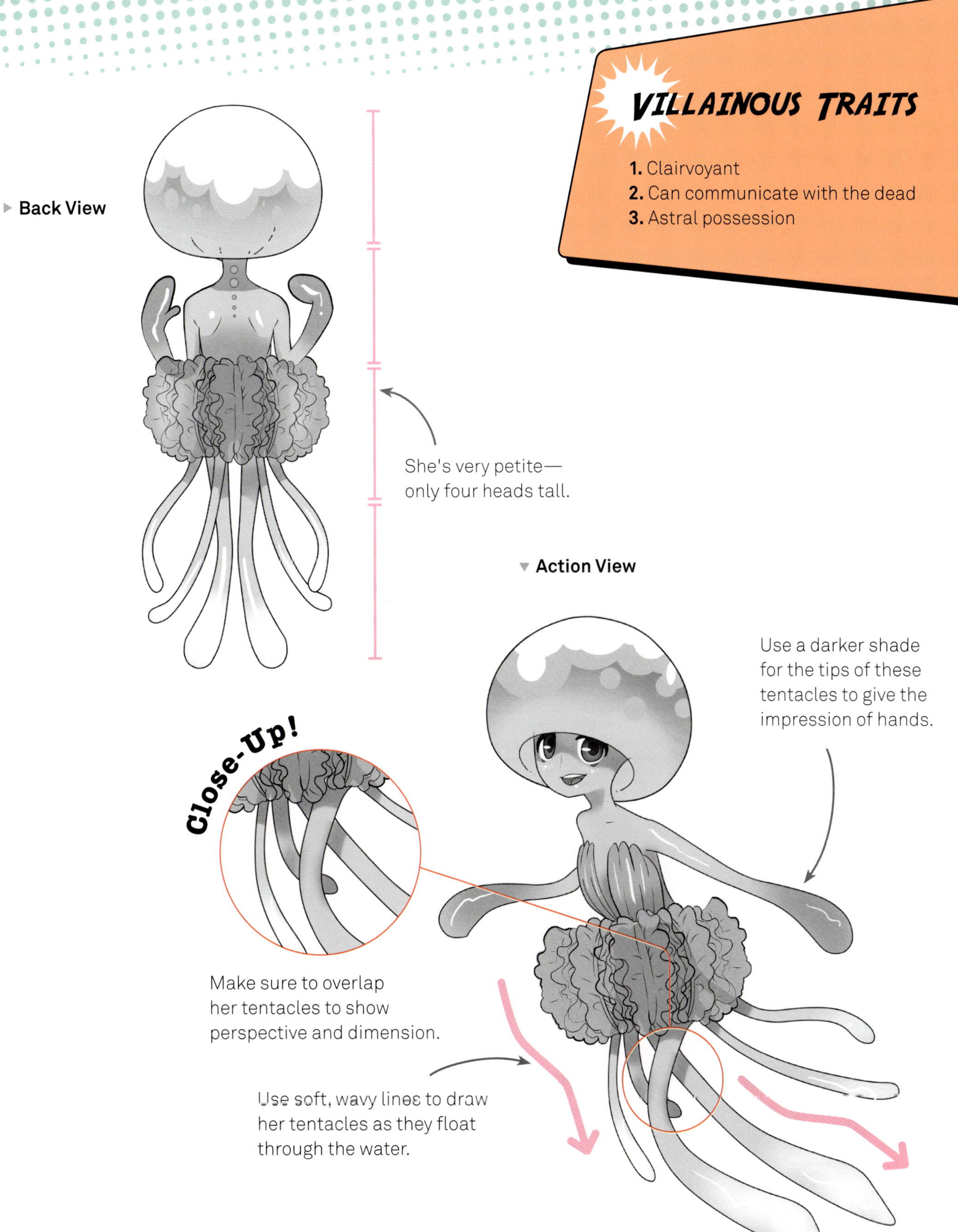
VILLAINOUS TRAITS
1. Clairvoyant
2. Can communicate with the dead
3. Astral possession
Back View
She's very petite—
only four heads tall.
Action View
Use a darker shade
for the tips of these
tentacles to give the
impression of hands.
Close-Up!
Make sure to overlap
her tentacles to show
perspective and dimension.
Use soft, wavy lines to draw
her tentacles as they float
through the water.

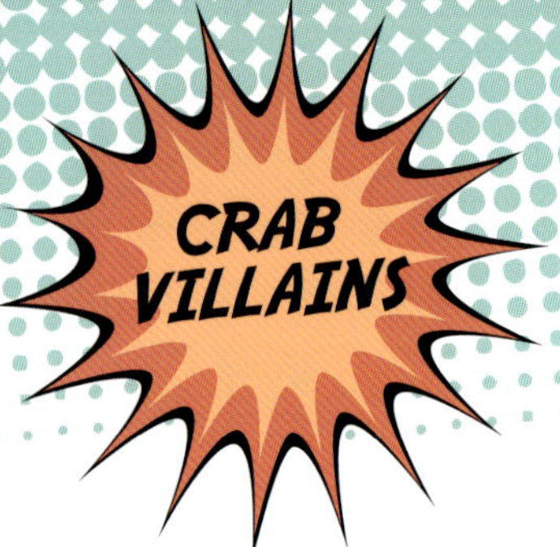

The Crusading Crustacean

This powerful crusader is one of the toughest villains in the underwater realm. His impenetrable shell and his inability to feel pain make him nearly impossible to defeat.

▼ **Front View**

COLOR TIP:

Use a dark shade for the hair, such as green or purple, to contrast with the predominantly red body.

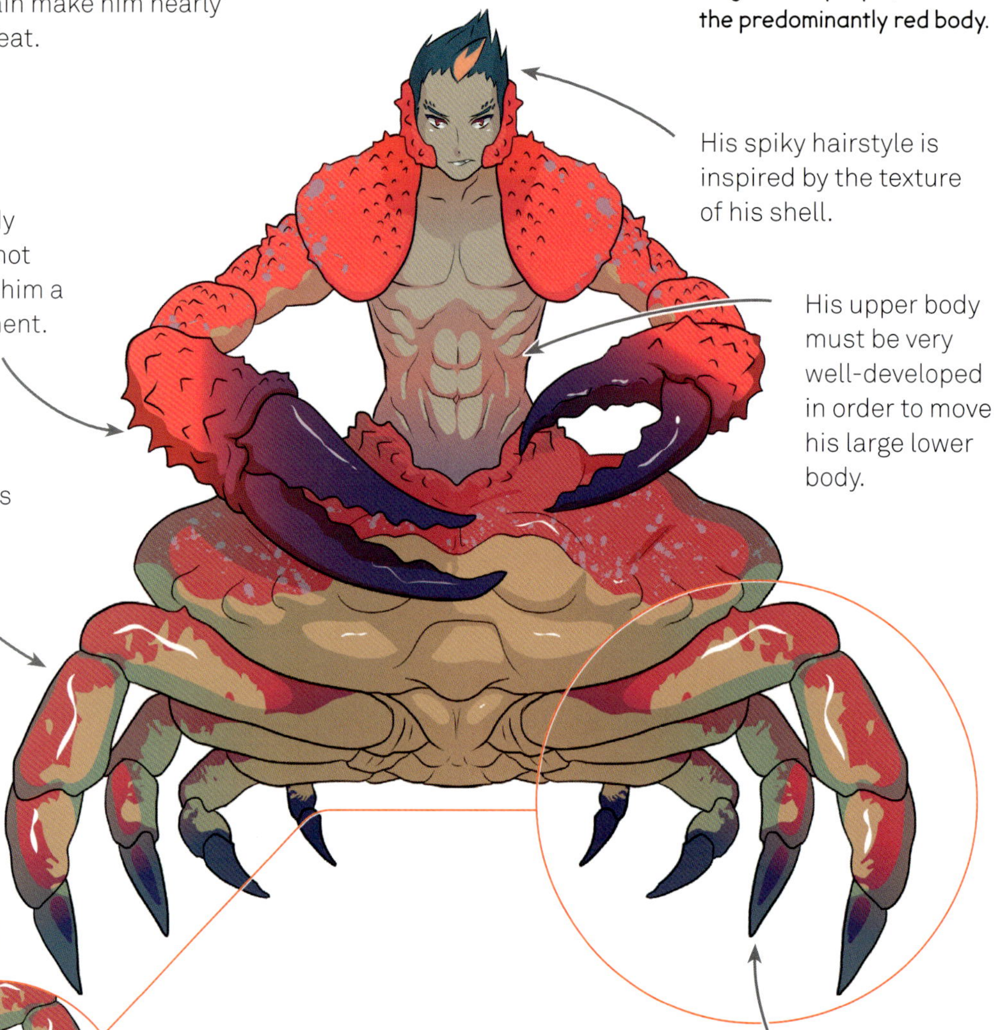

His spiky hairstyle is inspired by the texture of his shell.

His shell acts as impenetrable body armor. Crabs cannot feel pain, making him a formidable opponent.

His upper body must be very well-developed in order to move his large lower body.

Thin white highlights replicate the shiny surface of his shell.

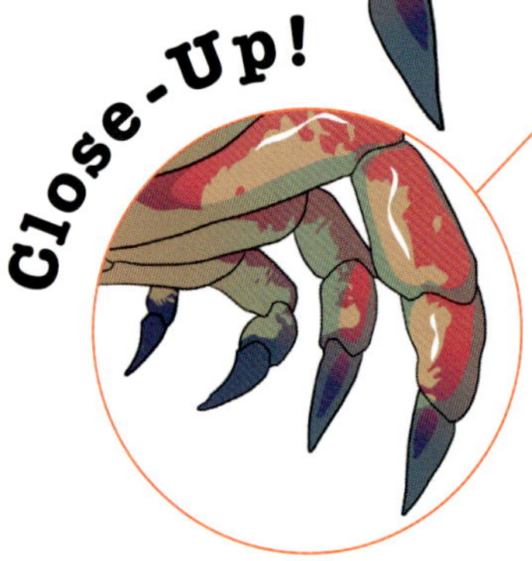

Close-Up!

Draw thick, muscular legs for a masculine look.

Add white highlights to capture the smooth, rigid texture of the shell.

COLOR TIP:

Use dark red or orange for the main color, then add gray to the tips of the legs for a realistic look.

VILLAINOUS TRAITS

1. Impenetrable shell
2. Cannot feel pain
3. Sharp pincers

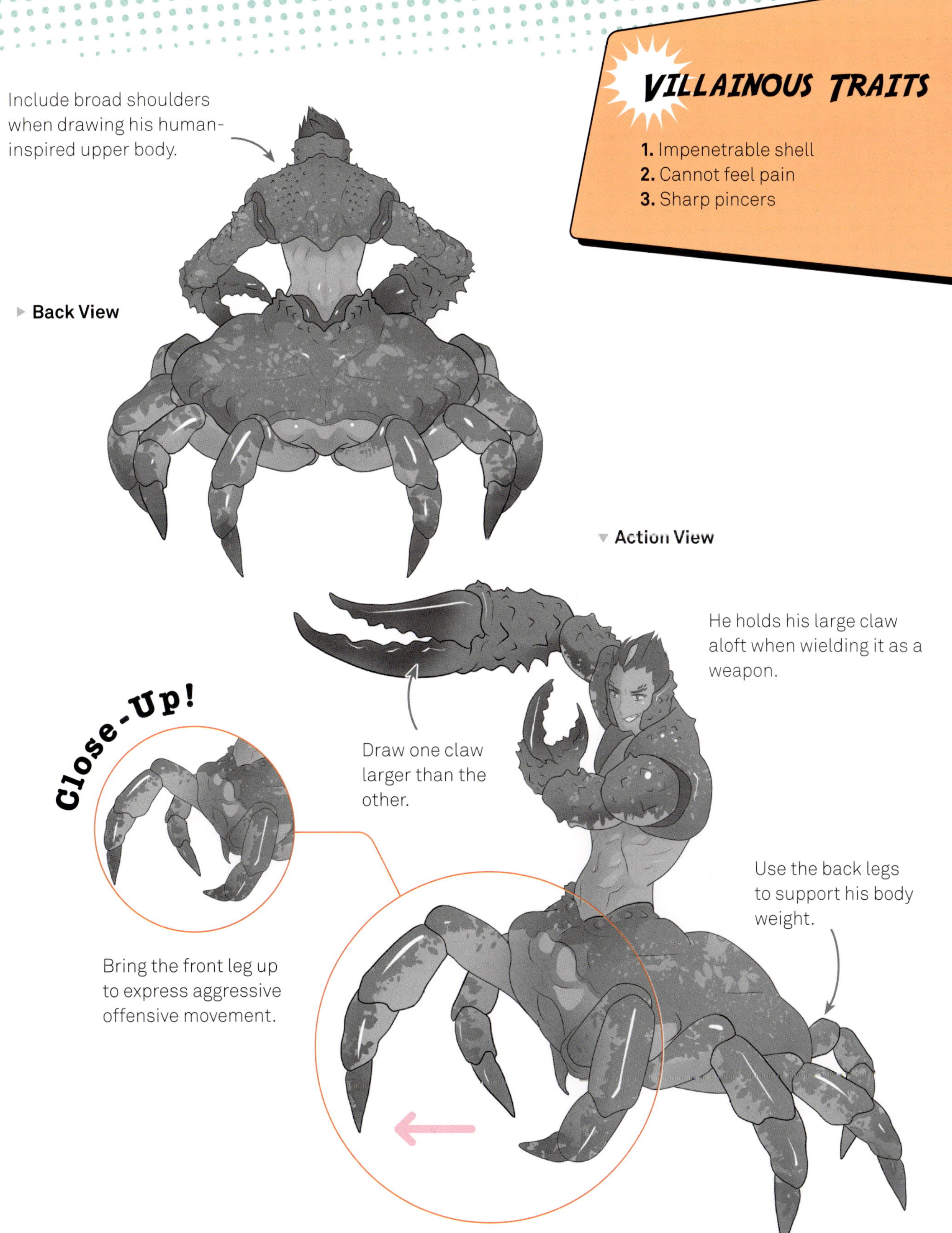

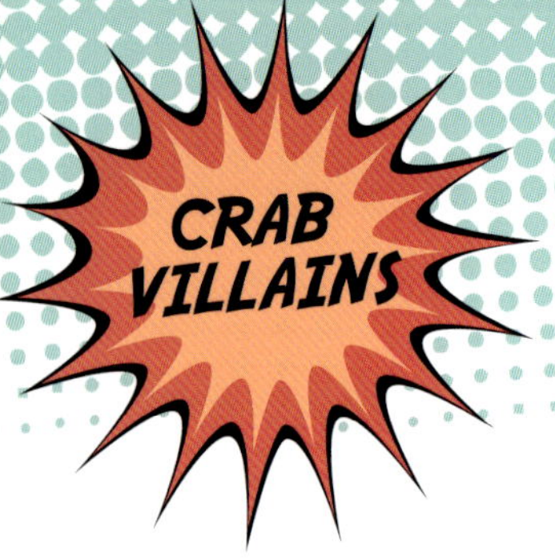

The Crab Countess

This untouchable beauty is a powerful female foe. She uses her looks to lure male victims into her grasp. Her only weakness is agoraphobia—she prefers to spend her time in narrow, cramped spaces.

▼ **Front View**

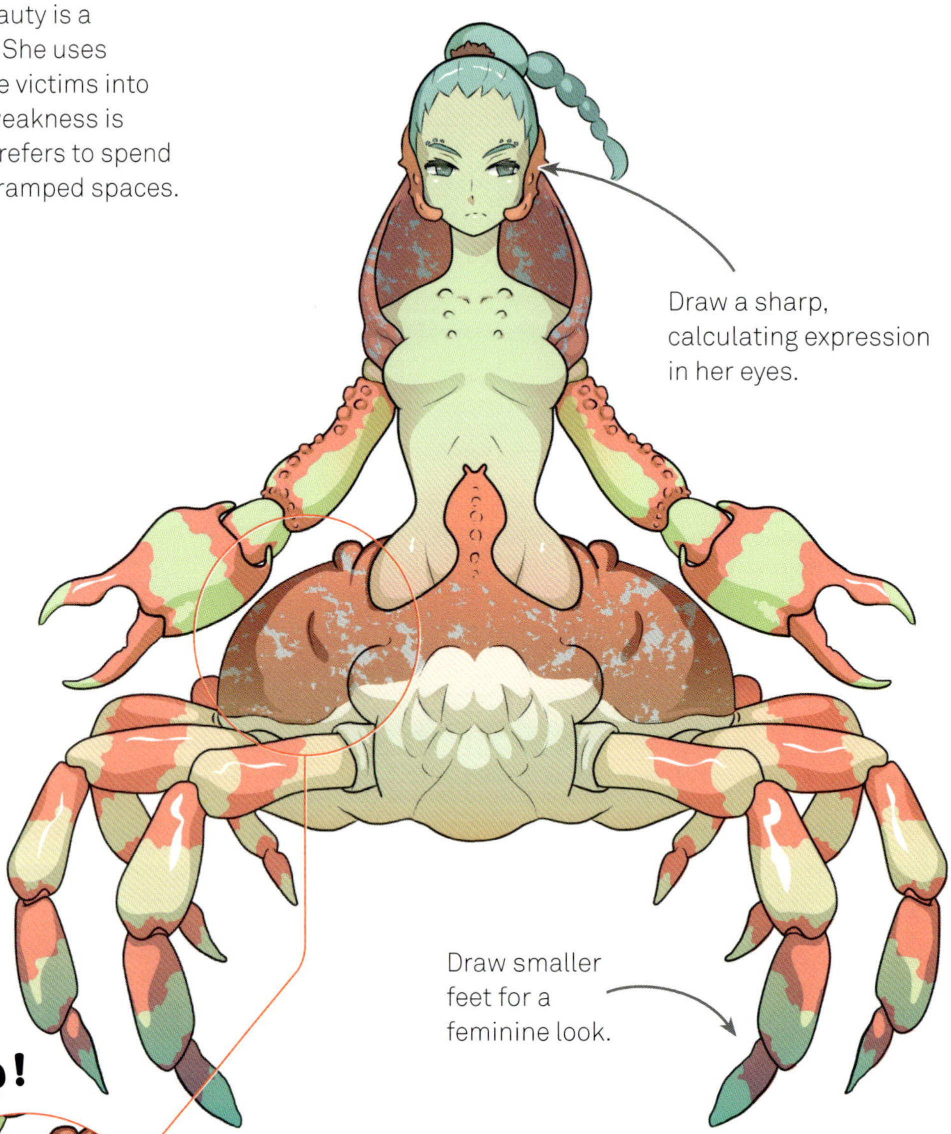

Draw a sharp, calculating expression in her eyes.

Make sure the human half of the body is in proportion to the crab half.

Draw smaller feet for a feminine look.

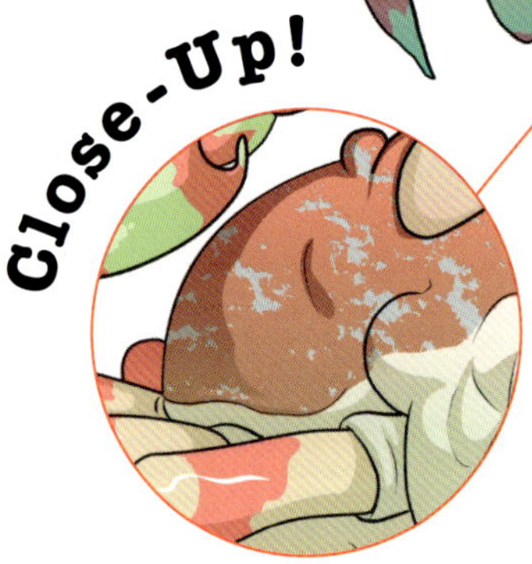

Close-Up!

Watch out ... she can walk frontwards, backwards and sideways!

Stipple an abstract camouflage pattern for a realistic-looking shell.

COLOR TIP:

Use a dark shade of orange as the main color, then add green accents throughout the shell.

VILLAINOUS TRAITS

1. Sadistic
2. Can regenerate severed limbs
3. Can move quickly in all directions

▶ Back View

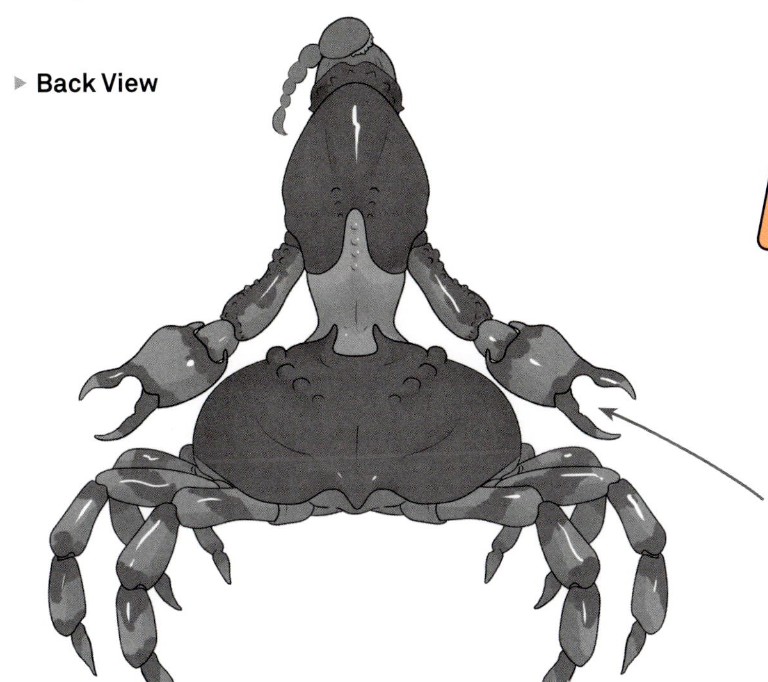

The durable shell protects her back and hips from attack. She uses her front legs as human-like arms.

Close-Up!

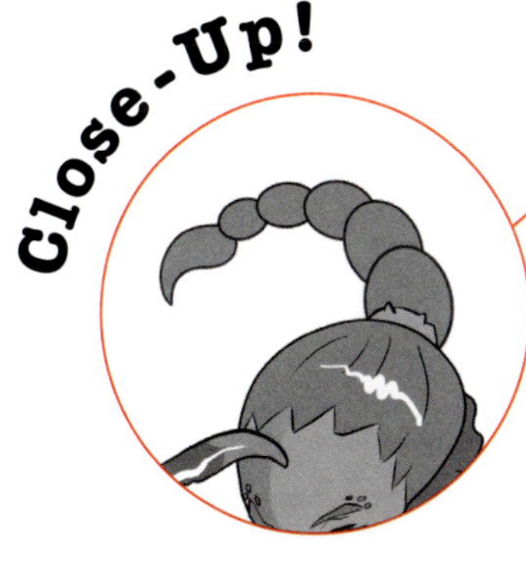

Her ponytail hairstyle is inspired by a scorpion's stinger. Her hair will swing as she moves.

▼ Action View

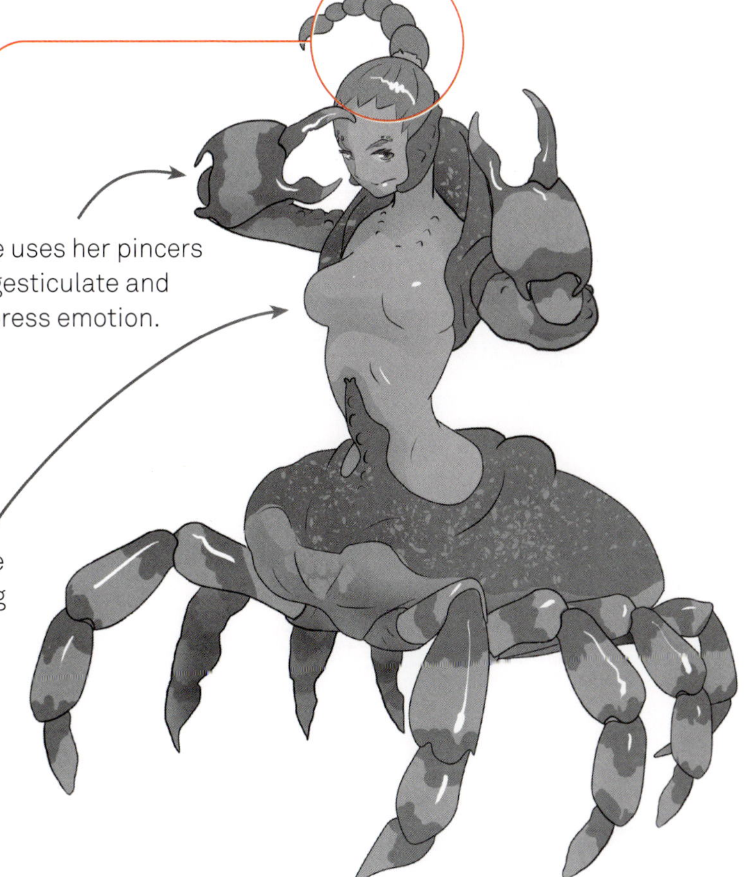

She uses her pincers to gesticulate and express emotion.

Incorporate feminine curves when drawing her torso.

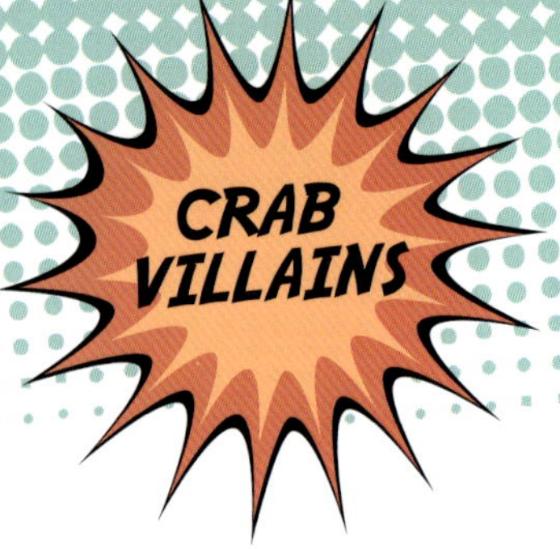

The Pinching Preteen

Don't underestimate this mischievous little monster—you need to take her seriously even though she's still a child. This hyperactive adolescent is very curious and is almost always up to no good!

▼ **Front View**

Large eyes and a fang tooth give her a mischievous look.

Since she is still an adolescent, her upper body has a boyish appearance.

Slim legs indicate her highly active lifestyle.

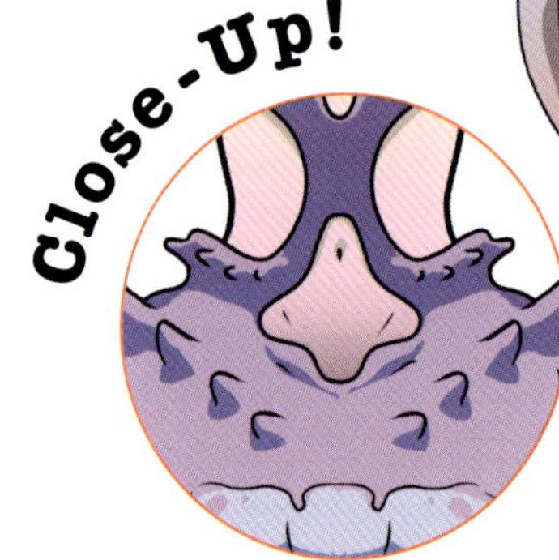

Include a belly button to increase the human element of the drawing.

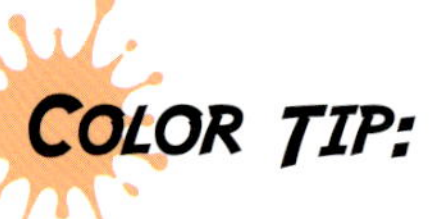

Use reddish shades of purple for the shell exterior and bluish shades for the underside.

VILLAINOUS TRAITS

1. Naughty
2. Daring
3. Sneaky and fast

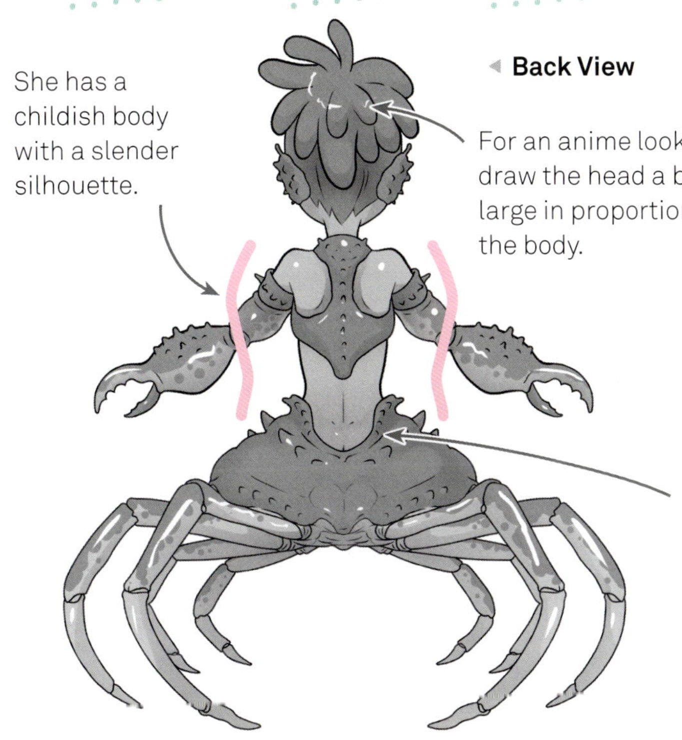

Back View

She has a childish body with a slender silhouette.

For an anime look, draw the head a bit large in proportion to the body.

When drawing the connection between the upper and lower body, it should look as if a human is riding on top of a crab.

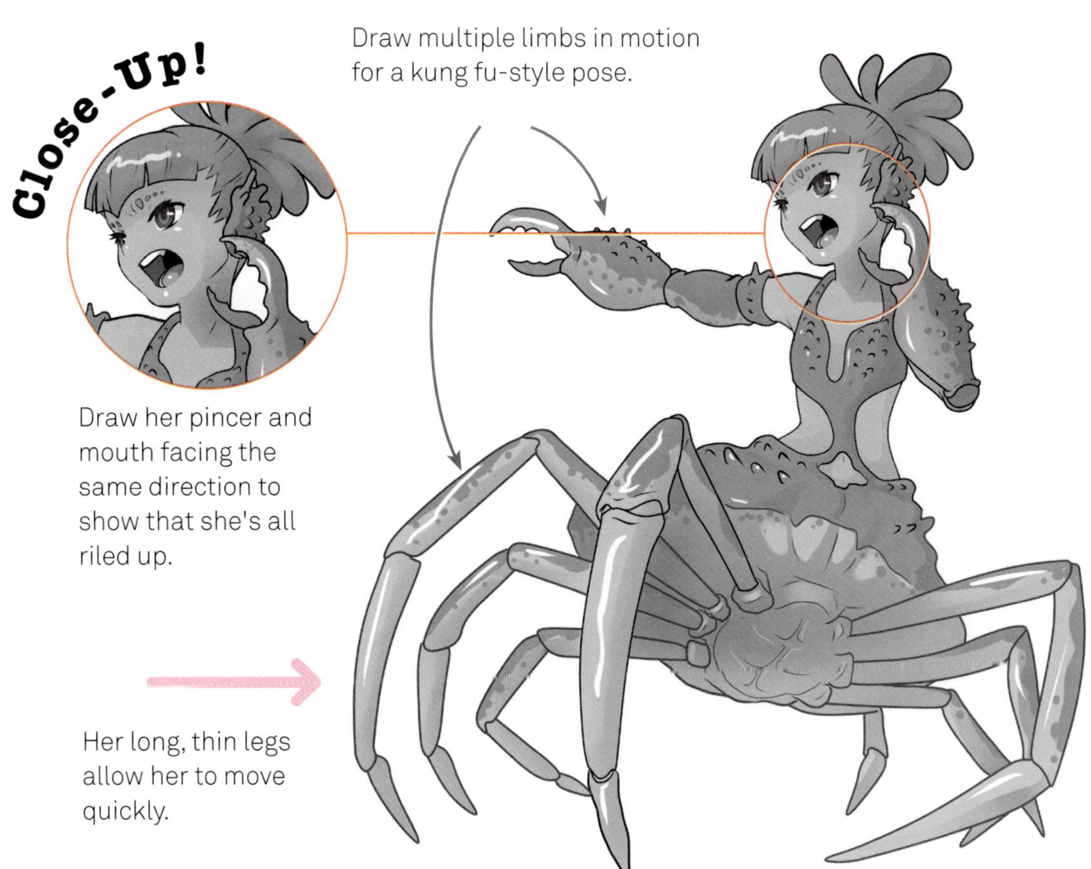

Action View

Draw multiple limbs in motion for a kung fu-style pose.

Draw her pincer and mouth facing the same direction to show that she's all riled up.

Her long, thin legs allow her to move quickly.

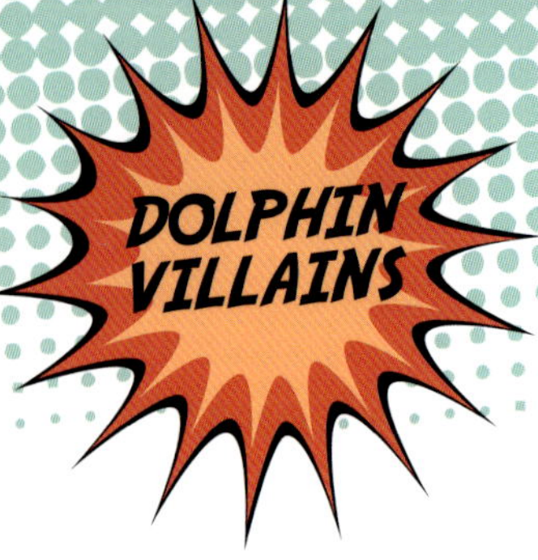

The Water Warlock

This enchanting dolphin character possesses unparalleled healing abilities, making him the envy and the target of many other villains. He uses dream and water manipulation to protect himself from attack.

▼ **Front View**

Use white highlights to capture the sleek surface of his skin.

COLOR TIP:

Blue and gray are classic color choices, but try adding accents of mint and turquoise.

Lean yet muscular body for maximum hydrodynamics

COLOR TIP:

A thin yellow line creates a boundary to divide the ventral and dorsal portions of his tail.

The curved shape of his tail allows him to move through the water with ease and grace.

VILLAINOUS TRAITS

1. Powerful healing abilities
2. Water manipulation
3. Dream manipulation

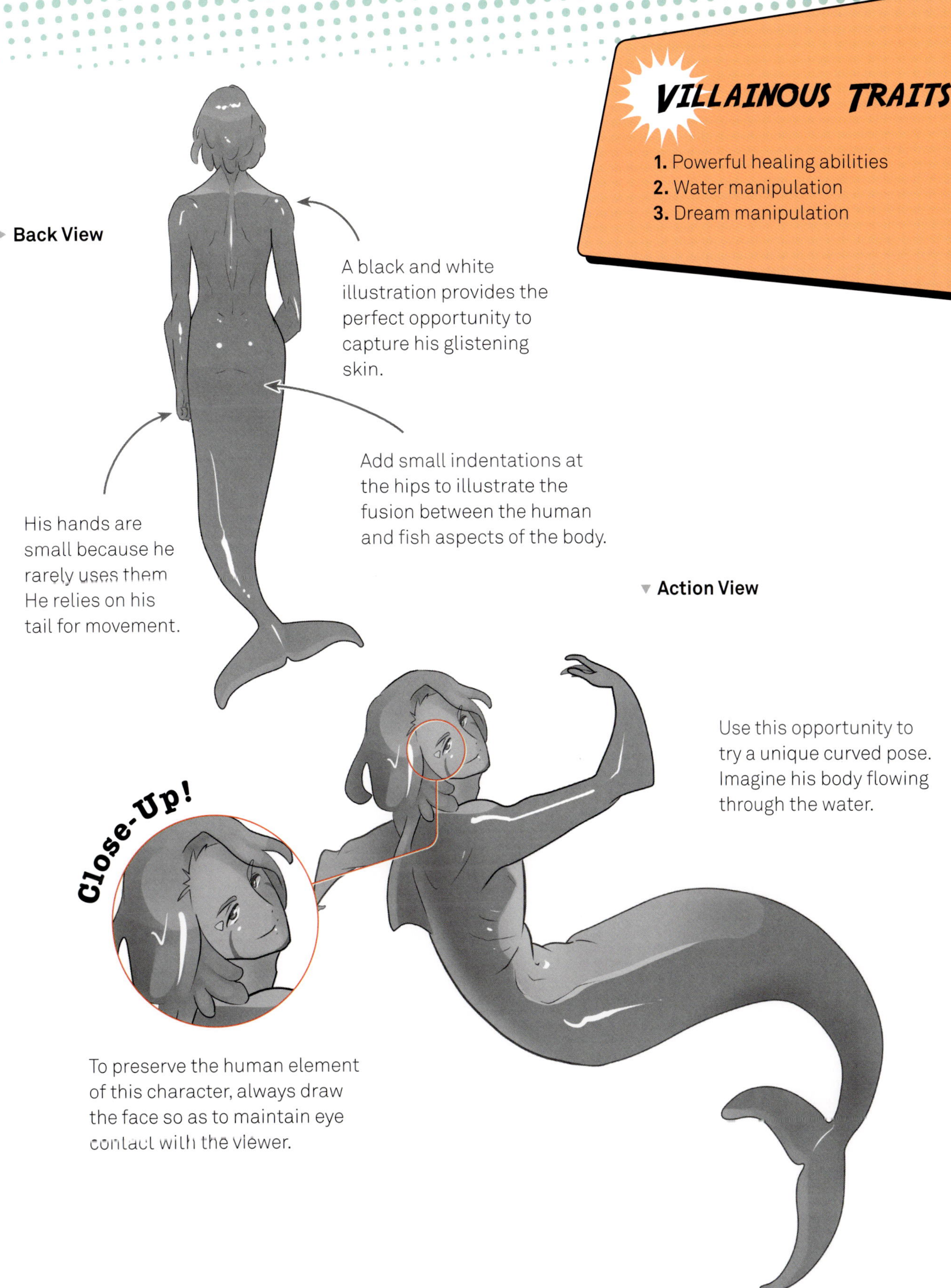

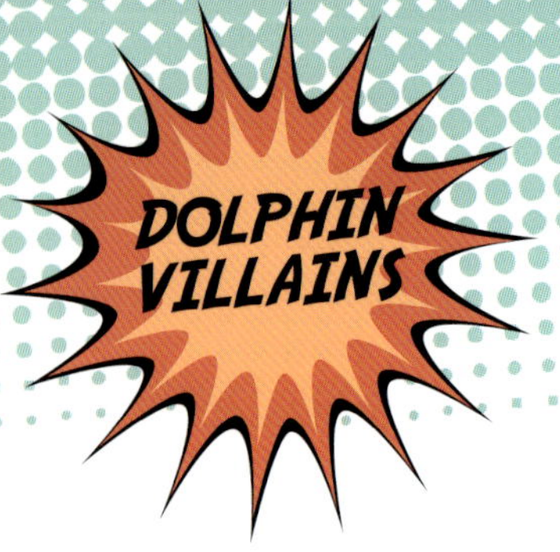

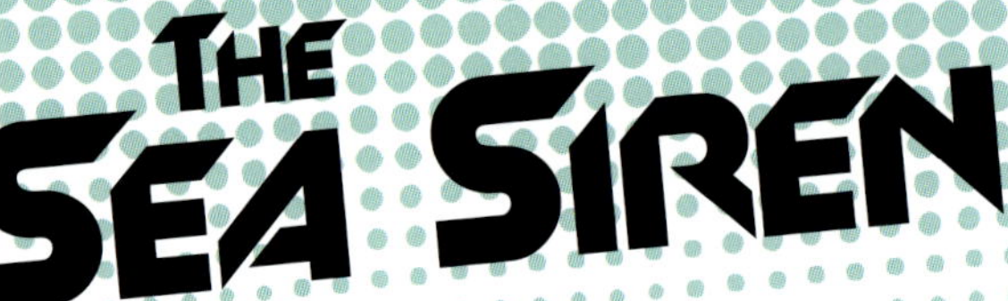

The Sea Siren

Much like a mermaid, this beautiful creature is known for her ability to bewitch unsuspecting sailors and make them fall in love. She's also renowned for her powers of telepathy and hypnotism.

▼ **Front View**

Beautiful, glossy hair

Soft, feminine figure

Include human features like a bellybutton and hip bones.

COLOR TIP:

Use a very pale pink for her stomach and darker shades for her tail and hair.

Close-Up!

Thin, long fingers suggest graceful movement.

COLOR TIP:

Use this opportunity to experiment with a less traditional color scheme. Pink is a natural choice because it symbolizes femininity.

VILLAINOUS TRAITS

1. Ultrasonic communication
2. Telepathy
3. Hypnotic dolphin call

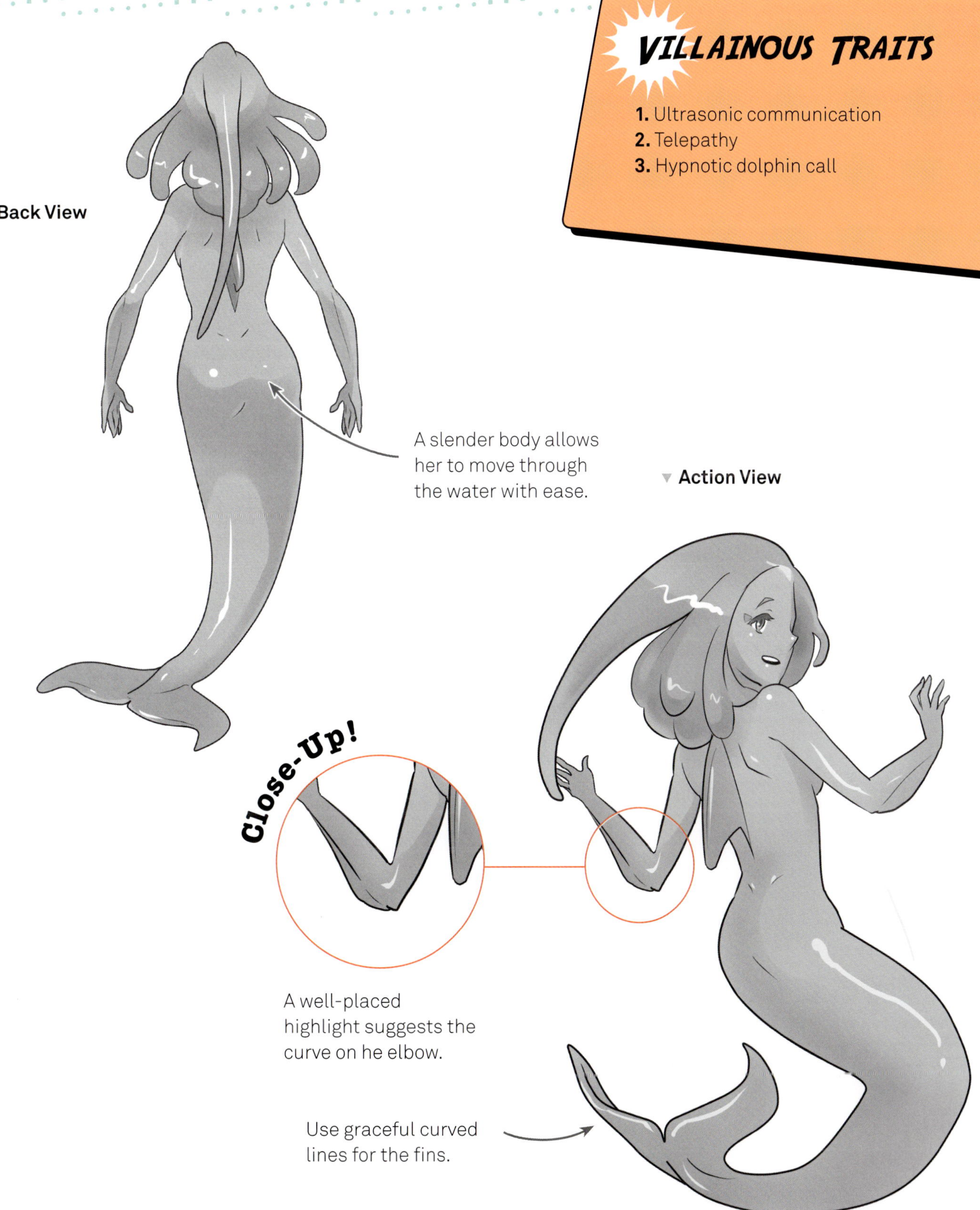

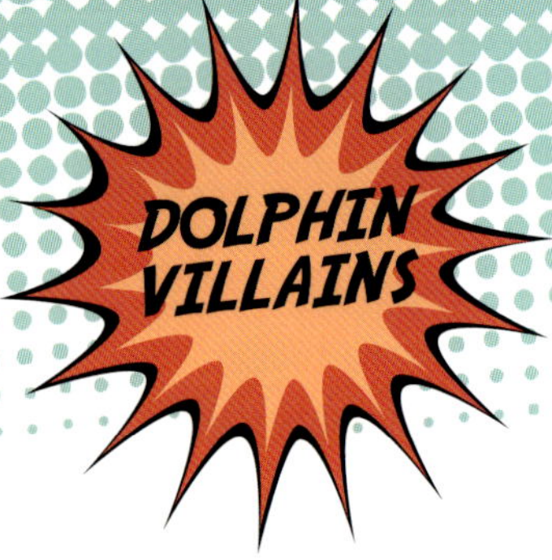

THE BRAINIAC

This precocious adolescent possesses an intelligence level 100 times higher than the average human, causing an inflated ego and delusions of grandeur. Dolphin hybrids don't develop their psychic abilities until they've fully matured, so his superiority complex will only get worse with age.

▼ **Front View**

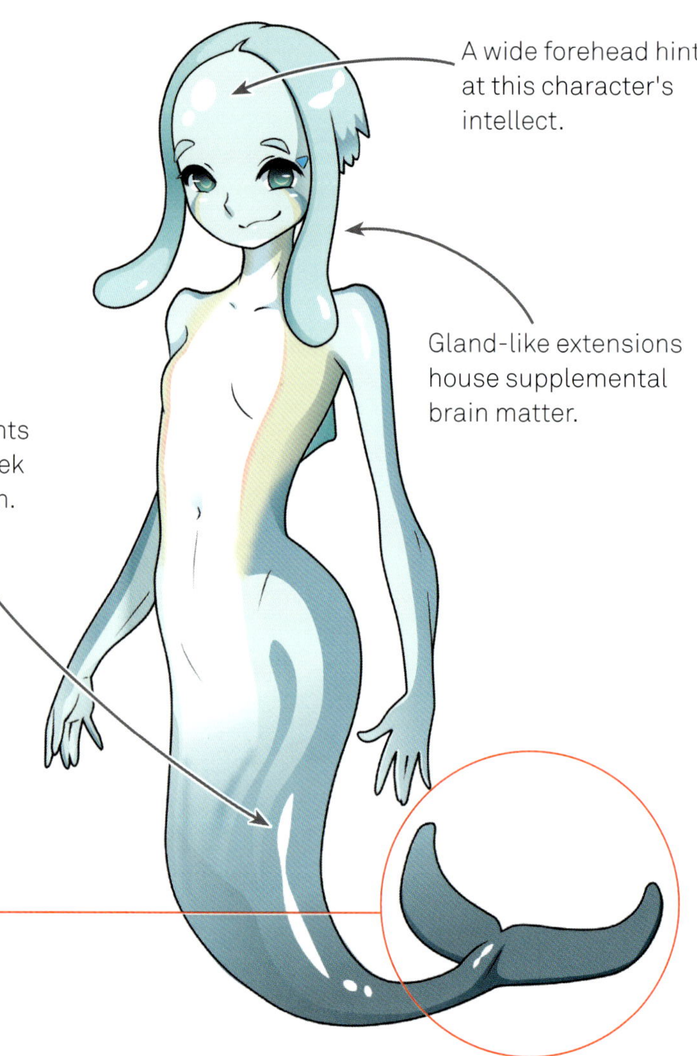

A wide forehead hints at this character's intellect.

Gland-like extensions house supplemental brain matter.

Use white highlights to capture the sleek surface of the skin.

Close-Up!

Draw a realistic dolphin tail. Position the fins parallel to the ground to give the impression that he is floating.

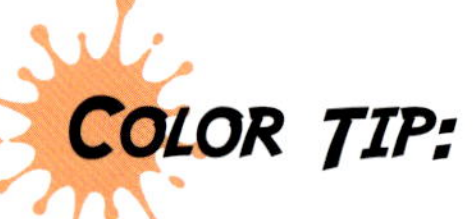

COLOR TIP:

Use a dolphin-blue color scheme, but experiment with saturation and highlights.

VILLAINOUS TRAITS

1. Genius level intelligence
2. Terrible ego
3. Strong swimmer—can travel to extremely deep parts of the ocean

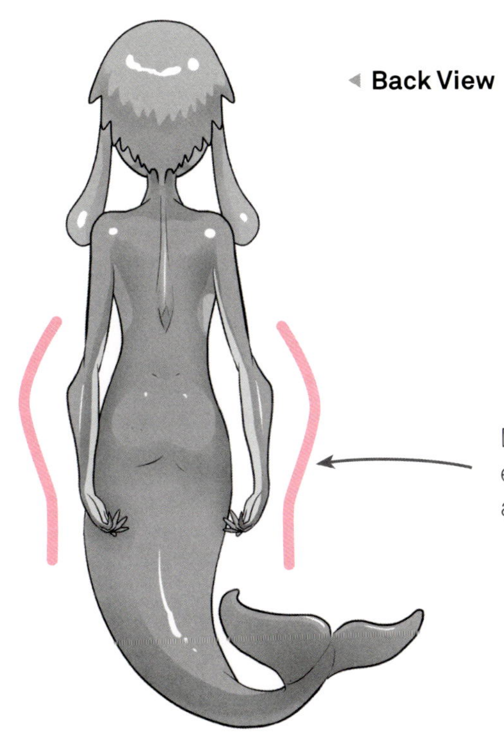

◀ **Back View**

Draw a narrow waist to emphasize the strength and power of his tail.

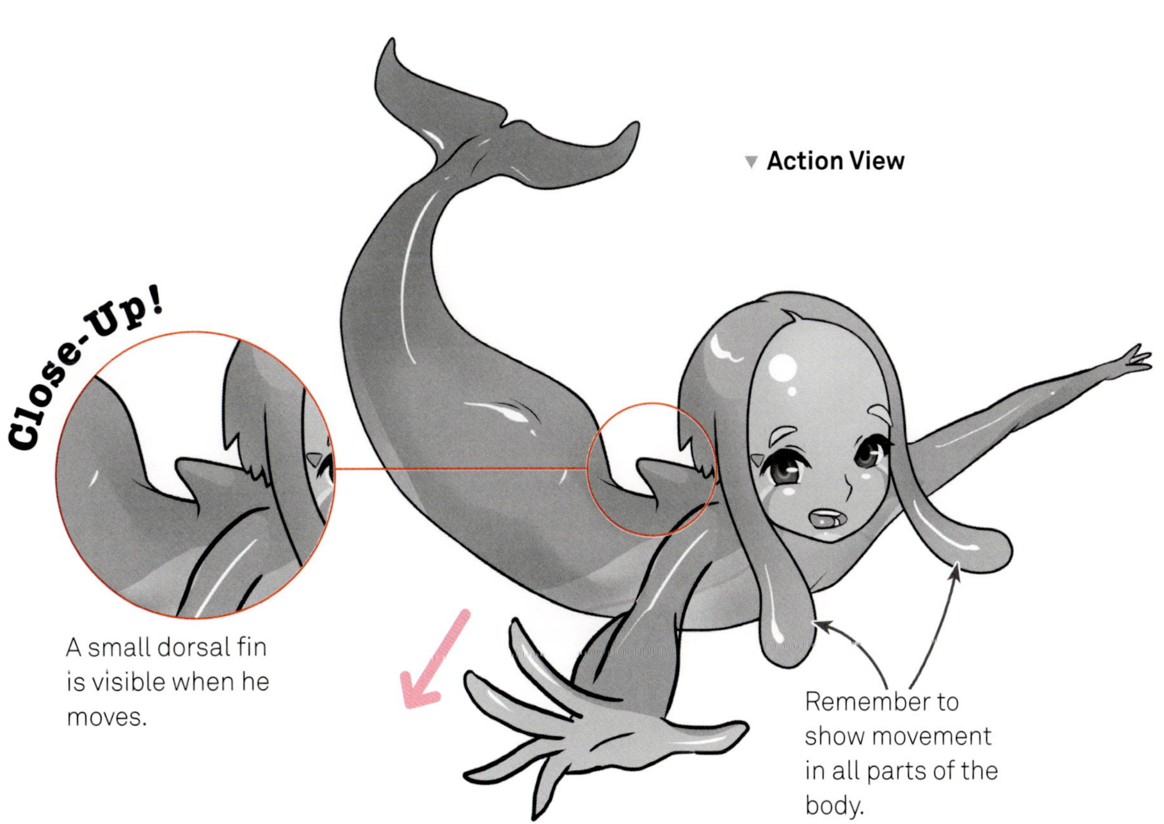

▼ **Action View**

A small dorsal fin is visible when he moves.

Remember to show movement in all parts of the body.

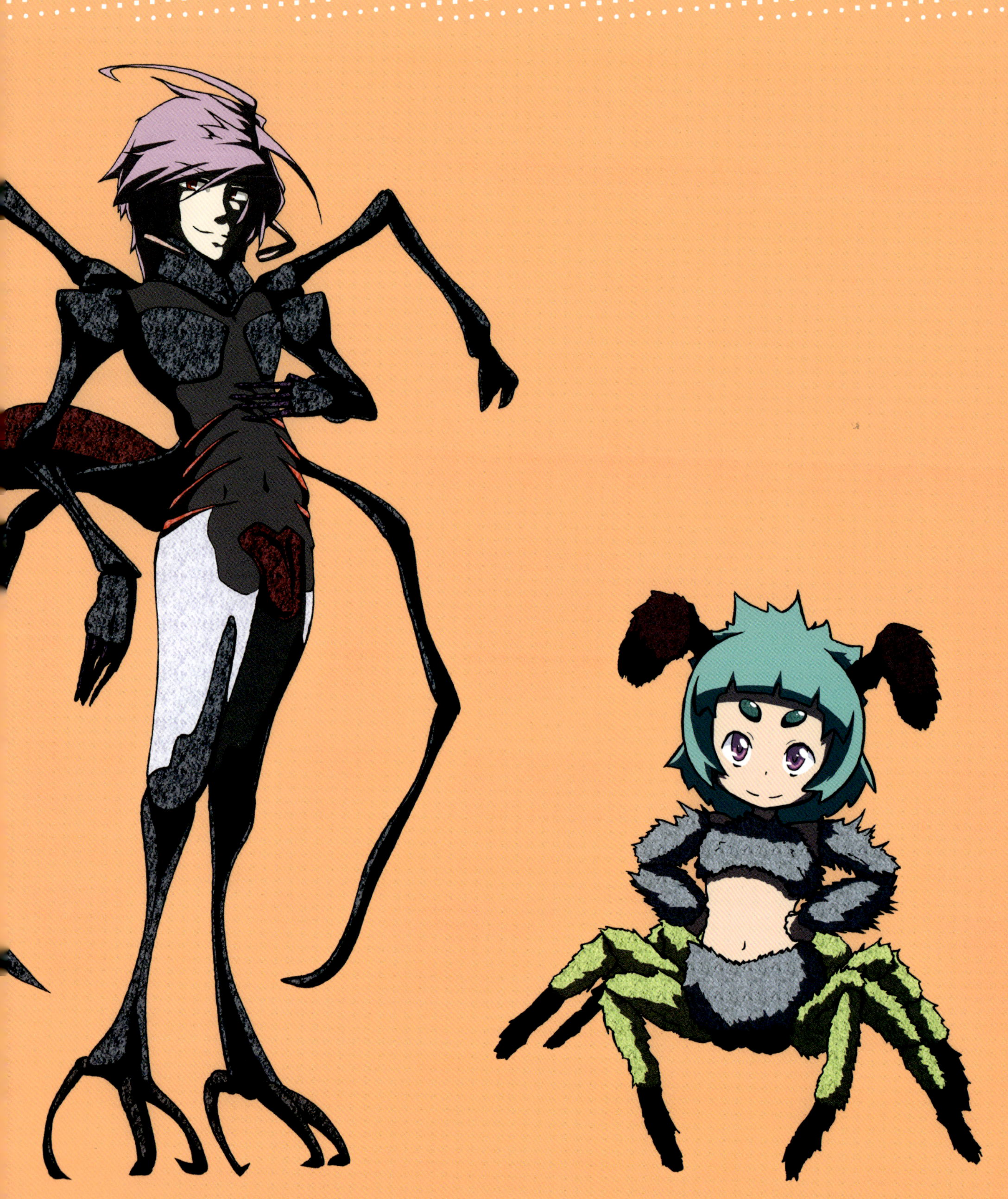

CHAPTER 3

INSECTS

Insects may be small, but there's a reason they've survived millions of years—they're tough! An insect's appearance transforms throughout the stages of life, so take this into account when drawing your characters.

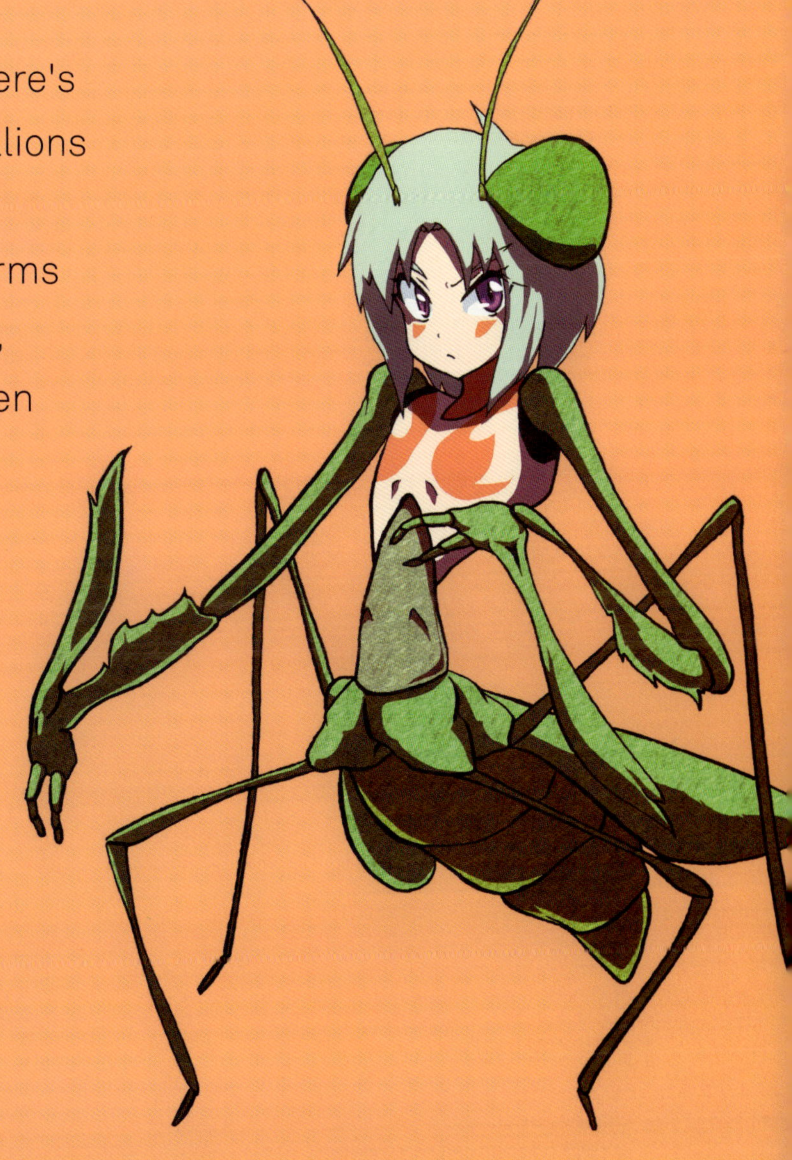

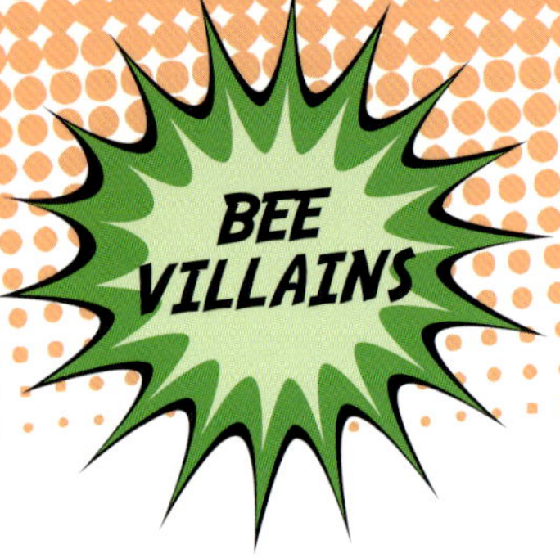

The Queen Bee

This powerful, mature female bee possesses complete control over her hive of worker bees. They will do her bidding upon command and even risk their own lives for her. She is highly seductive and uses her looks and abilities to obtain power over her victims.

Front View

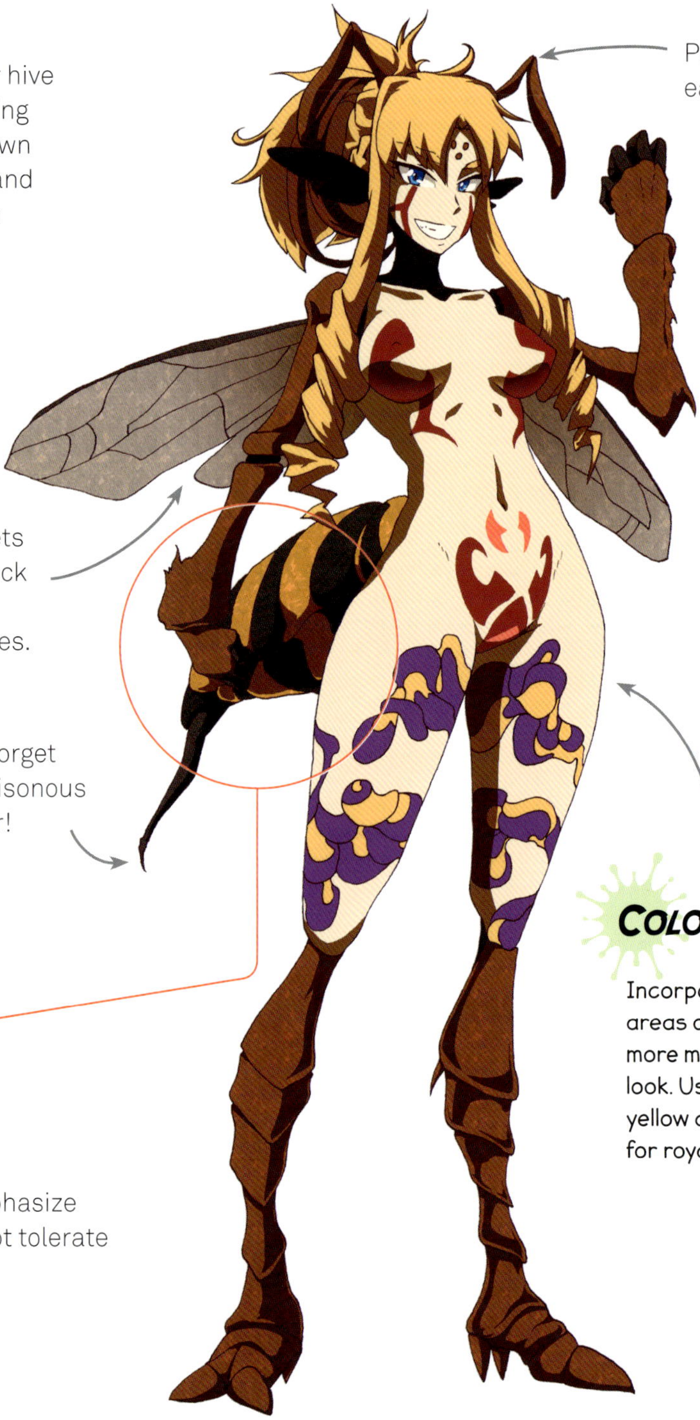

Pointy, elf-like ears

Bees have two sets of wings—the back ones are smaller than the front ones.

Don't forget her poisonous stinger!

Close-Up!

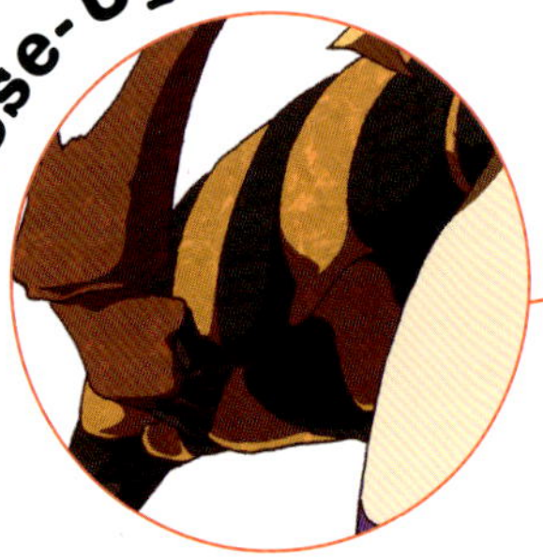

Draw a dramatically large tail to emphasize her queen bee status—she would not tolerate being confused for a worker bee!

COLOR TIP:

Incorporate larger areas of skin for a more mature, sexy look. Use bold purple, yellow and red accents for royal distinction.

COLOR TIP:

Honey bees are traditionally yellow and dark brown or black. Add colorful tattoo-inspired patterns to accentuate her body.

VILLAINOUS TRAITS

1. Emits pheromones to control other bees
2. Able to sting repeatedly without dying
3. Reproduces to form her own army when necessary

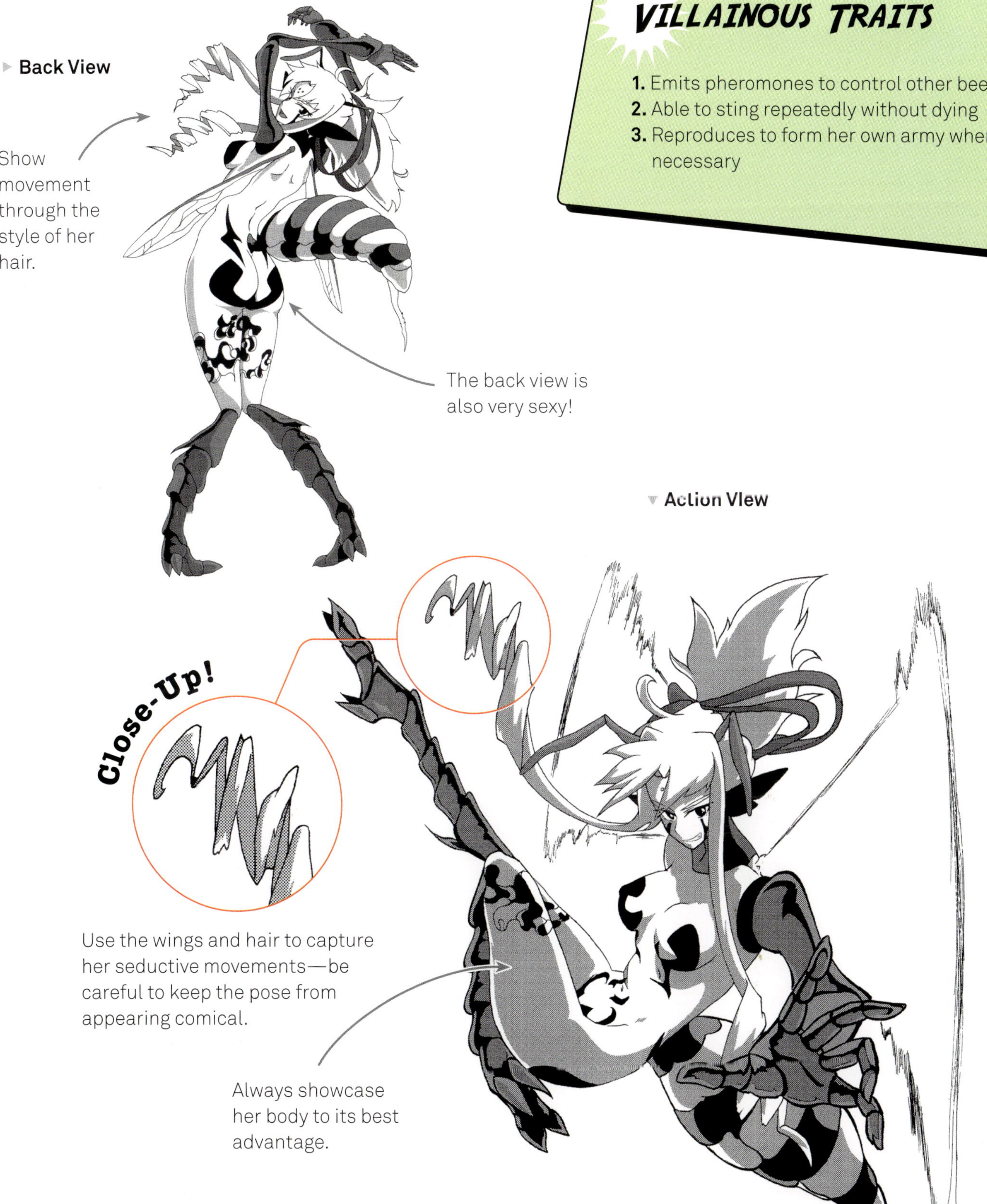

BEE VILLAINS

The Duplicitous Drone

As a drone, this bee's main role is to serve the queen. He's unhappy with his position within the hive, so he secretly works to undermine the queen. He uses his good looks and charisma to win others over to his cause. Because he does not possess a stinger like female worker bees, he is very insecure under the surface.

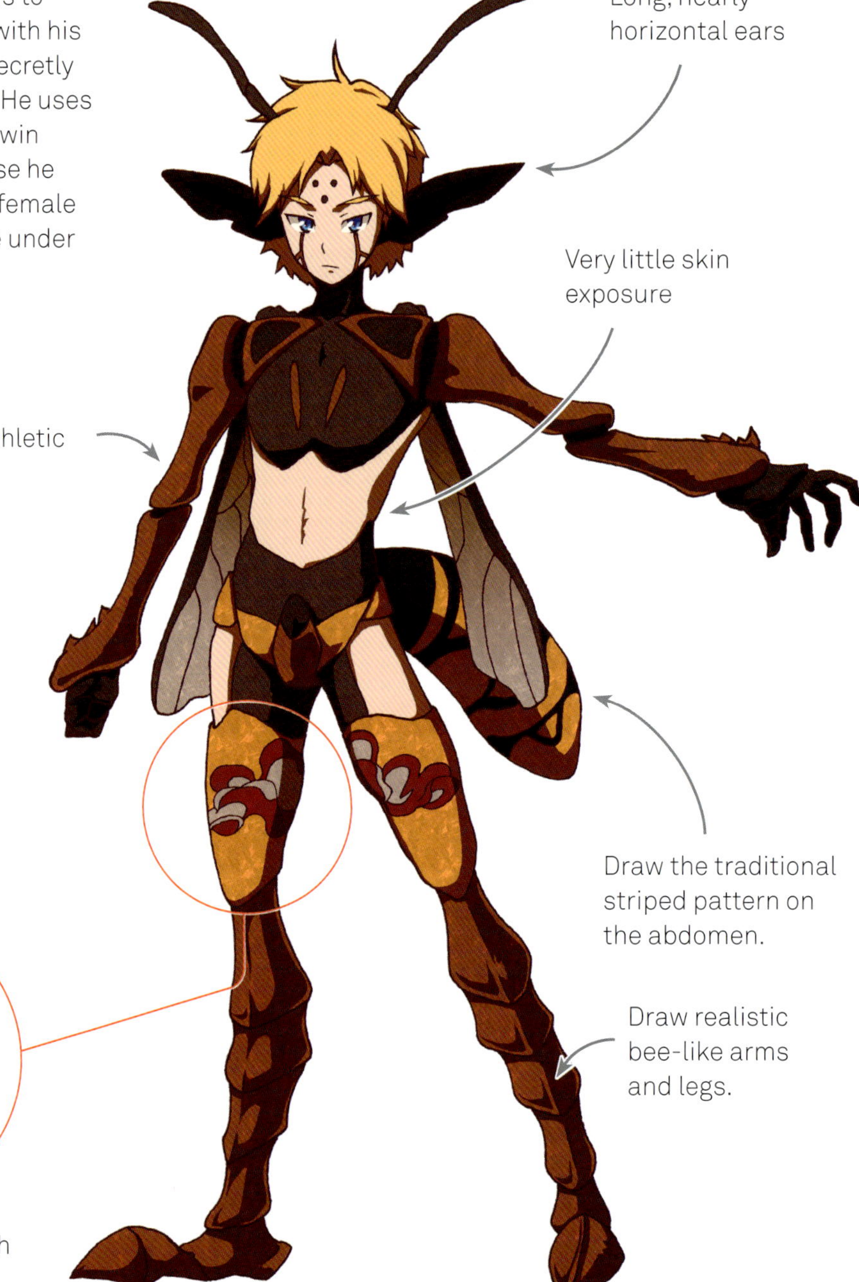

COLOR TIP:

Use golden yellow and rich shades of brown for the classic bee look.

VILLAINOUS TRAITS

1. Jealous and manipulative
2. Harbors delusions of grandeur
3. Charismatic

Back View

His body language expresses his love of freedom and resistance to authority.

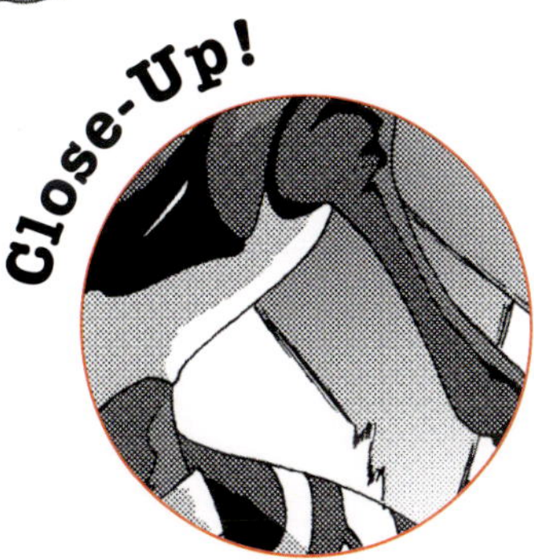

His back isn't perfectly straight while flying, but good posture accentuates the wing movement.

Action View

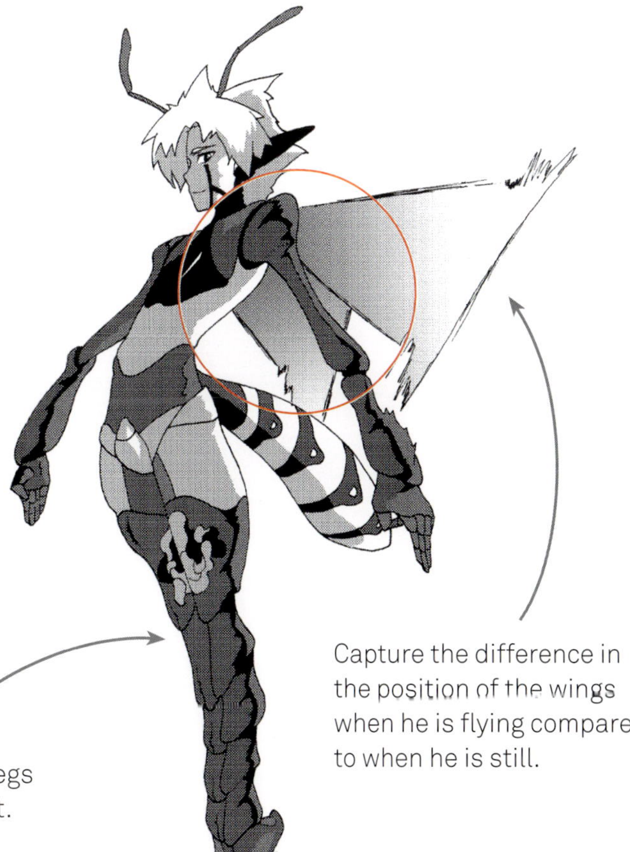

Highlight his good posture and long legs through movement.

Capture the difference in the position of the wings when he is flying compared to when he is still.

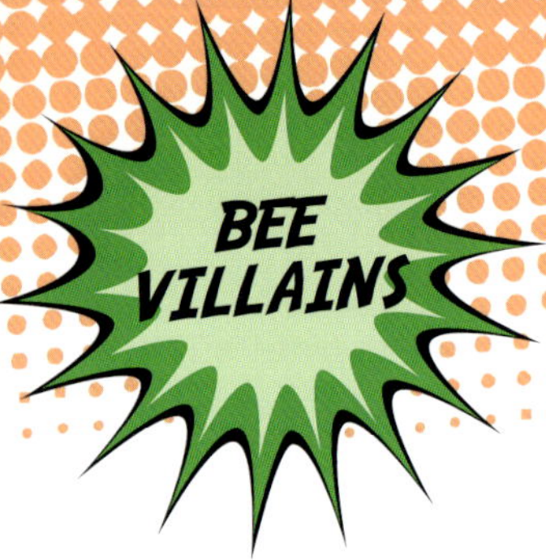

The Royal Pain

Since birth, this bee has been distinguished as the future queen. She has been showered with special attention, leading her to become a self-absorbed prima donna.

▼ Front View

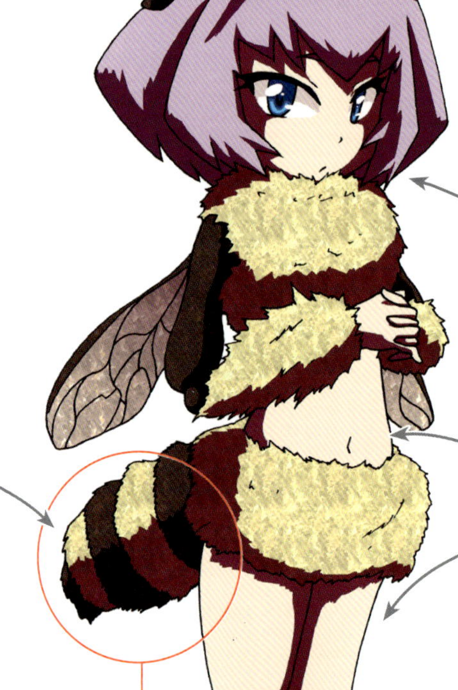

COLOR TIP:

Her purple hair and striking blue eyes give her a distinctive look.

She has not matured into a queen bee yet, but her calculating facial expression hints at her future position of power.

Her fuzzy tail is classic honey bee.

Soft, chubby figure shows her young age

Close-Up!

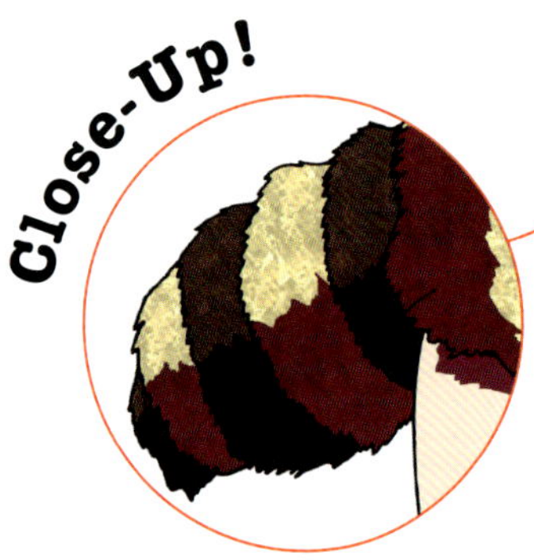

For a more sinister look, incorporate shadow when drawing the tail.

COLOR TIP:

Use yellow and dark brown, then add shadows to capture the furry texture of a honey bee.

VILLAINOUS TRAITS

1. Self-absorbed
2. Calculating
3. Spoiled

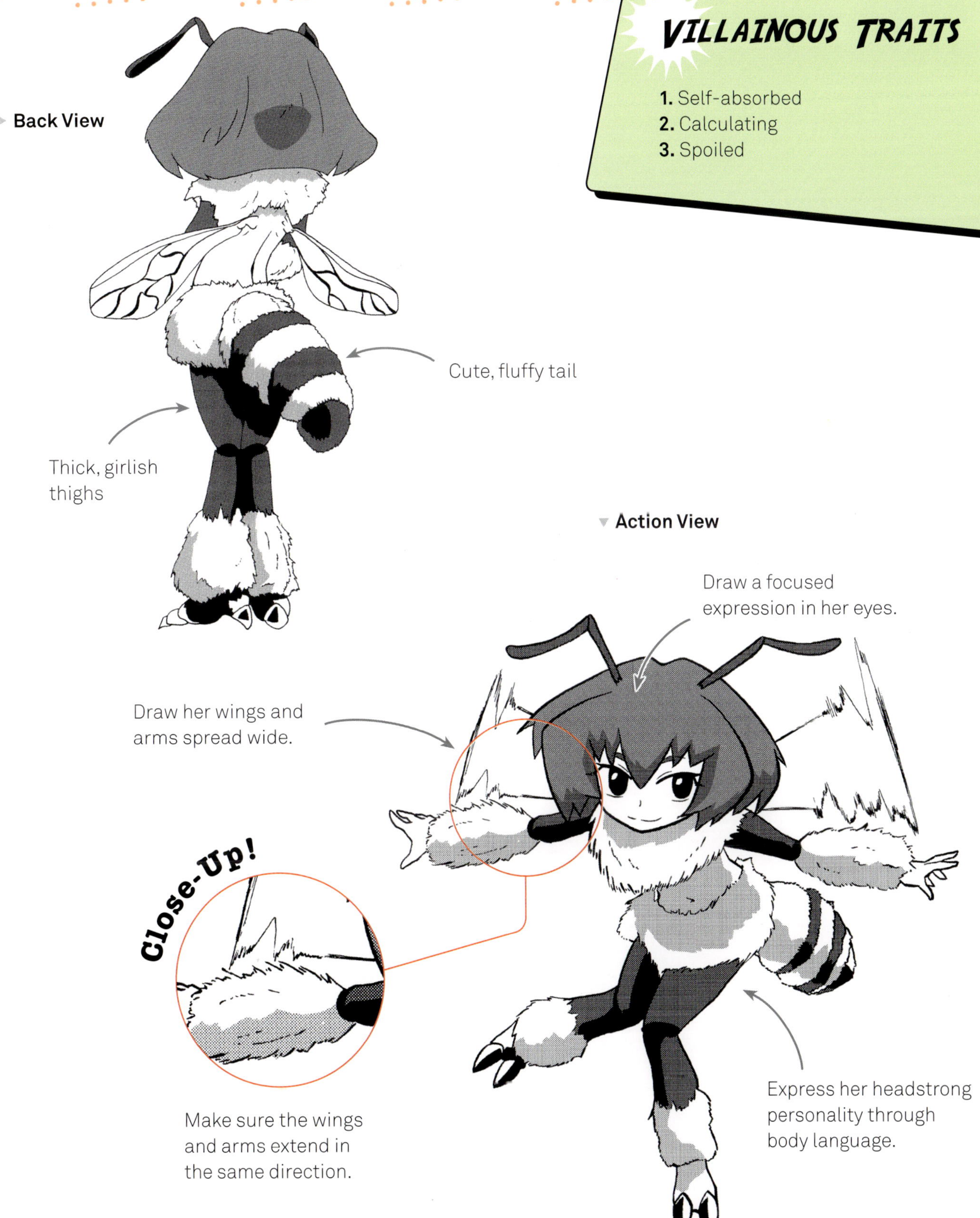

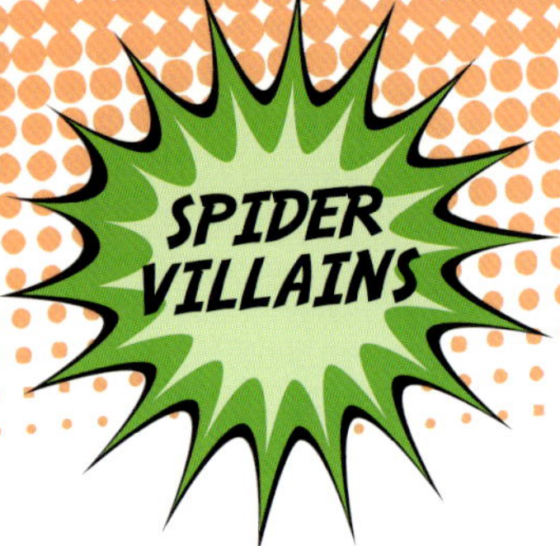

The Black Widow

This alluring arachnid is a skillful huntress who uses a web to catch her prey, then finishes them off with toxic venom. She's infamous for seducing mates, then eating them once she no longer has any use for them.

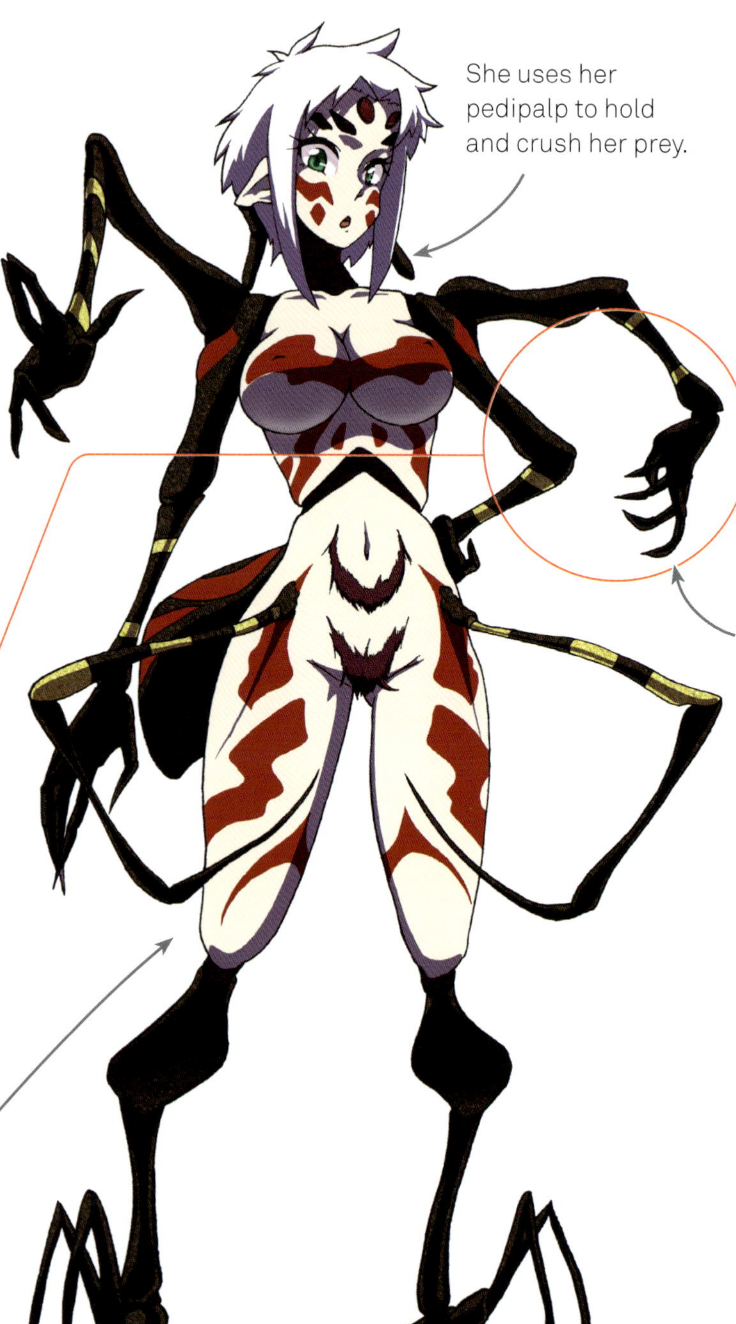

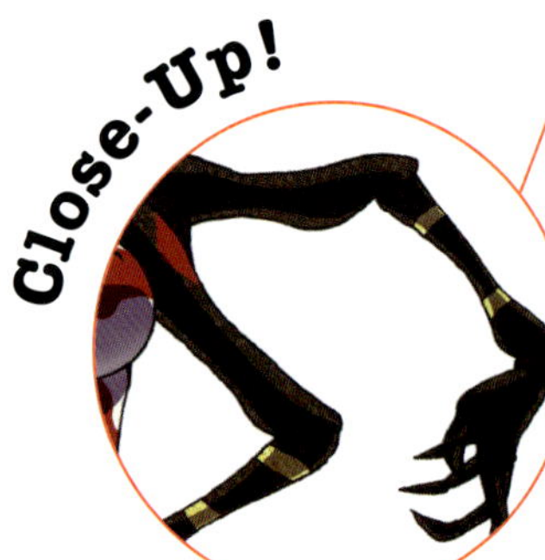

Use black, angular lines to make the legs look menacing.

Color Tip:

Use bold, vivid colors for this mature female character. Black and red work well as base colors, while yellow and white make excellent highlights.

VILLAINOUS TRAITS

1. Skilled huntress
2. Ruthless—known for eating her own mates
3. Possesses highly toxic venom

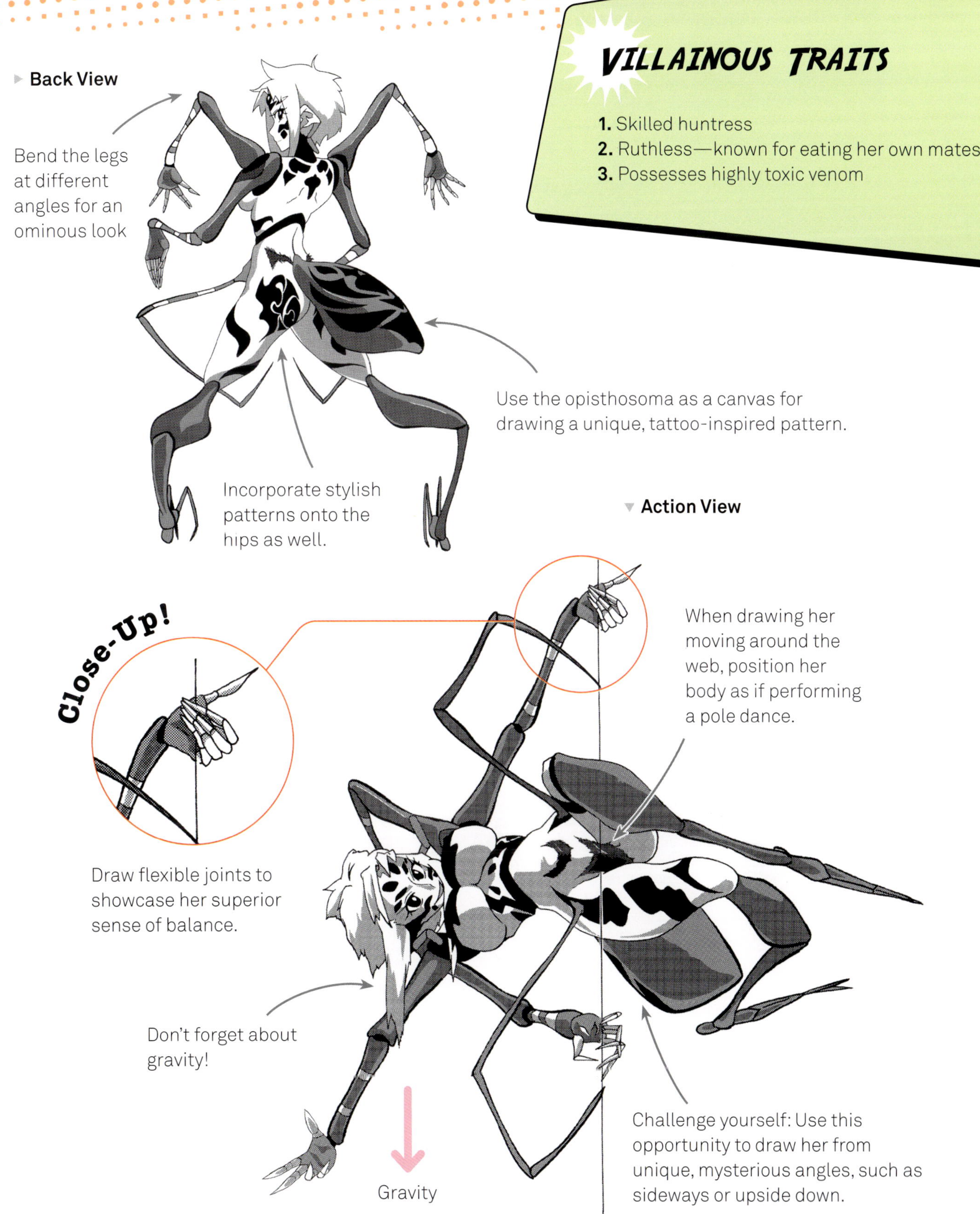

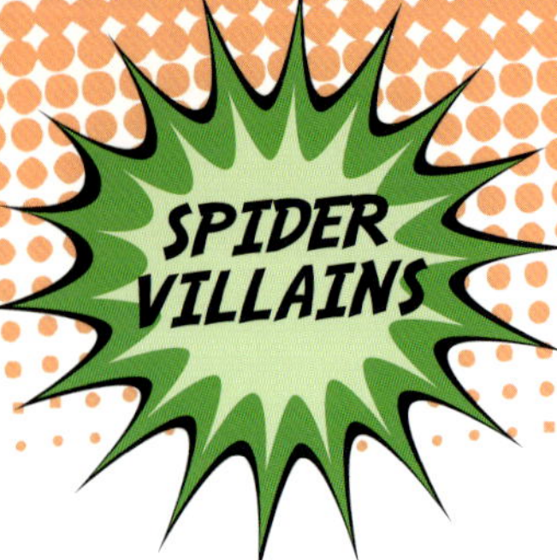

The Secret Agent Arachnid

Front View

Formerly a government asset, this secret agent spider has gone rogue. His superior athletic abilities and powers of web generation allow him to scale walls and jump from building to building with ease. He is also highly intelligent and can break just about any code.

COLOR TIP:

Use tones of dark red and blue, then add dimension with a stippled pattern.

Finger-like extensions allow for rapid movement.

Close-Up!

Extremely thin, angular legs emphasize the non-human aspects of this character.

Long, skinny legs and toe-like extensions allow him to land acrobatic jumps.

COLOR TIP:

Use more subtle colors—primary colors attract attention and this character likes to fly under the radar.

VILLAINOUS TRAITS

1. Extremely agile—can climb anything
2. Stealthy
3. Excellent analytical skills

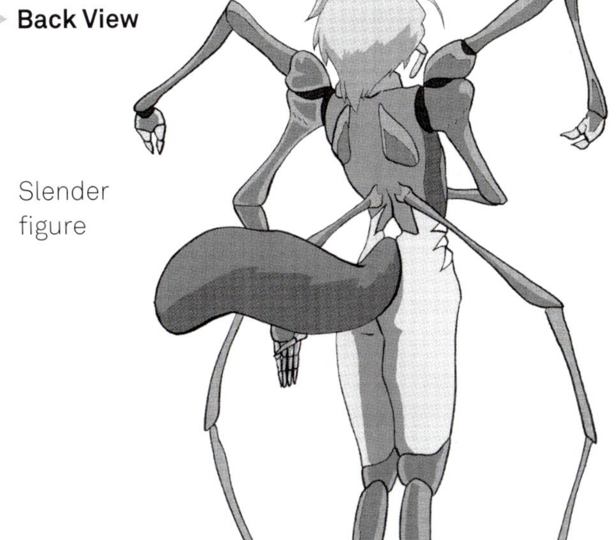

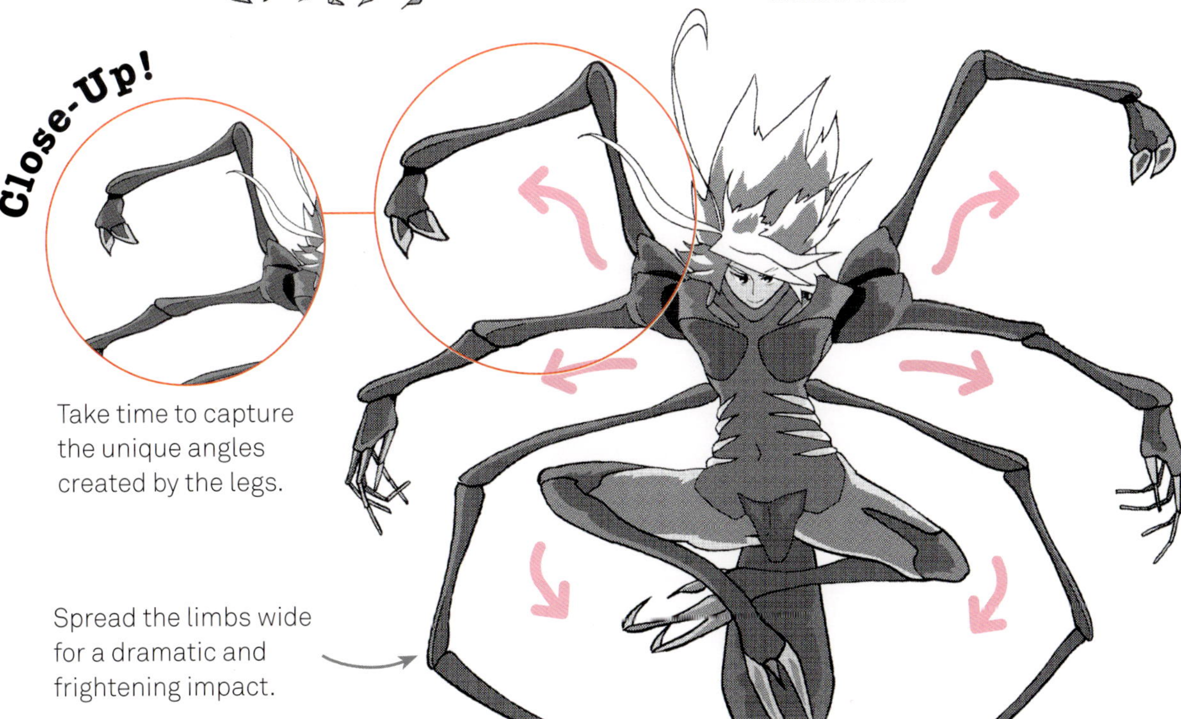

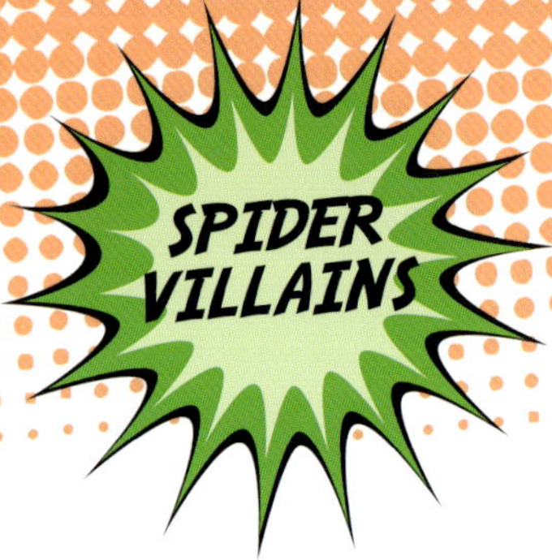

The Toddler Tarantula

Although she may be small, this young arachnid is quite fierce. She's quick and smart—a dangerous combination! She's renowned for trapping those who underestimate her in a web that's nearly impossible to escape.

▼ **Front View**

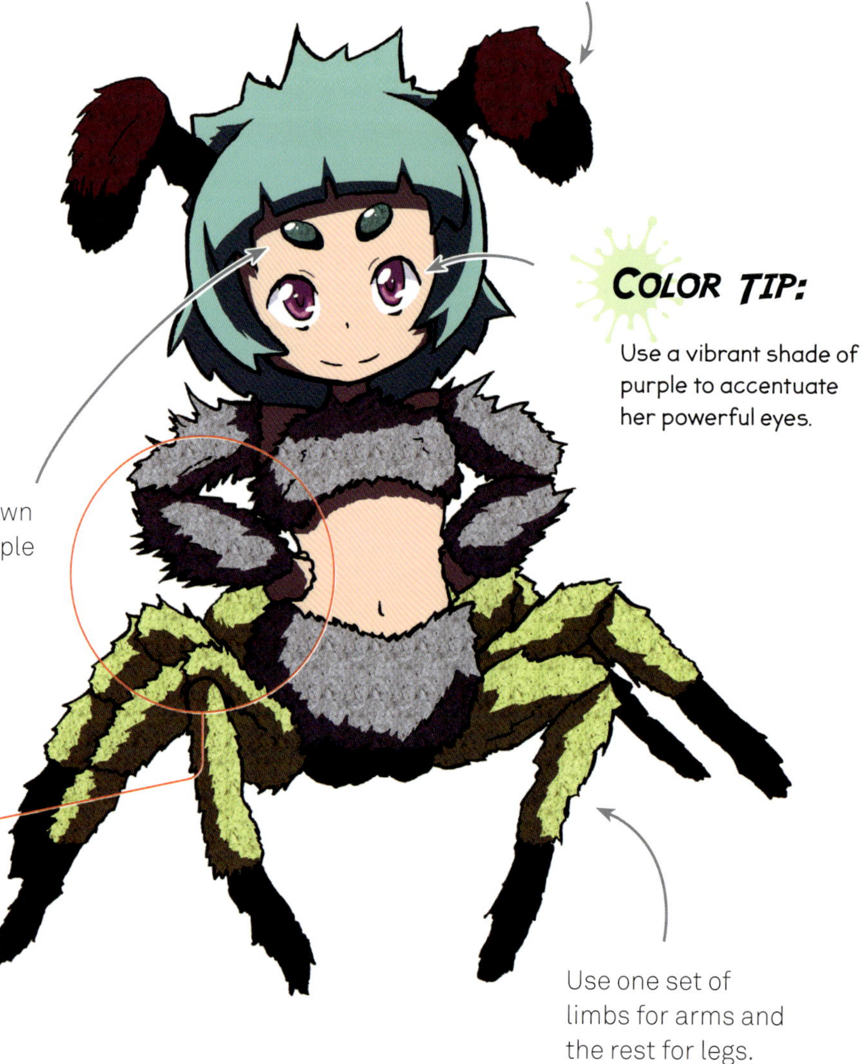

Unlike insects with antennae, spiders have pedipalp, which they use for catching prey.

Color Tip:

Use a vibrant shade of purple to accentuate her powerful eyes.

Spiders are known for having multiple sets of eyes.

Position the human-like torso on top of the spider legs.

Use one set of limbs for arms and the rest for legs.

Color Tip:

Use neutral grays and greens for the body—this will make the dark purple accents pop.

VILLAINOUS TRAITS

1. Extremely protective
2. Acute sense of smell
3. Superstitious

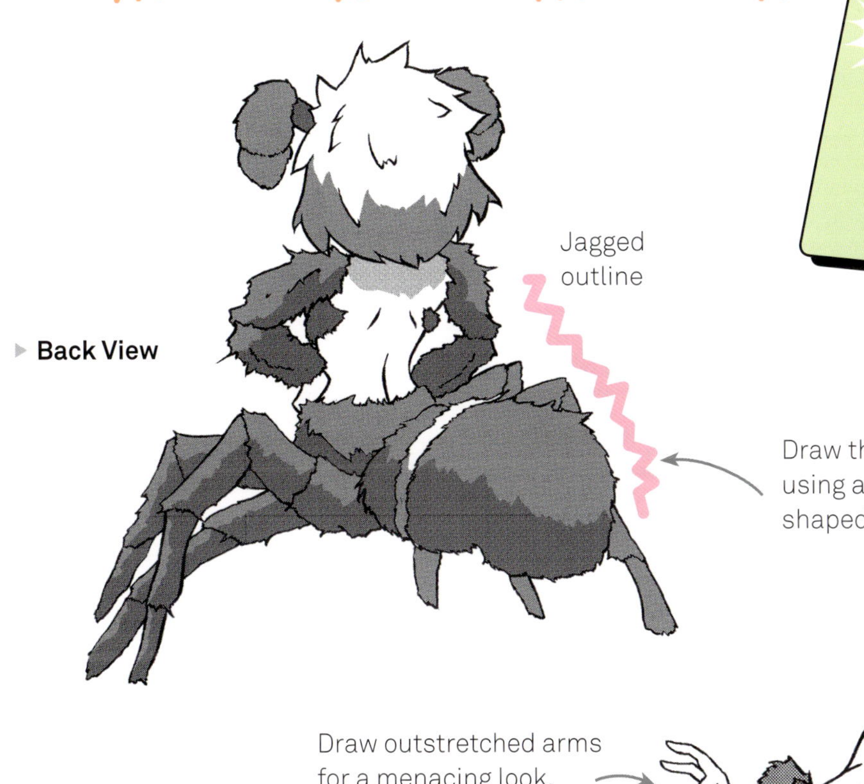

▸ **Back View**

▾ **Action View**

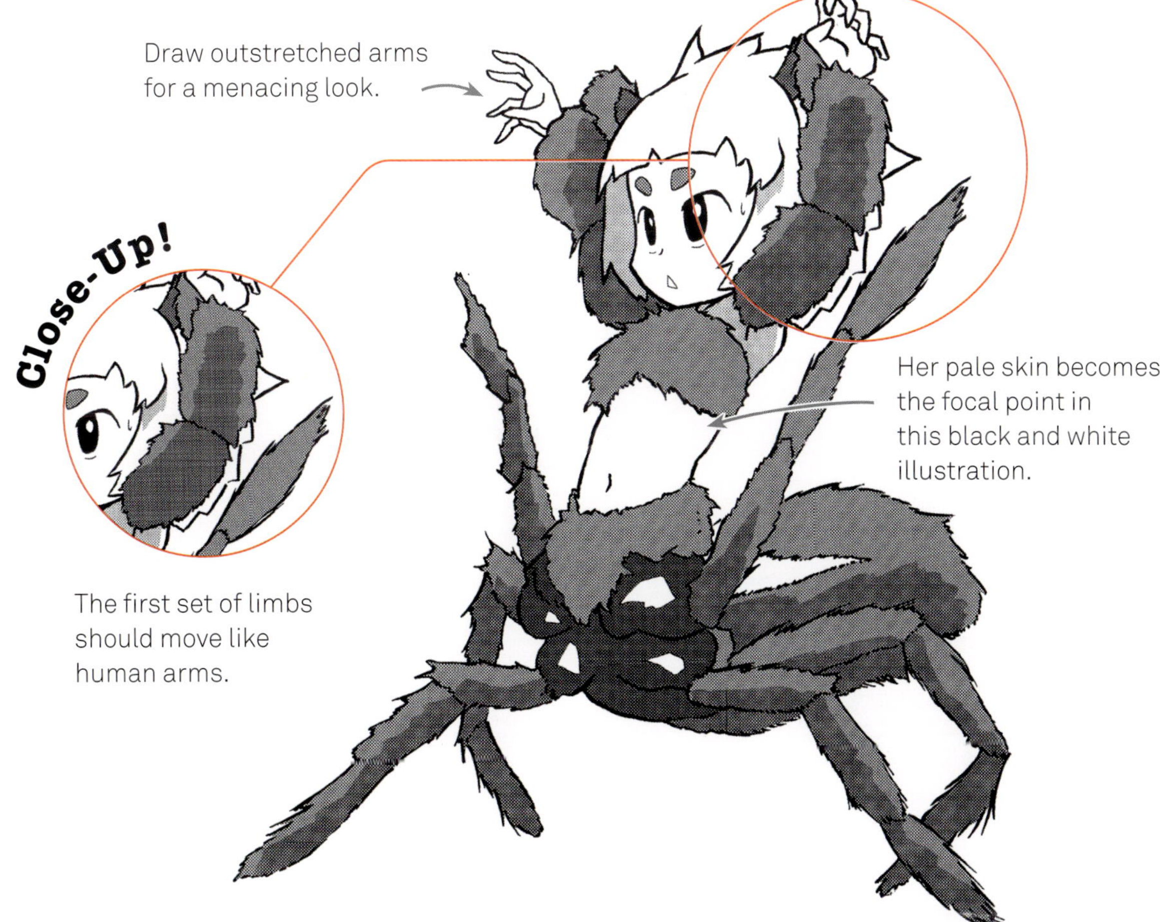

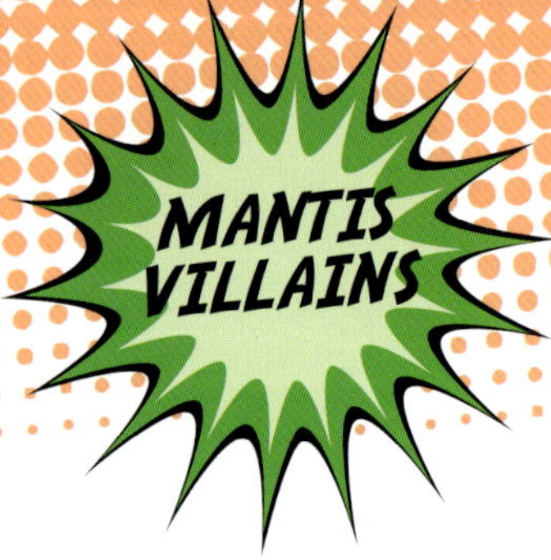

THE MANEATER

This strong female mantis is larger than her male counterparts. She possesses large, sharp hooks on her forearms, which she uses to cut her victims to pieces. She is infamous for biting the heads off males after mating.

Front View

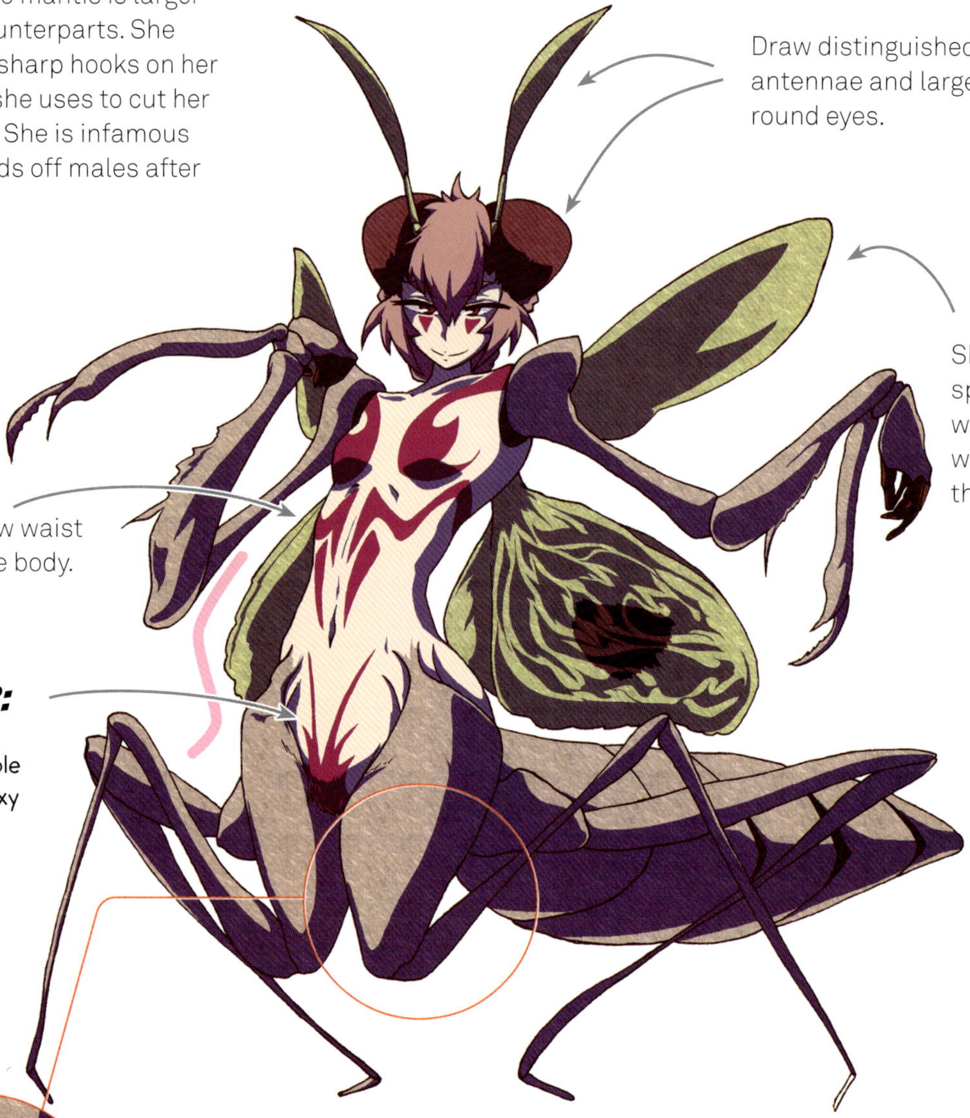

Draw distinguished antennae and large, round eyes.

She will spread her wings wide when feeling threatened.

Draw a narrow waist for a feminine body.

COLOR TIP:

Use vibrant purple accents for a sexy look.

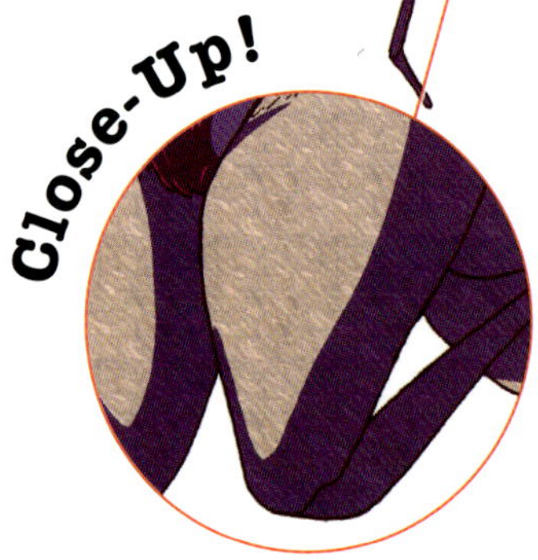

Close-Up!

Incorporate shadow for an ominous effect.

COLOR TIP:

Use green as a base color, then add seductive purple and maroon accents.

VILLAINOUS TRAITS

1. Aggressive and quick-tempered
2. Large, sharp hooks
3. Cannibalistic—bites the heads off her male mates

▸ **Back View**

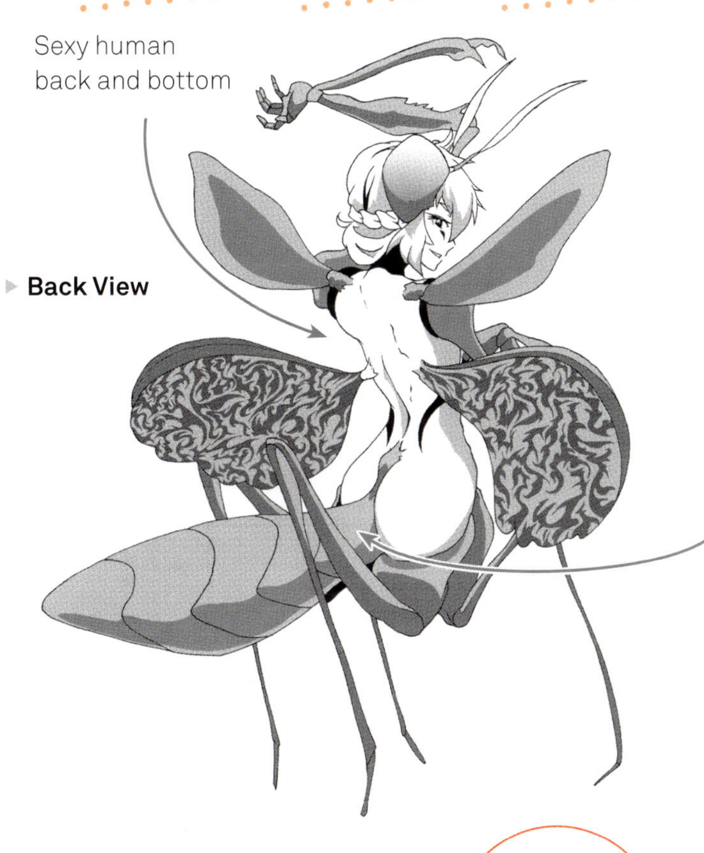

▾ **Action View**

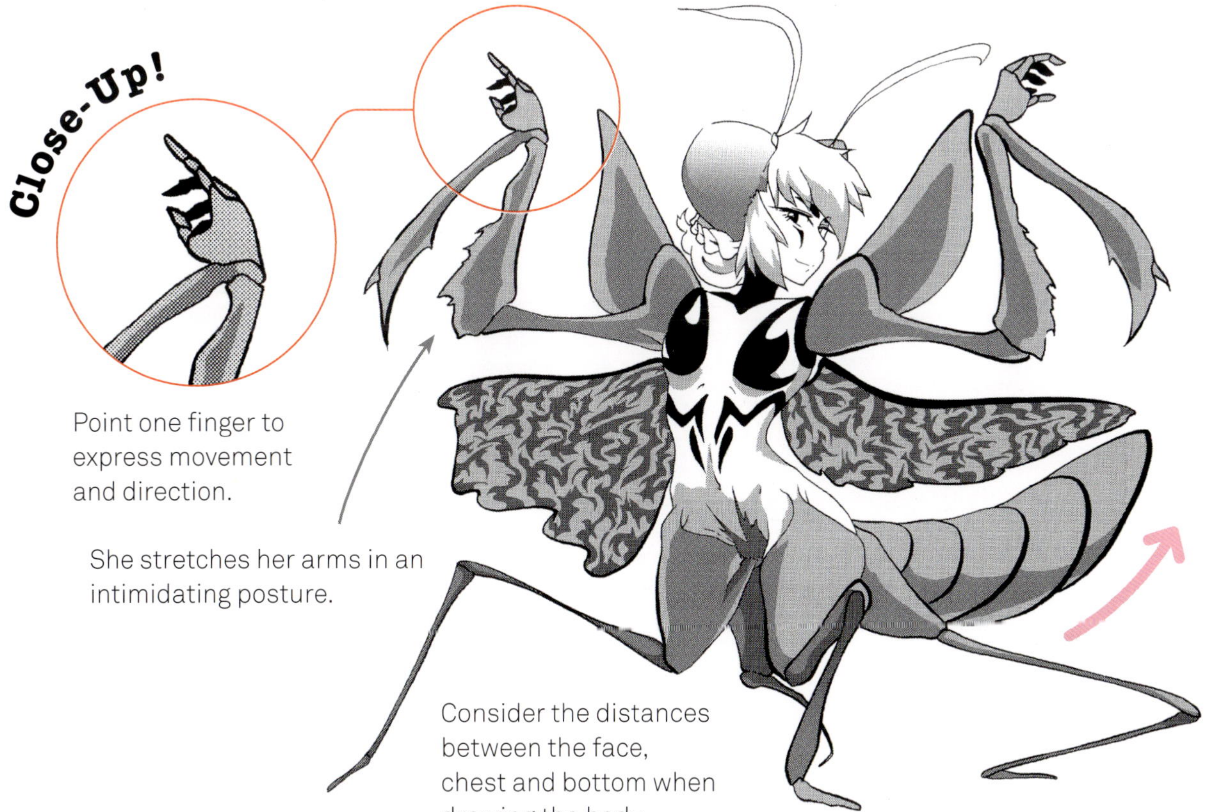

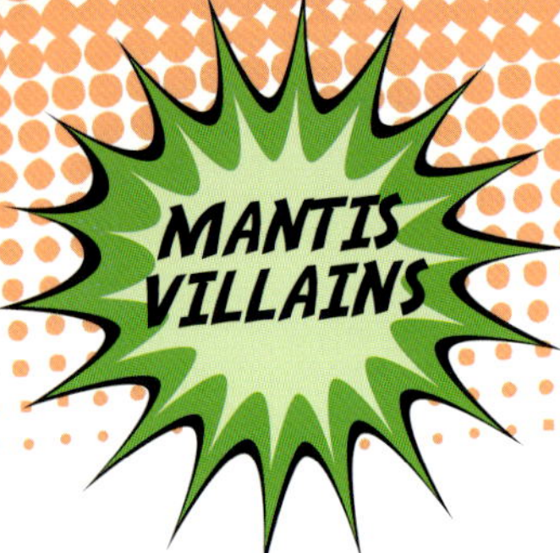

The Manipulative Mantis

In the mantis world, females are more physically powerful, so this evil insect has honed his psychological weapons and hypnotic skills in order to gain power.

▼ Front View

He proudly displays his mantis hooks.

Close-Up!

This signature mantis pose shows off his dangerous hooks.

The antennae and large, round ears inspired by a mantis' eyes serve as focal points.

Long, willowy legs allow him to jump great distances at a moment's notice.

COLOR TIP:

Use shades of green for the classic mantis look. Reddish-purple accents add a nice contrast to the green.

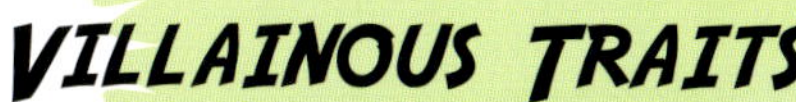

VILLAINOUS TRAITS

1. Agile
2. Vain
3. Hypnotic powers

▸ **Back View**

Scale is important! Don't make the hooks too large in proportion to the rest of the body.

Think of his human torso as a tree trunk, then add the legs and wings, just like branches.

▾ **Action View**

Since this pose is drawn from an aerial view, sketch long, straight antennae in the foreground.

Close-Up!

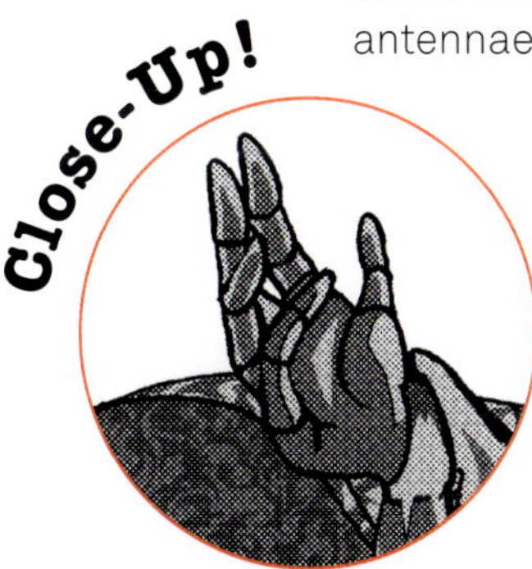

Draw a realistic human hand casting a hypnotic spell.

Draw thin legs extending in the direction in which he's moving. When drawing insects on the move, the legs are the most important element.

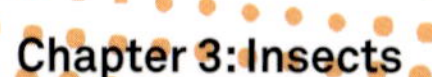

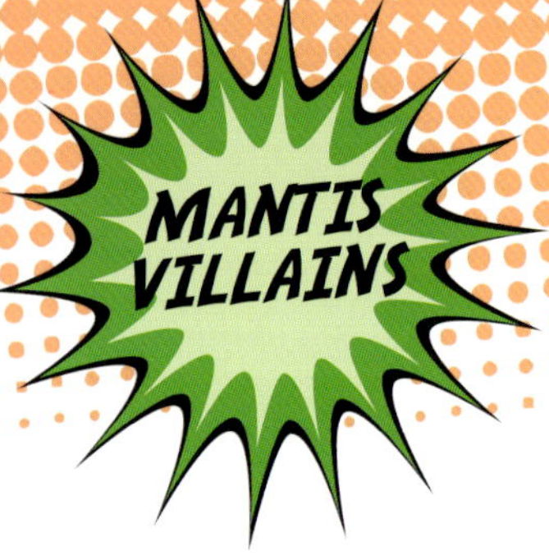

The Praying Pest

Spoiled by her parents, this naughty mantis teen has become the bully of the insect world. She preys upon weaker, smaller victims to mask her own insecurities. Her lethal hooks are her prized possessions.

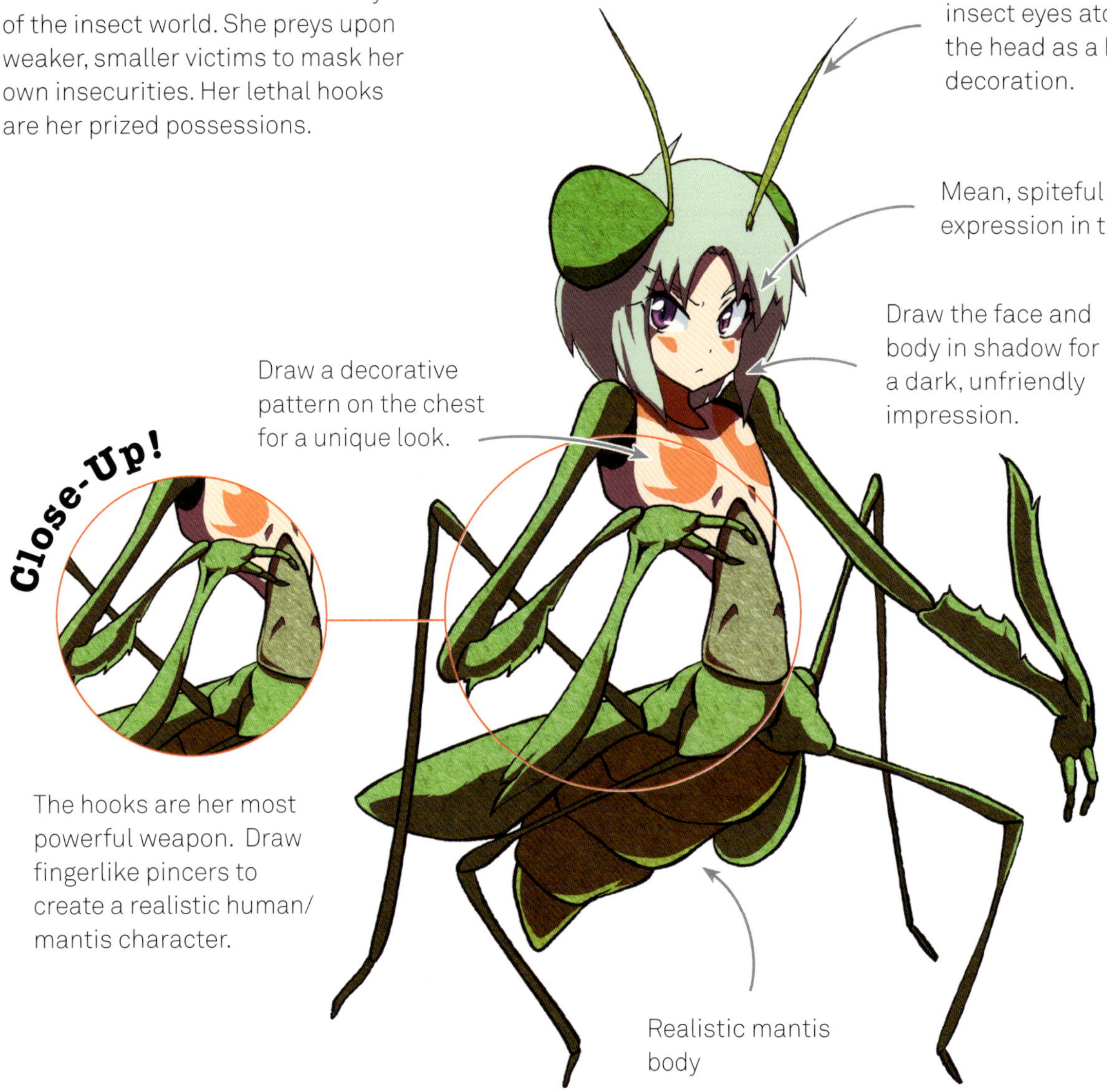

Front View

Position the antennae and characteristic insect eyes atop the head as a hair decoration.

Mean, spiteful expression in the eyes

Draw the face and body in shadow for a dark, unfriendly impression.

Draw a decorative pattern on the chest for a unique look.

Close-Up!

The hooks are her most powerful weapon. Draw fingerlike pincers to create a realistic human/mantis character.

Realistic mantis body

Color Tip:

Use shades of green since mantises are known for their camouflaging abilities. Use light purple for shadow accents.

VILLAINOUS TRAITS

1. Bossy
2. Self-centered
3. Kung fu master of the insect world

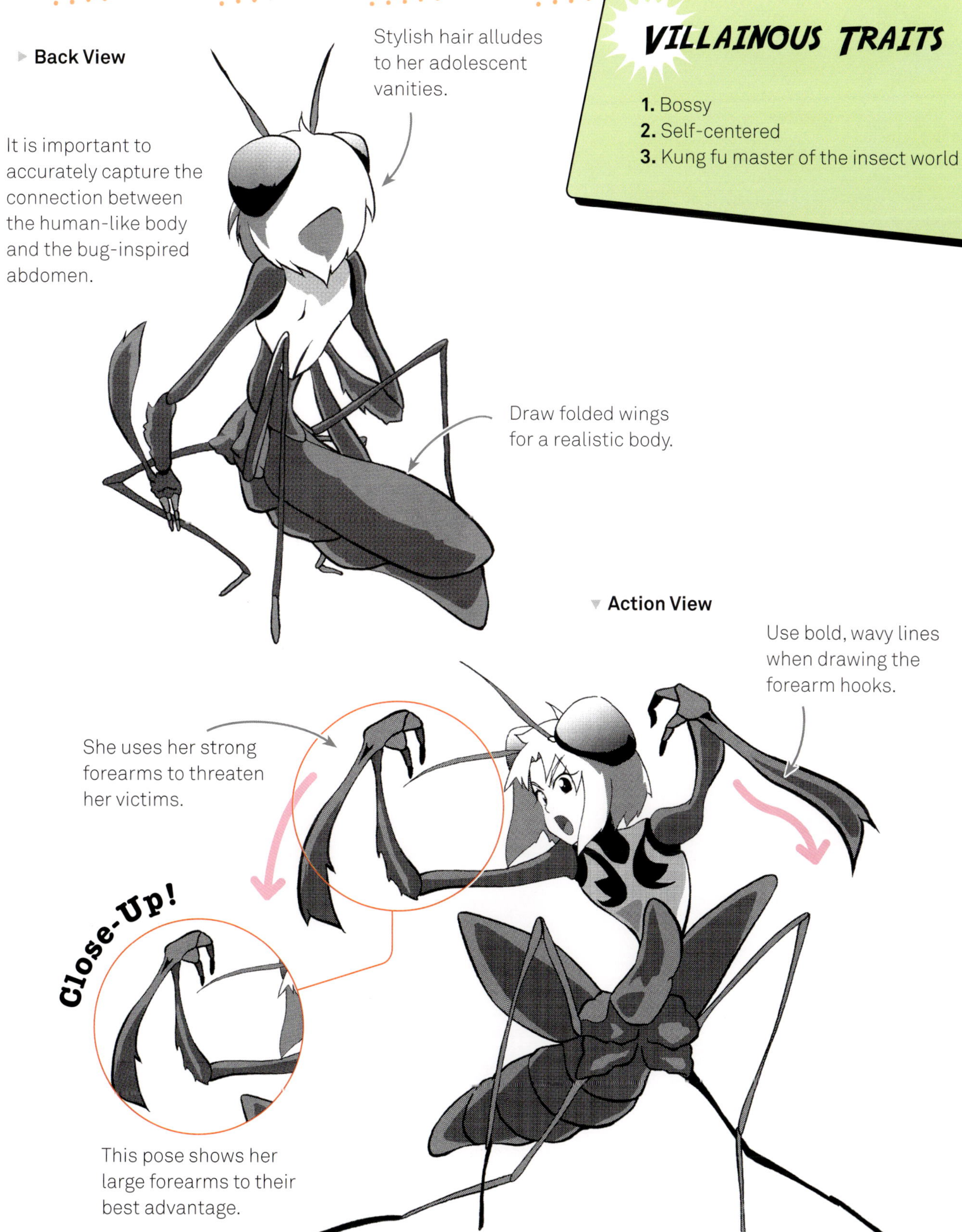

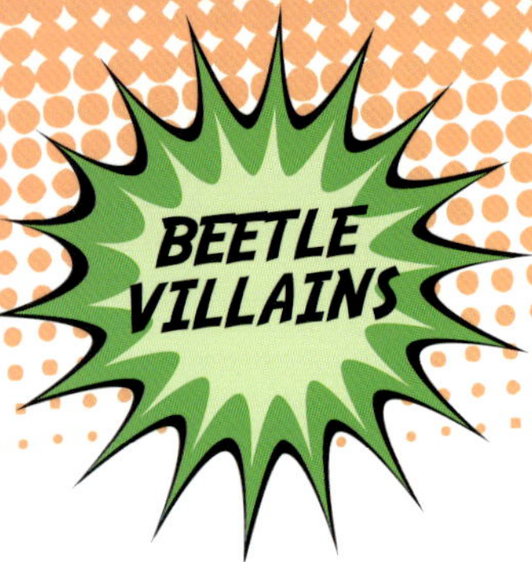

The Beetle Bot

This insect villain possesses extremely unique capabilities: He can appear as an unassuming beetle, then transform into a killer robot. Revered as the "Lord of the Beetles," he can call upon the world's billions of beetles to swarm and attack at his command.

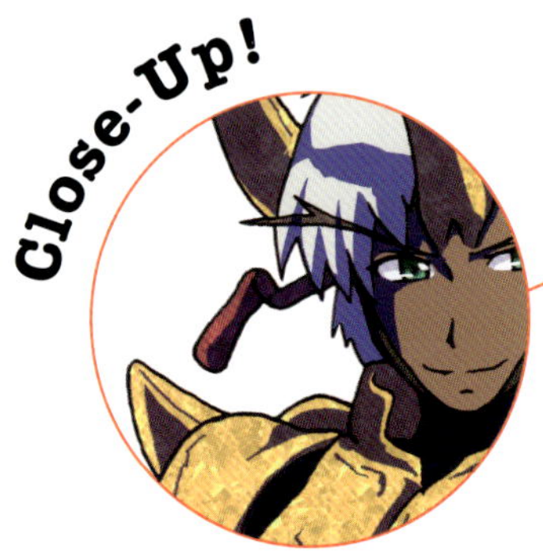

Make sure to draw large, imposing horns to capture the viewer's attention. Use shadow to create a metallic appearance.

▼ Front View

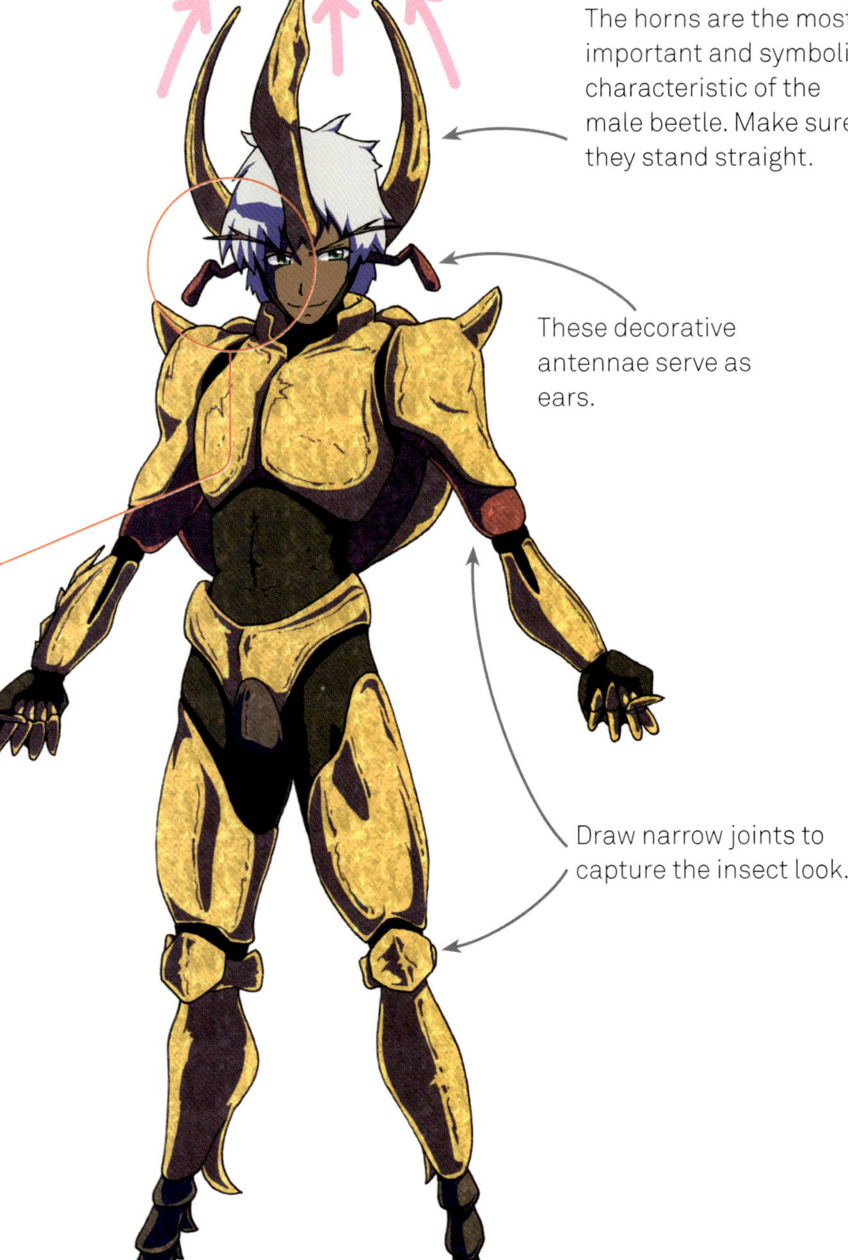

The horns are the most important and symbolic characteristic of the male beetle. Make sure they stand straight.

These decorative antennae serve as ears.

Draw narrow joints to capture the insect look.

Color Tip:

The majority of beetles are dark brown or black, but try using bold, majestic colors like gold and purple to emphasize his strength and status.

VILLAINOUS TRAITS

1. Transformation
2. Sharp horns
3. Exoskeleton armor

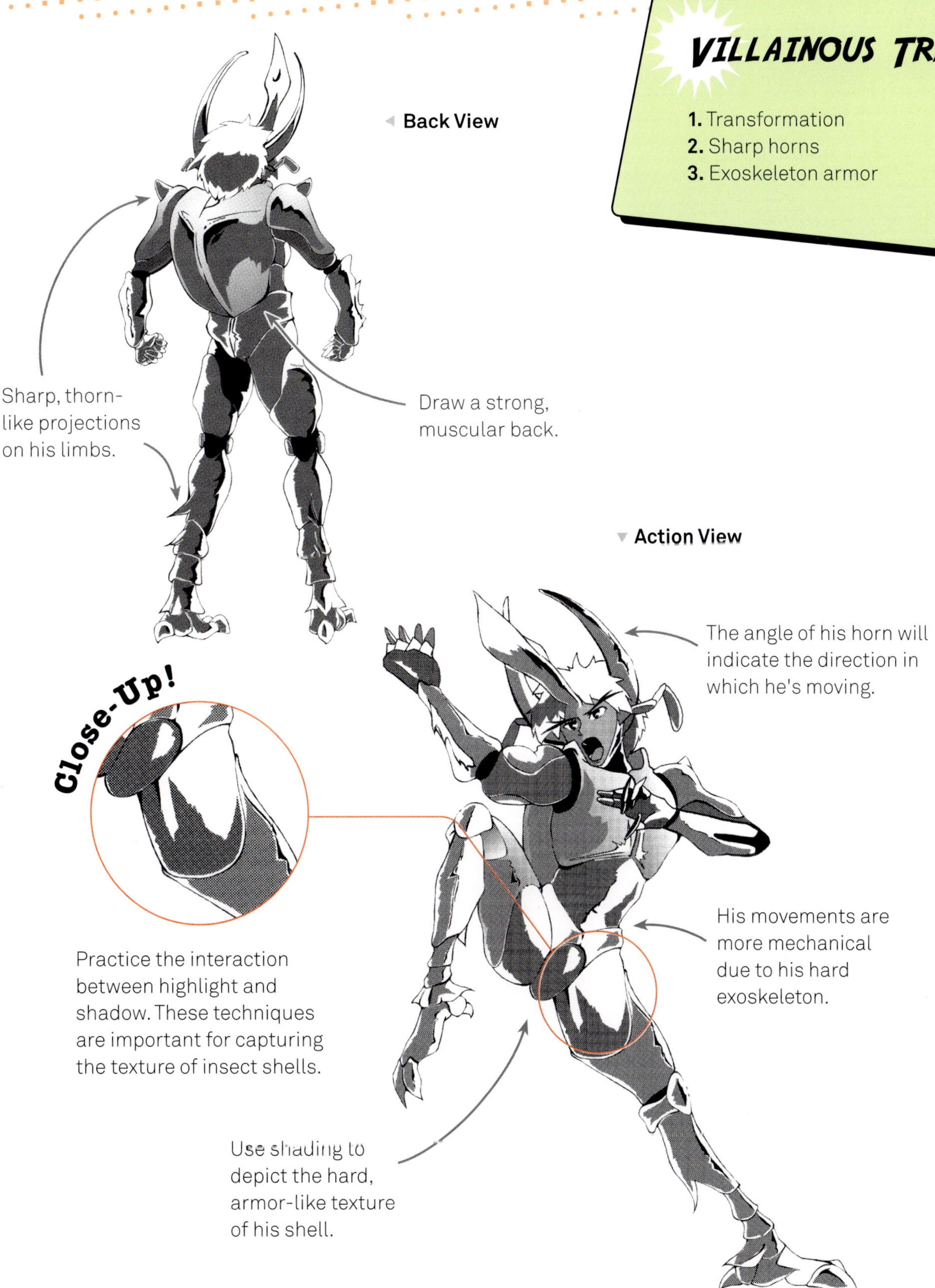

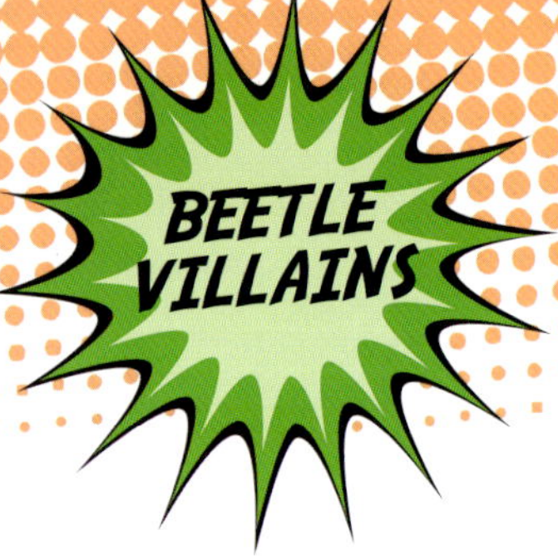

The Beetle Babe

This powerful female beetle is a strong and formidable opponent. She's able to camouflage herself in almost any setting and can sense imminent danger. If she does come under attack, she possesses an impenetrable armored shell for protection.

▼ Front View

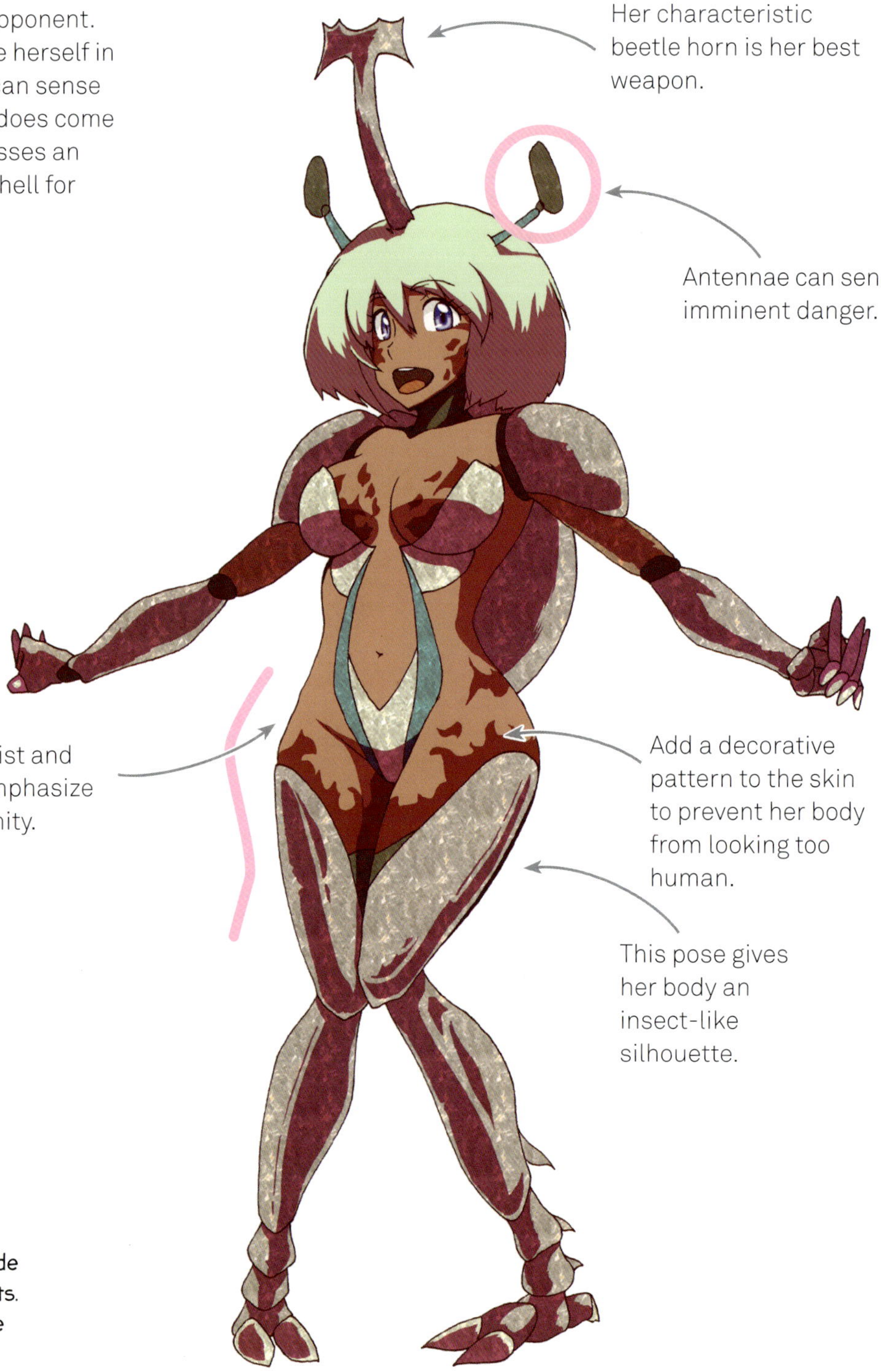

Her characteristic beetle horn is her best weapon.

Antennae can sense imminent danger.

Narrow waist and full hips emphasize her femininity.

Add a decorative pattern to the skin to prevent her body from looking too human.

This pose gives her body an insect-like silhouette.

Color Tip:

For the main color, opt for a shade of brown with red and purple tints. Add metallic accents to replicate a beetle's iridescent shell.

VILLAINOUS TRAITS

1. Danger-sensing antennae
2. Impenetrable armored shell
3. Lethal horn

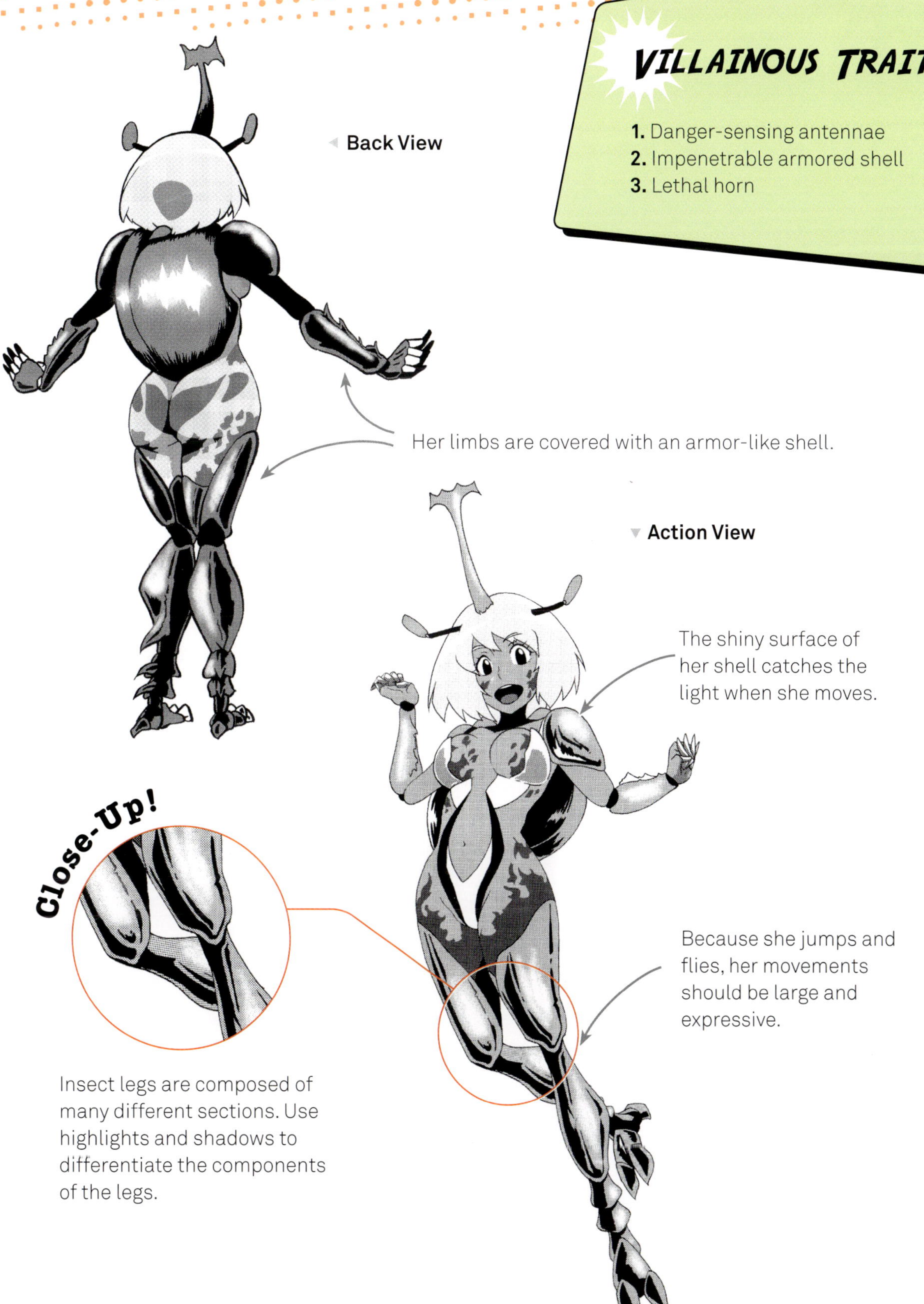

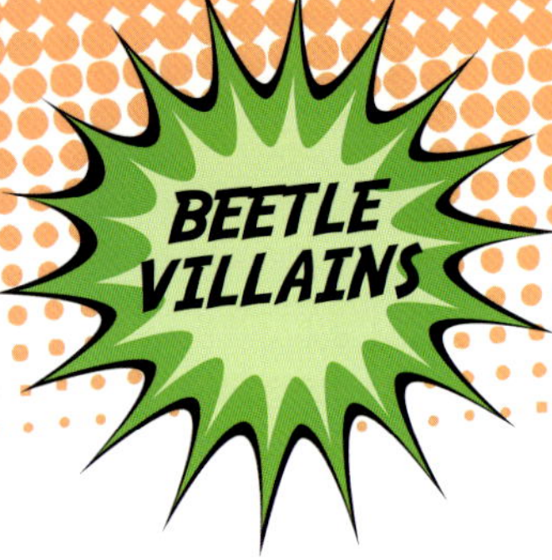

THE PETULANT PUPA

Inspired by the adolescent stage of the insect life cycle, this character is more annoying than evil. As a spoiled child, this character has developed a terrible temper.

Front View

Helmet-inspired headwear is appropriate for this character's age.

For the classic insect look, the eyes should be large in proportion to the mouth.

Stack several round sections on top of each other to achieve the caterpillar body shape.

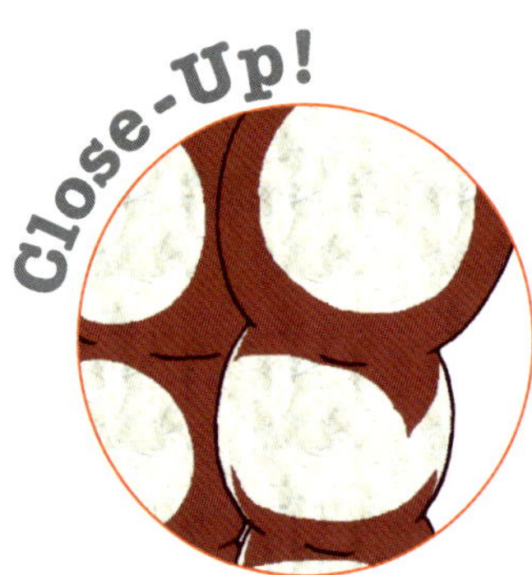

Shading is the key to capturing the silhouette of the round sections.

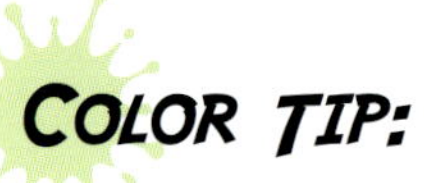

COLOR TIP:

For a natural look, use white as the main color, then add contrasting brown shadows.

VILLAINOUS TRAITS

1. Volatile temper
2. Spoiled
3. Protective shell

▼ Back View

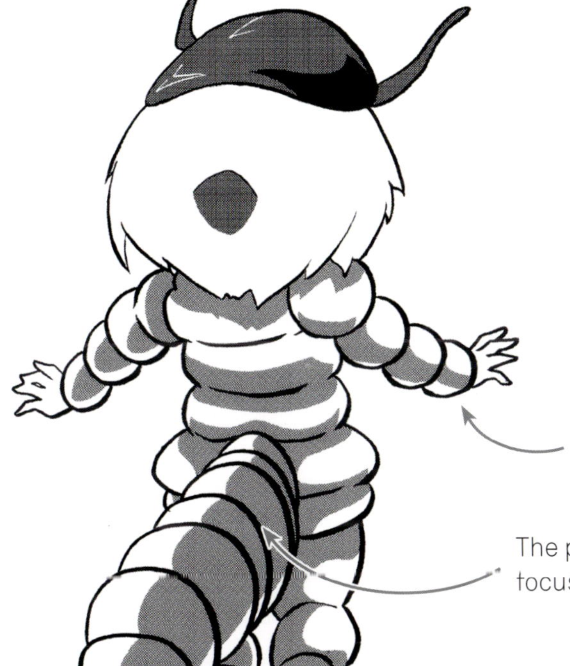

Use round shapes for the arms and legs.

The perspective is focused on the tail.

▼ Action View

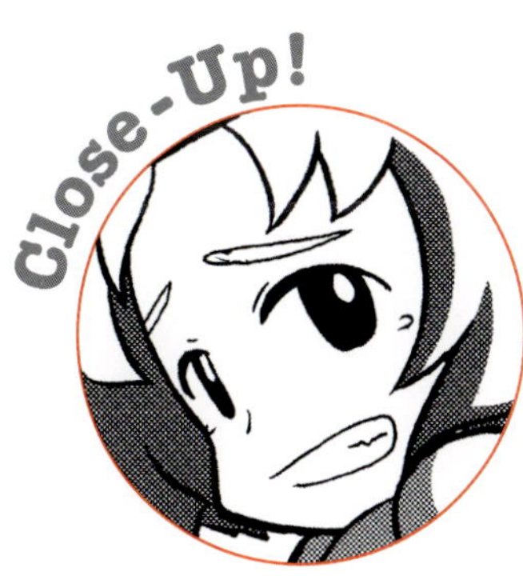

Tears, knit eyebrows and twisted mouth convey that this character is in the middle of a temper tantrum of epic proportions.

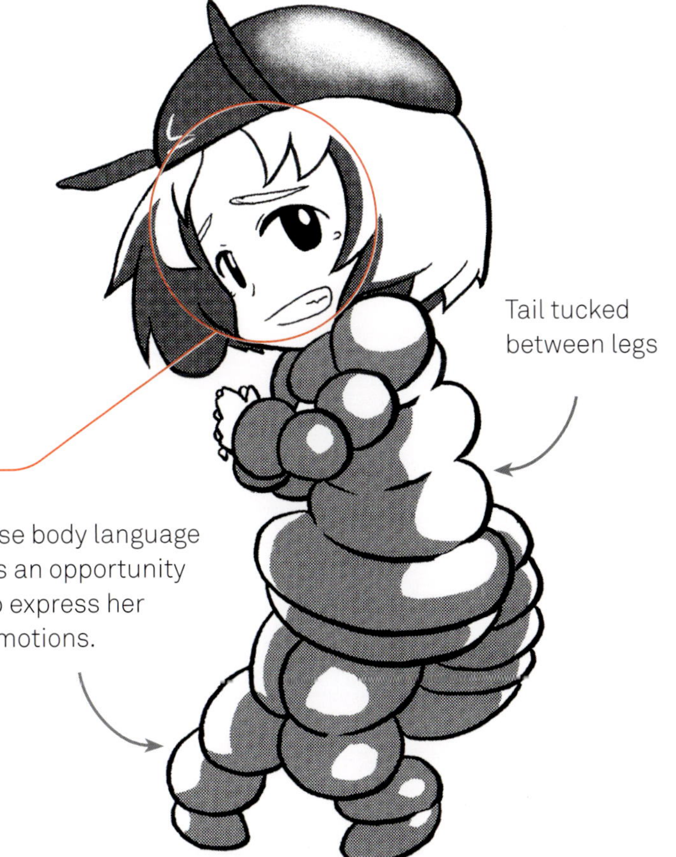

Use body language as an opportunity to express her emotions.

Tail tucked between legs

THE CHARM IS IN THE DETAILS

From the head to the toes, it's all about the details.

Have you ever heard the expression: "God is in the details?" Well, we like to say "the charm is in the details." Details are the perfect opportunity to add creative touches that emphasize a character's personality and motivations.

For example, the clothing of the The Chosen One featured on page 50 includes tentacle-inspired design elements. The character would be a lot less interesting if she were wearing a more traditional human girl's dress.

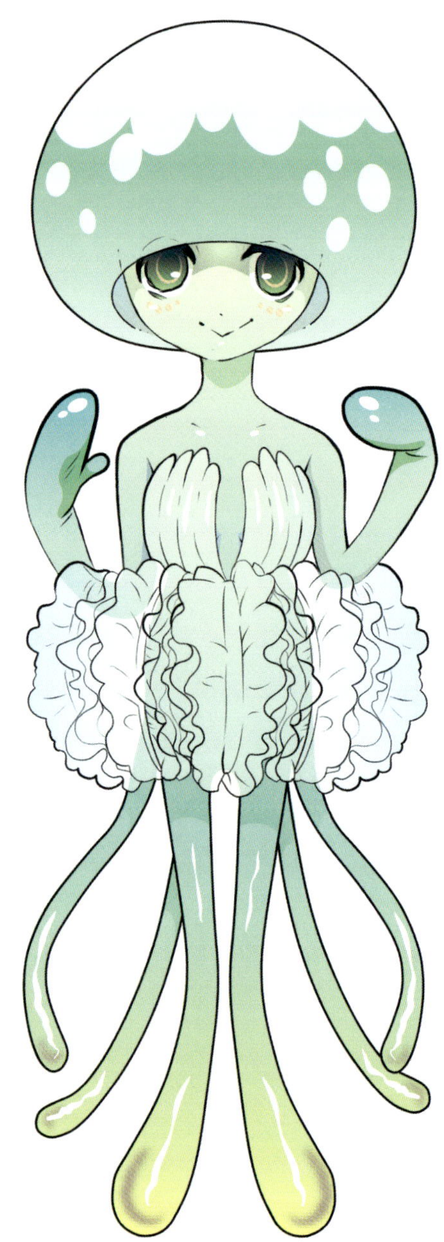

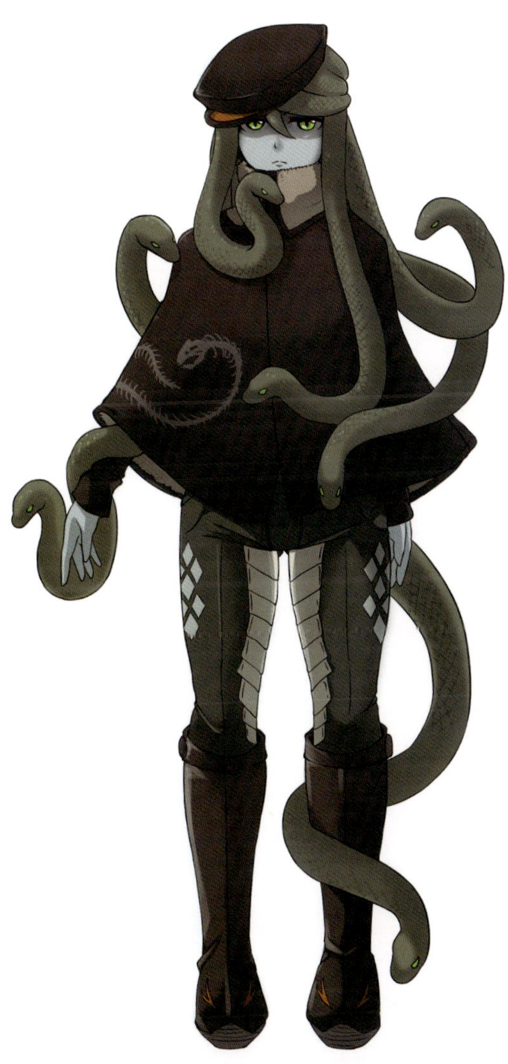

Clothing is one of the easiest and most obvious ways to incorporate details about your character. Try using body language and facial expressions to convey more subtle details about the character's personality. Notice how the Feline Fatale on page 16 coyly wraps her furry tail around her legs, while her ears stand at alert. What do these details reveal about her personality?

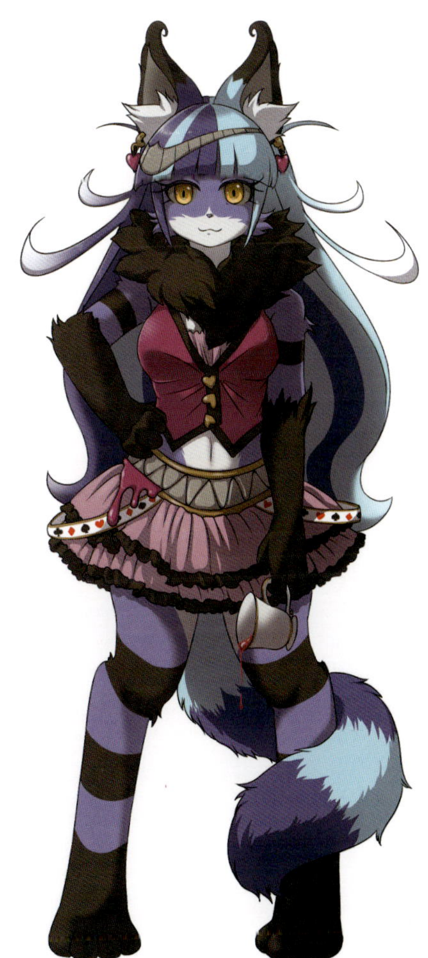

Another great example involves the Serpentine Seductress from page 32. From her snakeskin leggings to her snake-shaped boots, reptilian influences are visible in nearly every aspect of her outfit.

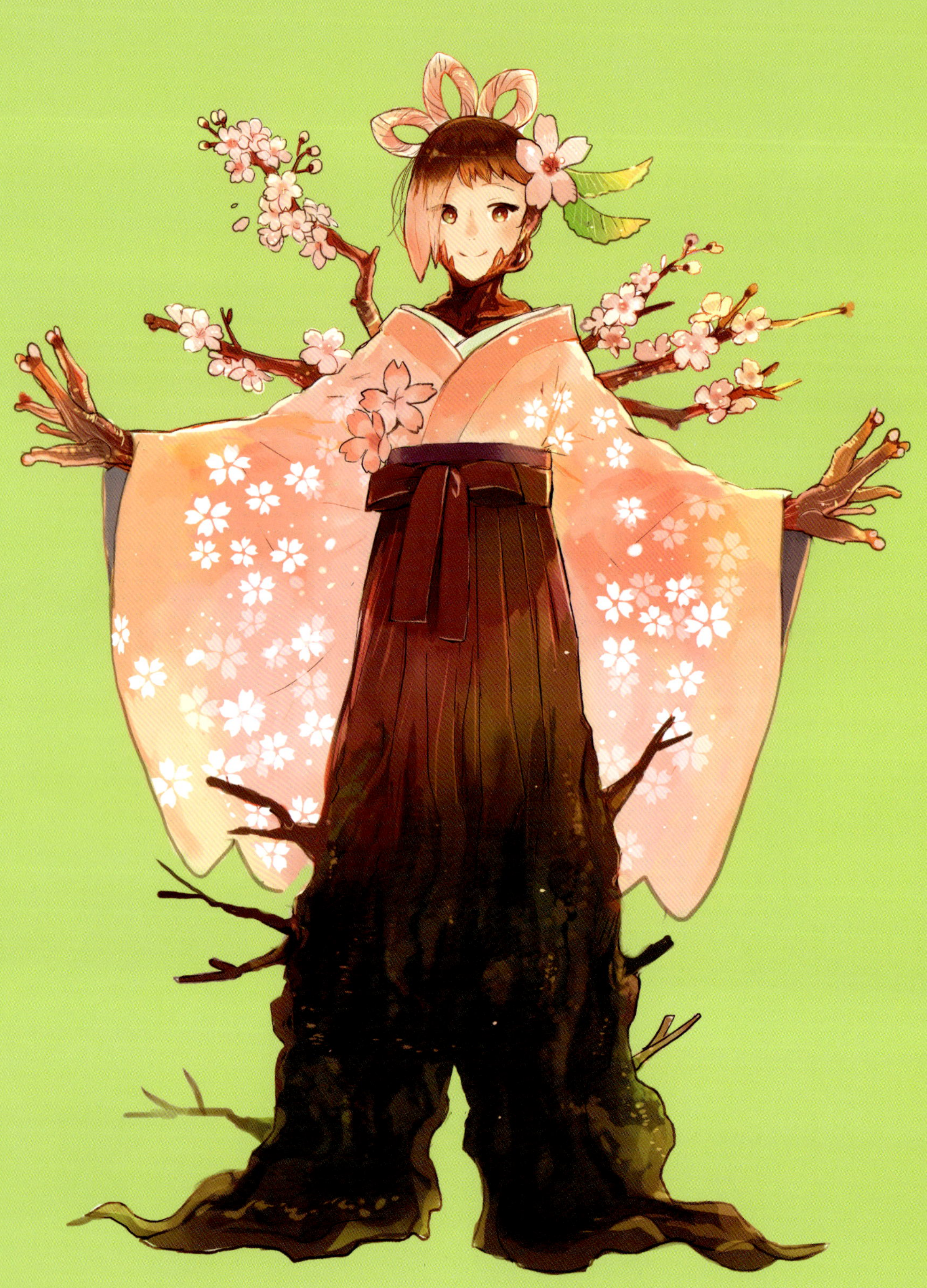

CHAPTER 4

PLANTS

The key to drawing plant-inspired villains lies in the hands and feet. If you draw a character with a plant body and human hands and feet, it tends to have a cosplay look, which you want to avoid. Instead, try drawing branch and stem-shaped limbs.

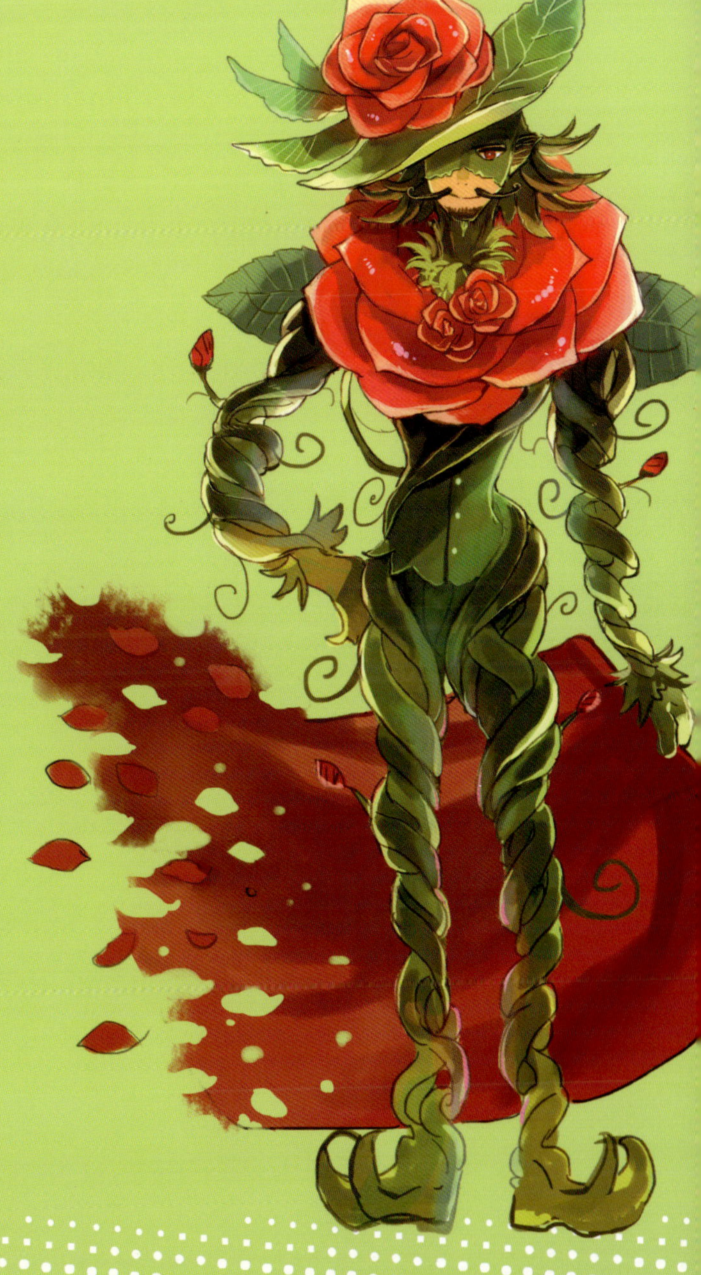

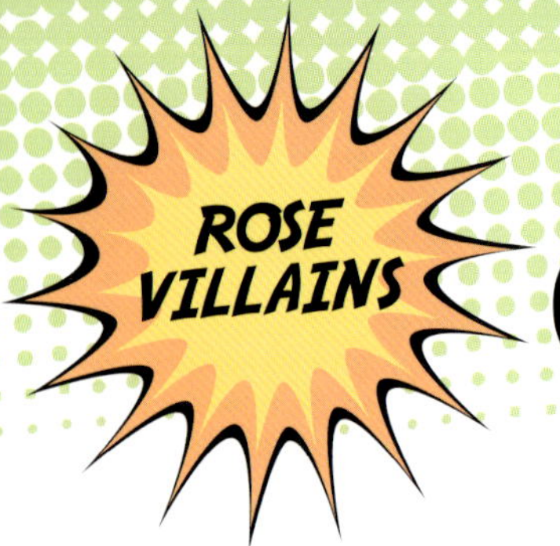

The Queen of Thorns

This beautiful and elegant rose queen rules the botanic world. She is known for being graceful and noble, but she's extremely passionate and can become quite dangerous when enraged. She uses her powerful vines to snare and strangle her dissidents ... and watch out for those thorns!

▼ **Front View**

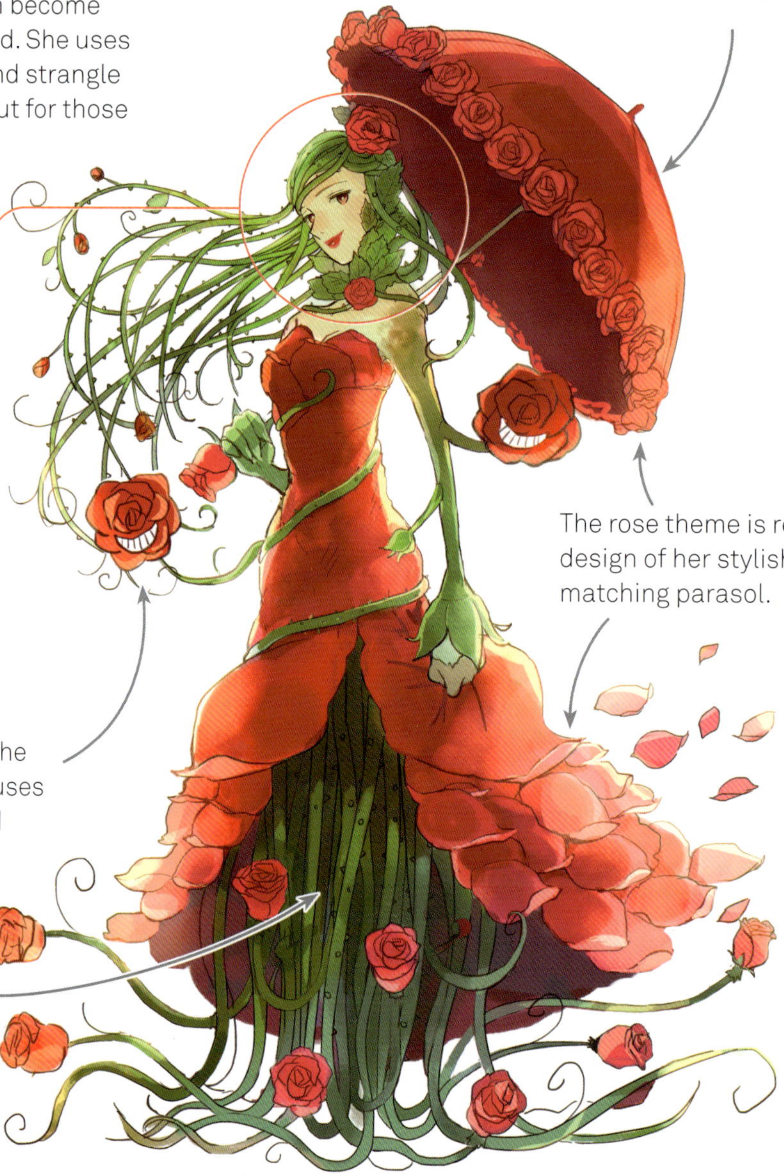

Her ladylike parasol suggests a classy, refined personality.

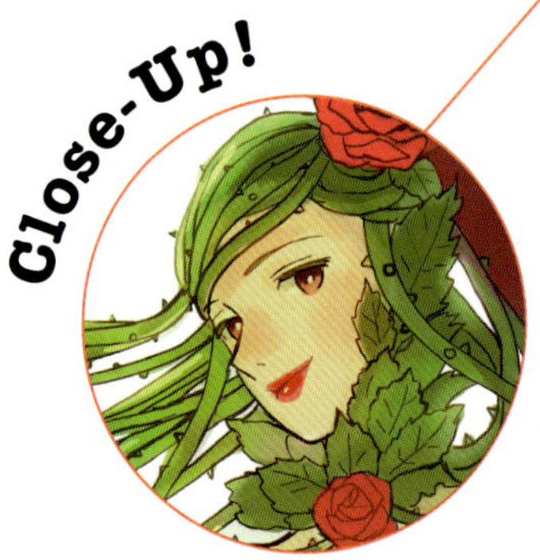

Close-Up!

Draw elegant, dainty facial features.

The rose theme is reflected in the design of her stylish gown and matching parasol.

Look closely: The roses blooming at the ends of the vines have mouths! She uses her vines to entangle and then devour her victims.

Instead of legs, she uses her vines to climb and move.

COLOR TIP:

In addition to being the most popular rose color, red is a symbol of passion and strength.

VILLAINOUS TRAITS

1. Sharp thorns
2. Strangling vines
3. Powers of season manipulation

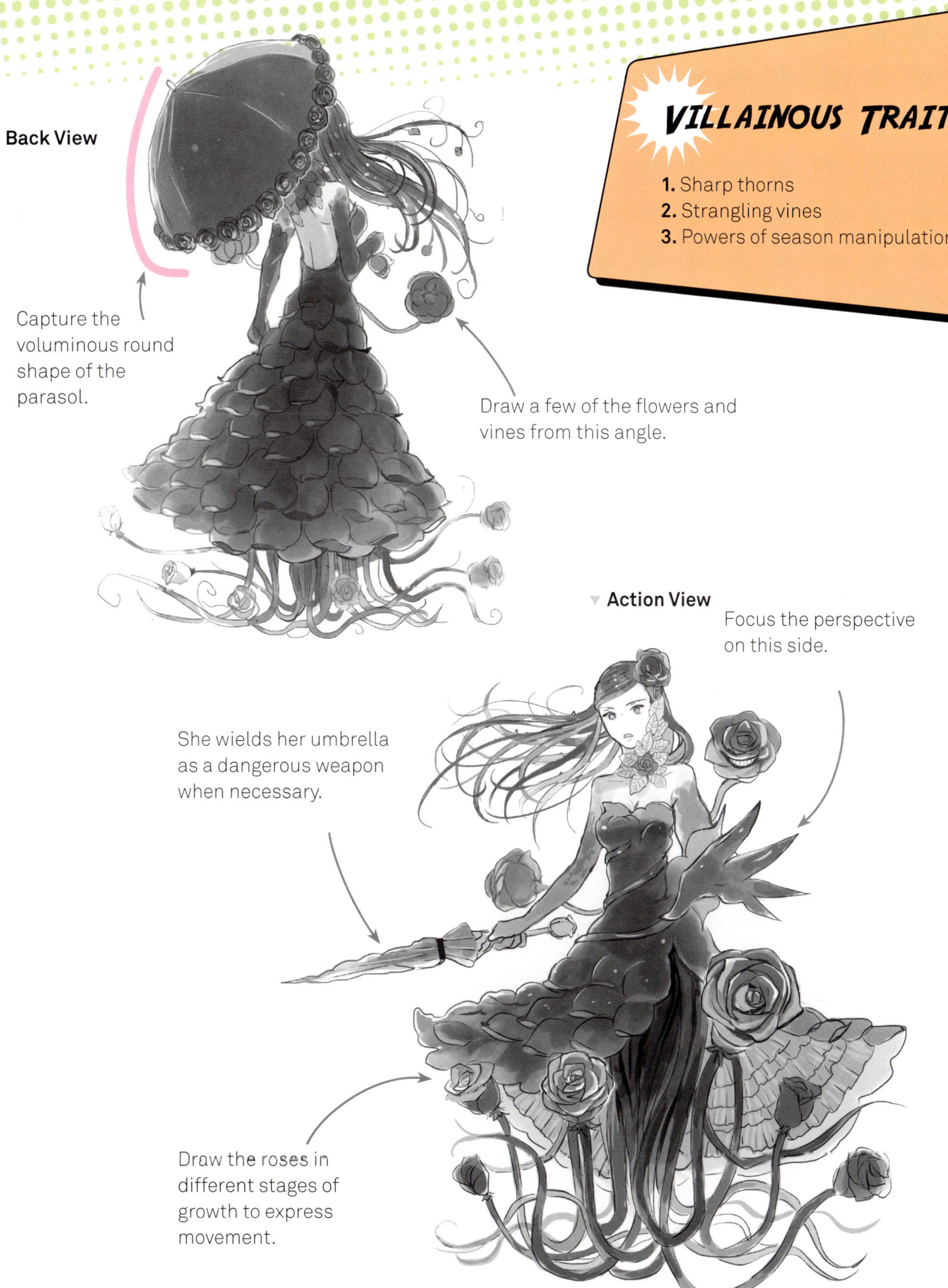

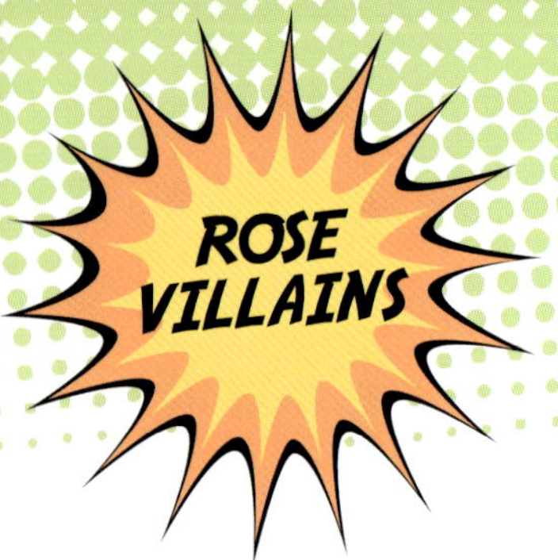

The Blooming Bullfighter

This brave bullfighter has a tragic past filled with great loss. He's become addicted to danger and goes around picking fights with anyone and everyone who stands in his way.

▼ **Front View**

A large leaf forms the base of his sombrero-style hat. Use soft yellow highlights to add dimension.

Sinuous vines and budding flowers add depth.

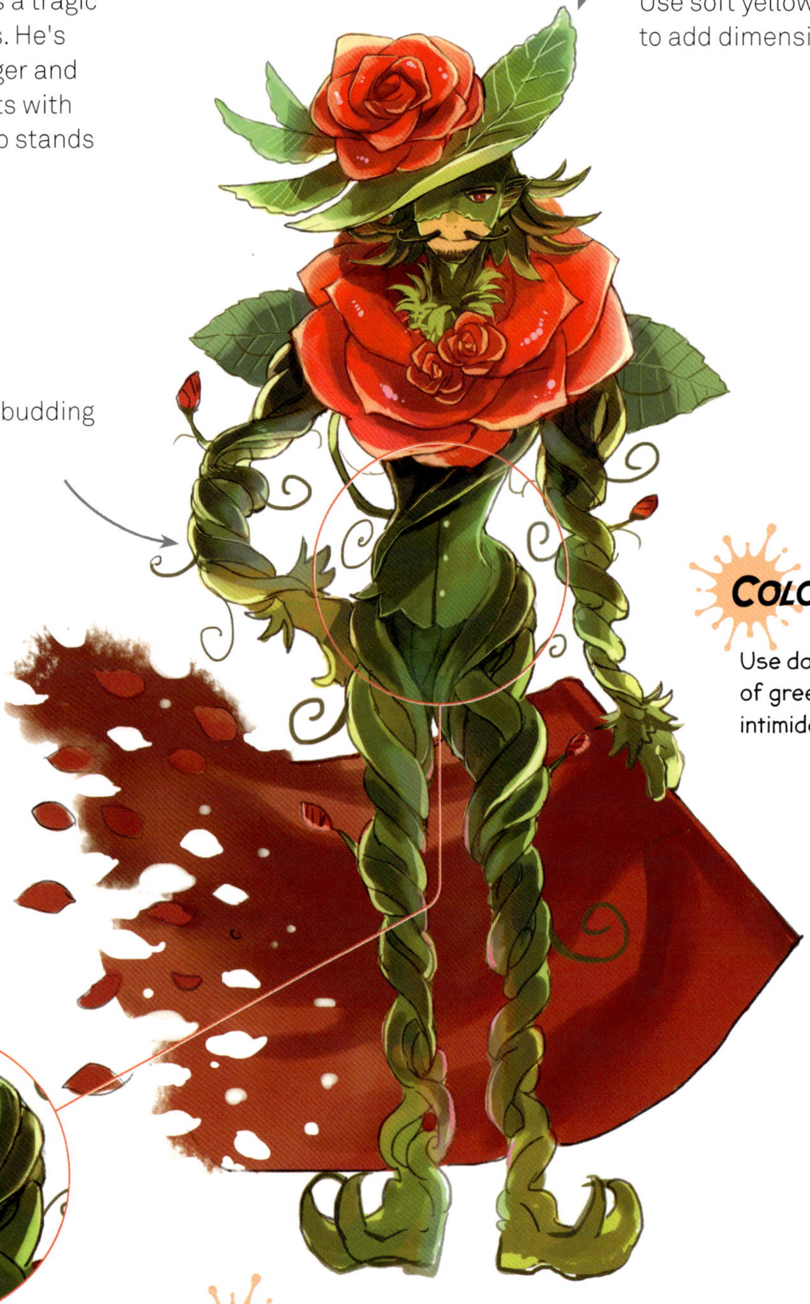

COLOR TIP:

Use dark shades of green for a more intimidating look.

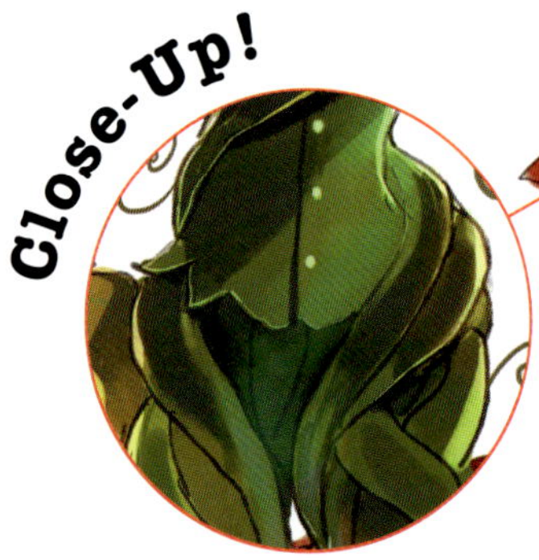

Close-Up!

Incorporate small details from a matador's costume, such as this traditional vest.

COLOR TIP:

The gradated shades of green emphasize the twisting silhouette of the vines. The surface area of the red cape should equal the amount of green used in the illustration in order to provide impactful contrast.

VILLAINOUS TRAITS

1. Ladies' man
2. Addicted to danger
3. Poisonous petals that can be used to sedate victims

▶ Back View

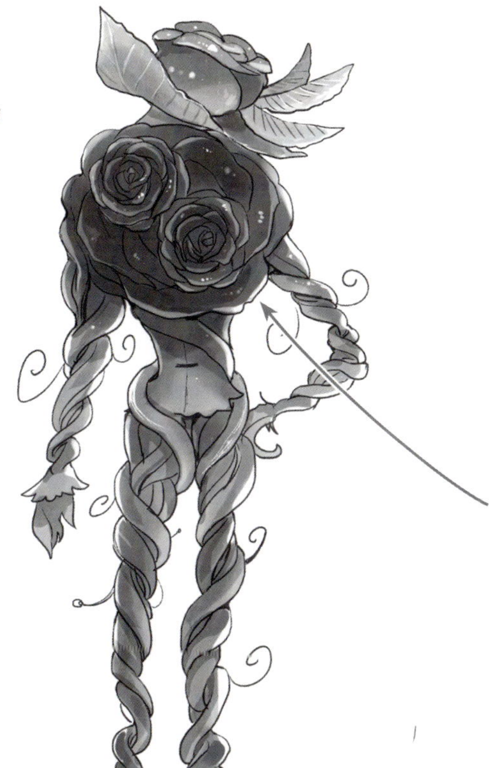

This view creates a lonely cowboy impression that hints at a sad past.

▼ Action View

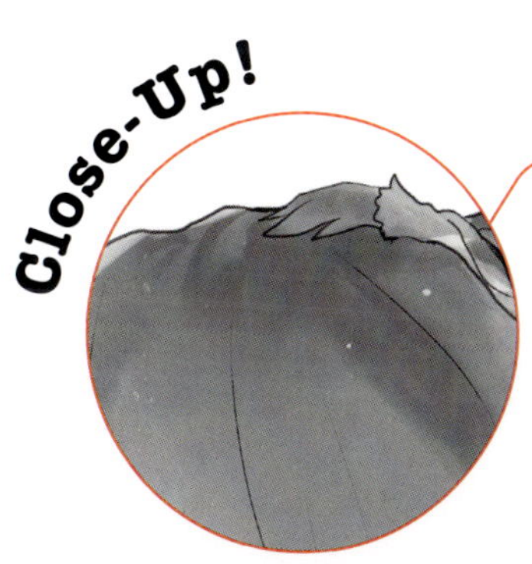

Focus on the lines of movement when drawing the cape. The petals floating in the breeze also add movement.

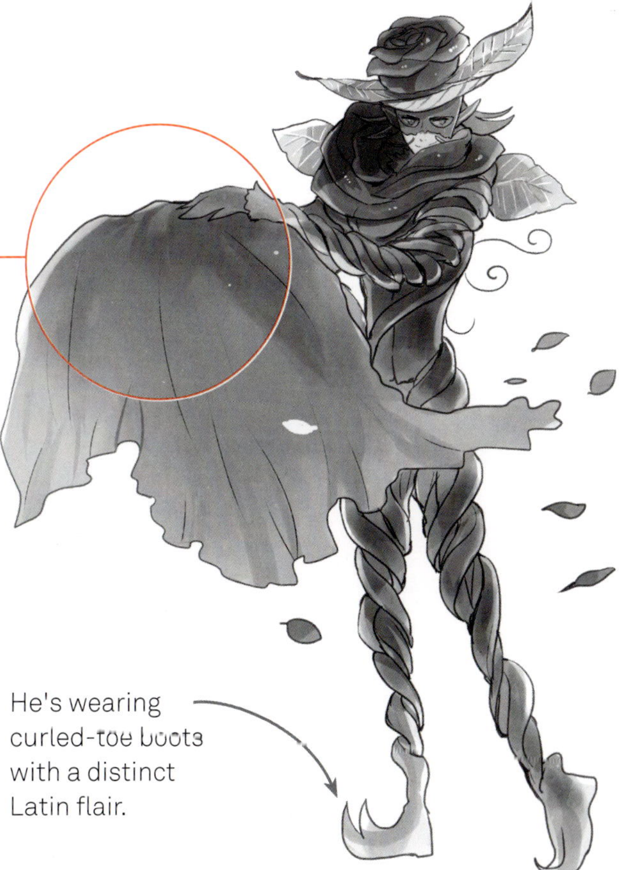

He's wearing curled-toe boots with a distinct Latin flair.

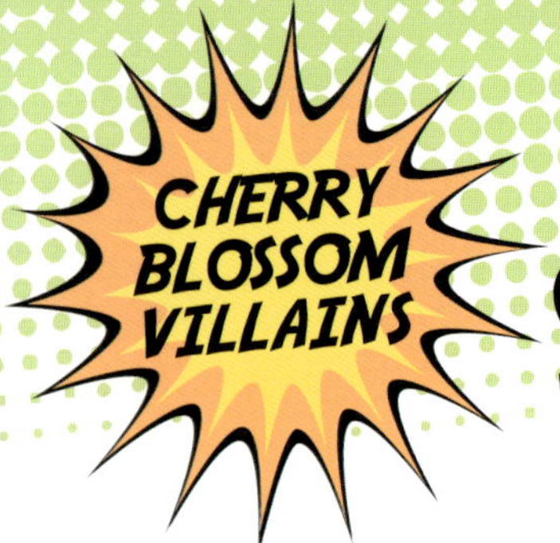

THE SAKURA SORCERESS

This graceful beauty is a powerful witch who can control the emotions of those around her. Although she is normally a pacifist, she can use her massive branches and trunk to thrash her enemies.

▼ **Front View**

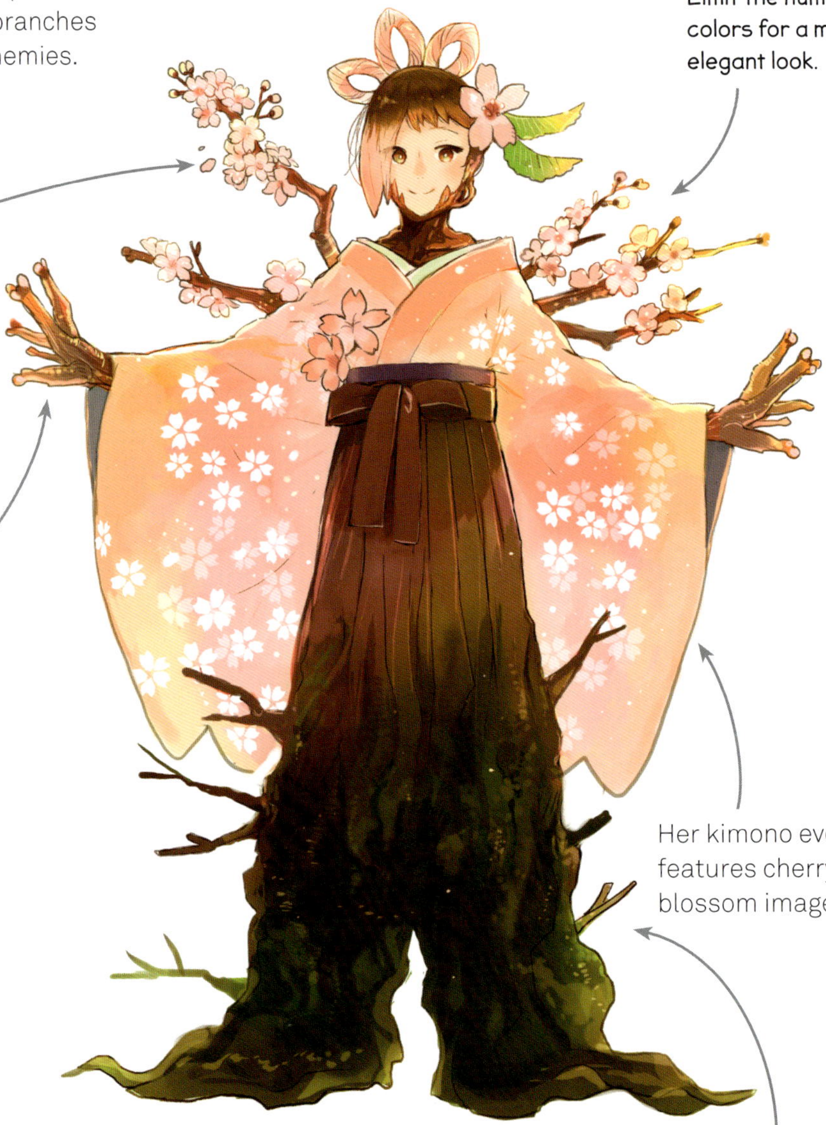

COLOR TIP:

Limit the number of colors for a muted, elegant look.

Incorporate as many cherry blossoms as possible.

Draw thin, branch-like fingers with small blossoms at the tips.

Her kimono even features cherry blossom imagery.

COLOR TIP:

Use more muted shades of pink for an elegant look. White serves as a striking accent color when set against the dark tree trunk.

The bottom of her *hakama* (traditional Japanese pants) gradually transforms into a tree trunk with roots.

VILLAINOUS TRAITS

1. Sorceress
2. Aura vision
3. Can control the emotions of those around her

◂ Back View

Her branches intersect in a striking radial pattern.

▾ Action View

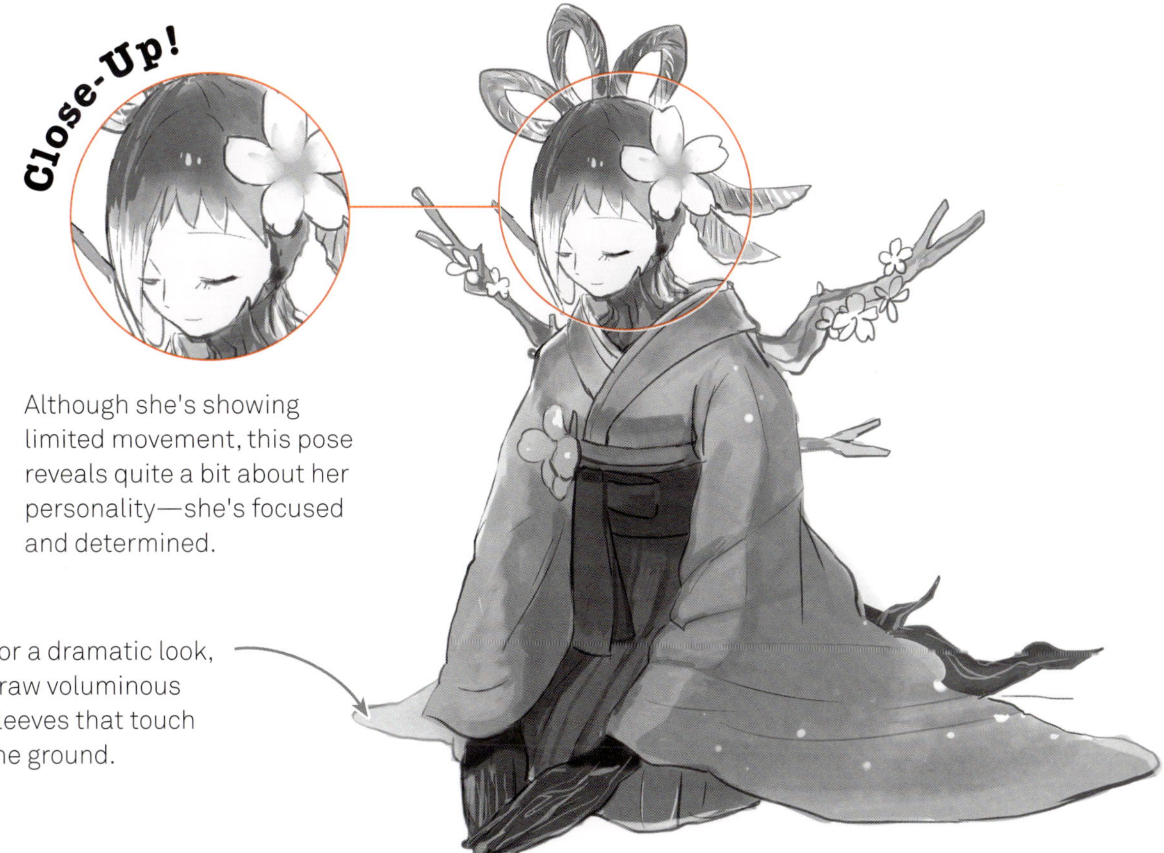

Although she's showing limited movement, this pose reveals quite a bit about her personality—she's focused and determined.

For a dramatic look, draw voluminous sleeves that touch the ground.

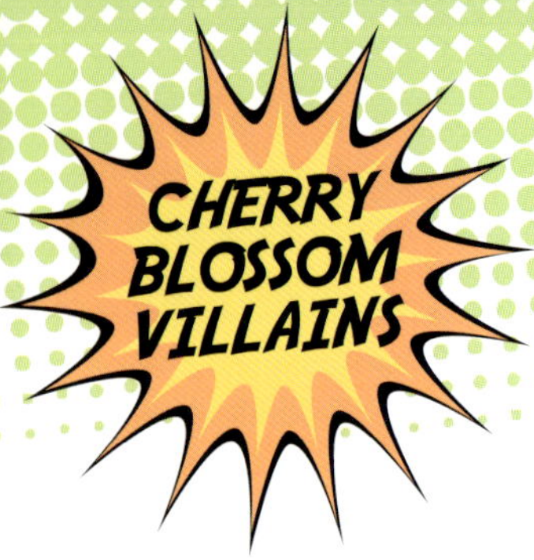

THE WOODLAND WARRIOR

This handsome loner is a fierce warrior. He possesses a strong sense of justice and is not afraid to sacrifice his life for his cause. He lives in the remote mountains of Japan.

▼ **Front View**

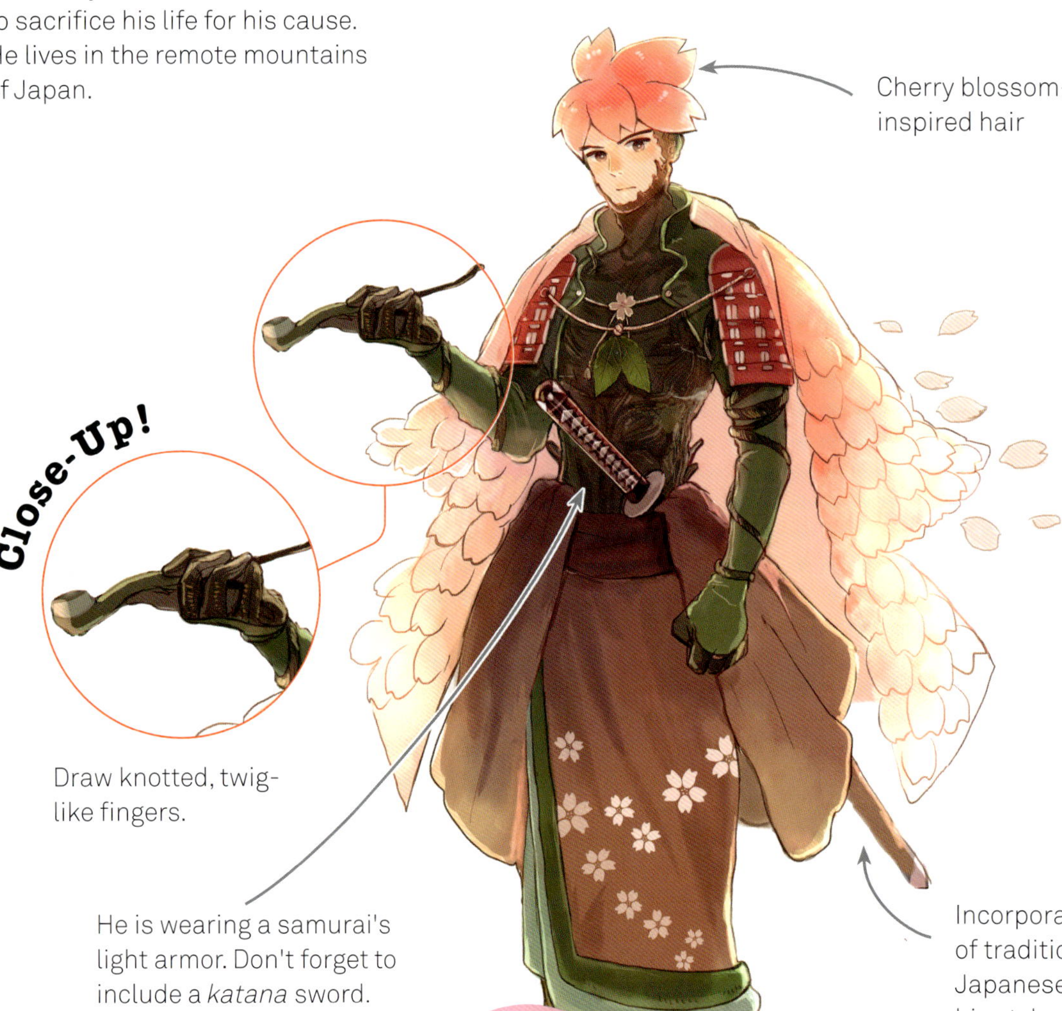

Cherry blossom-inspired hair

Draw knotted, twig-like fingers.

He is wearing a samurai's light armor. Don't forget to include a *katana* sword.

Incorporate elements of traditional Japanese culture into his style of dress.

He is a go-getter—draw realistic human shoes instead of plant-inspired ones.

COLOR TIP:

Use dark greens and browns as the main colors, then add cherry blossom pink as an accent. The earthy tones evoke a strong, mature cherry tree and represent masculinity.

VILLAINOUS TRAITS

1. Smokes a Japanese *kiseru* pipe—the smoke from which can put his victims in a trance
2. Skilled martial artist
3. Stubborn

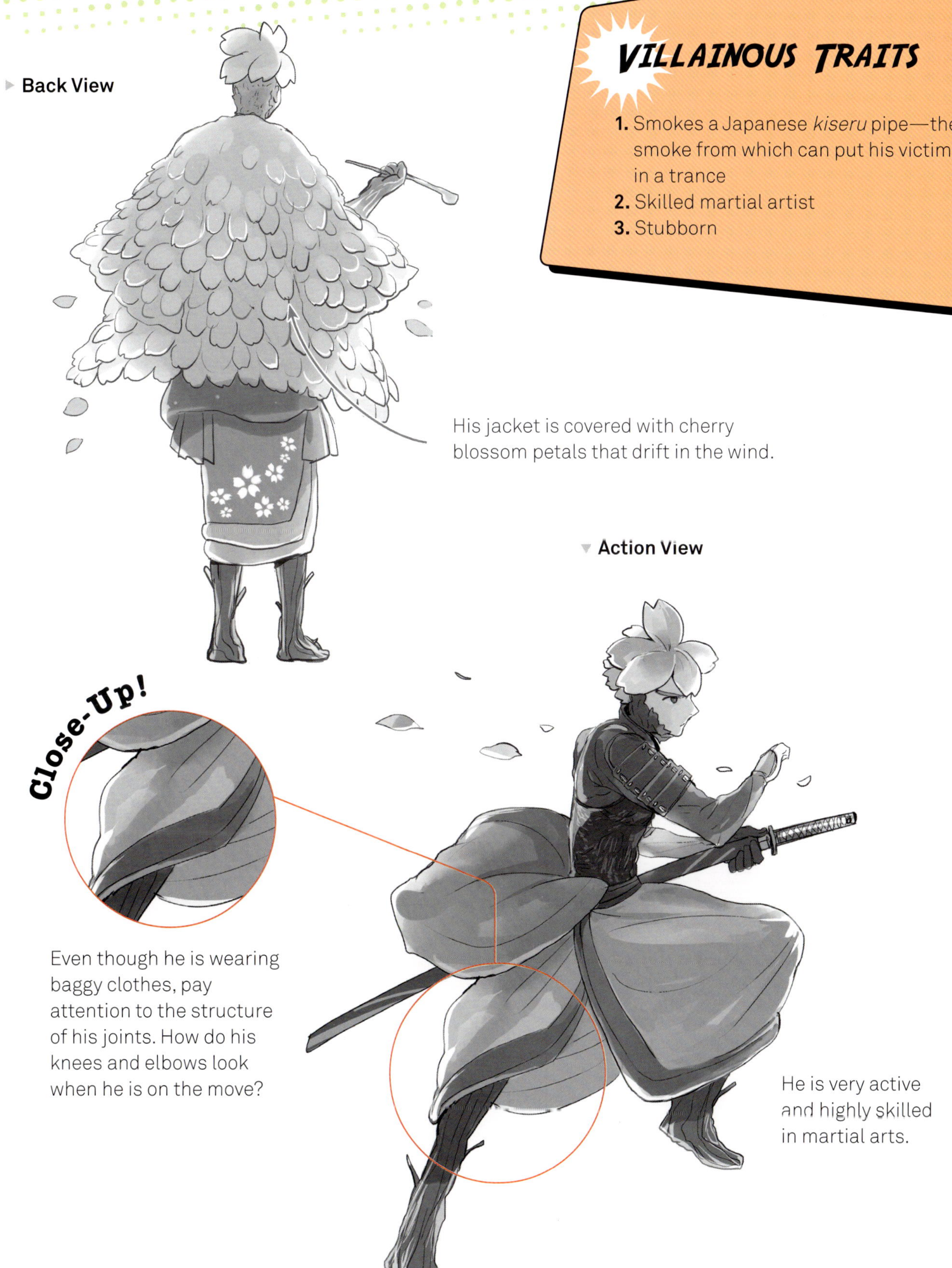

His jacket is covered with cherry blossom petals that drift in the wind.

Even though he is wearing baggy clothes, pay attention to the structure of his joints. How do his knees and elbows look when he is on the move?

He is very active and highly skilled in martial arts.

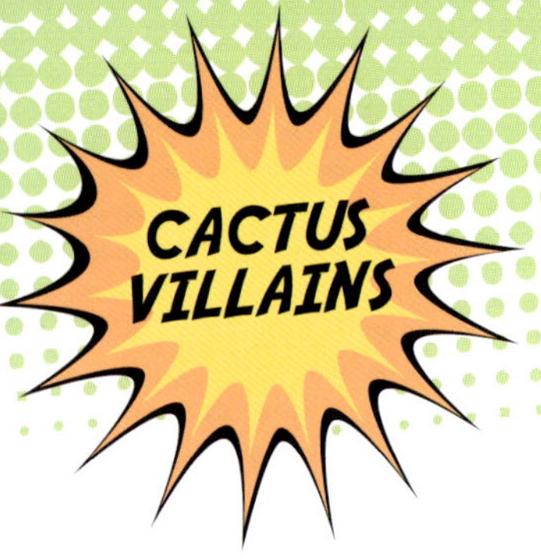

THE PRICKLY PIN-UP

This vintage-inspired villain is straight out of the Wild West. She is a passionate feminist who is not afraid of any man. In addition to possessing sharp spines, she has multiple limbs and is highly armed.

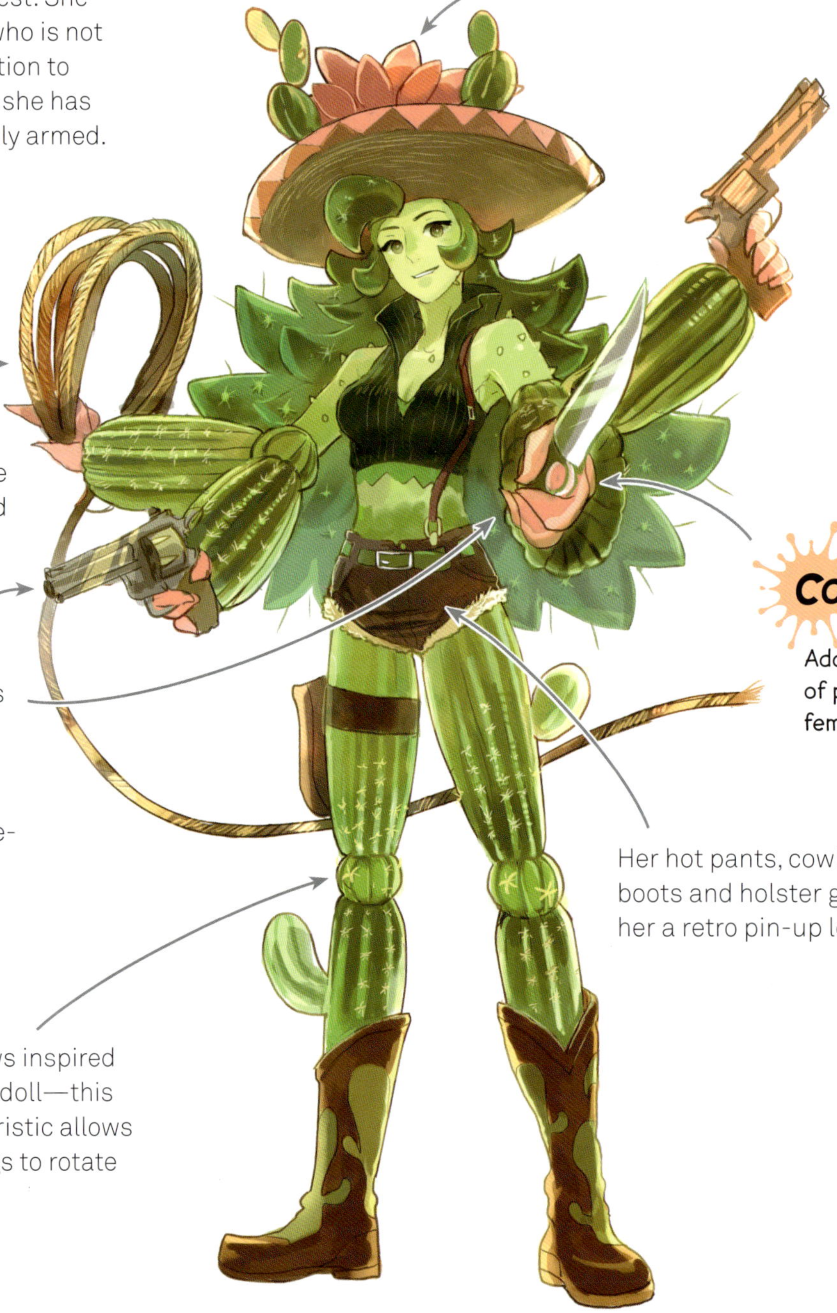

Front View

Stylish sombrero hat

She uses her multiple cactus hands to wield a variety of weapons.

She uses weapons commonly seen in western horse operas—a lasso, dagger and double-barrelled pistols.

Knees and elbows inspired by a ball-jointed doll—this unique characteristic allows her arms and legs to rotate 360°.

Her hot pants, cowboy boots and holster give her a retro pin-up look.

COLOR TIP:

Add some hints of pink for a feminine look.

COLOR TIP:

Use green as the dominant color, then add splashes of brown and pink.

VILLAINOUS TRAITS

1. Sharp spines
2. Multiple arms make her quick and dangerous
3. Drought-resistant

Back View

Her back is inspired by a flat cactus variety.

Action View

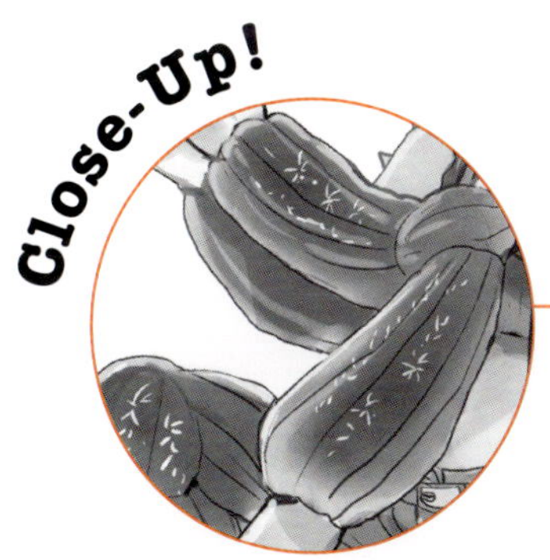

Close-Up!

Incorporate realistic cactus details so it doesn't look like she's wearing a costume.

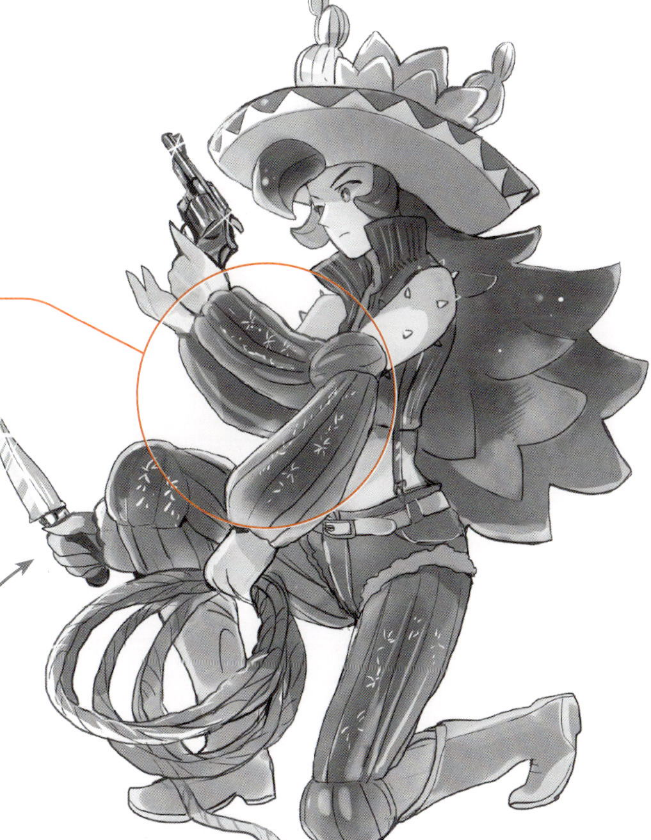

Her multiple arms make her a dangerous foe.

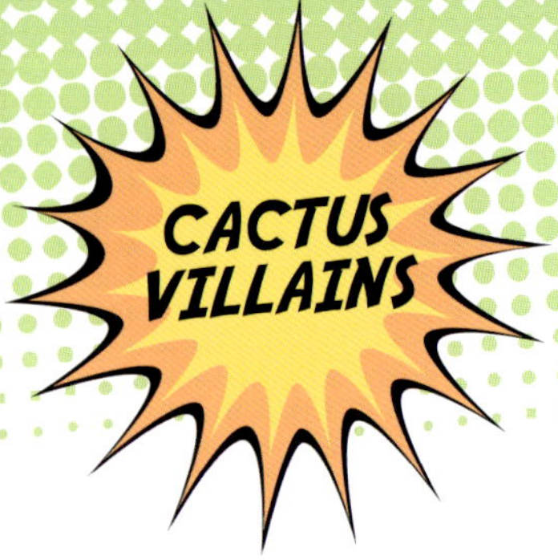

EL LUCHADOR

Inspired by a Mexican *lucha libre* wrestler, this cactus villain possesses incredible strength. With a passionate disposition, he often loses control of his temper and destroys everything in his path.

Front View

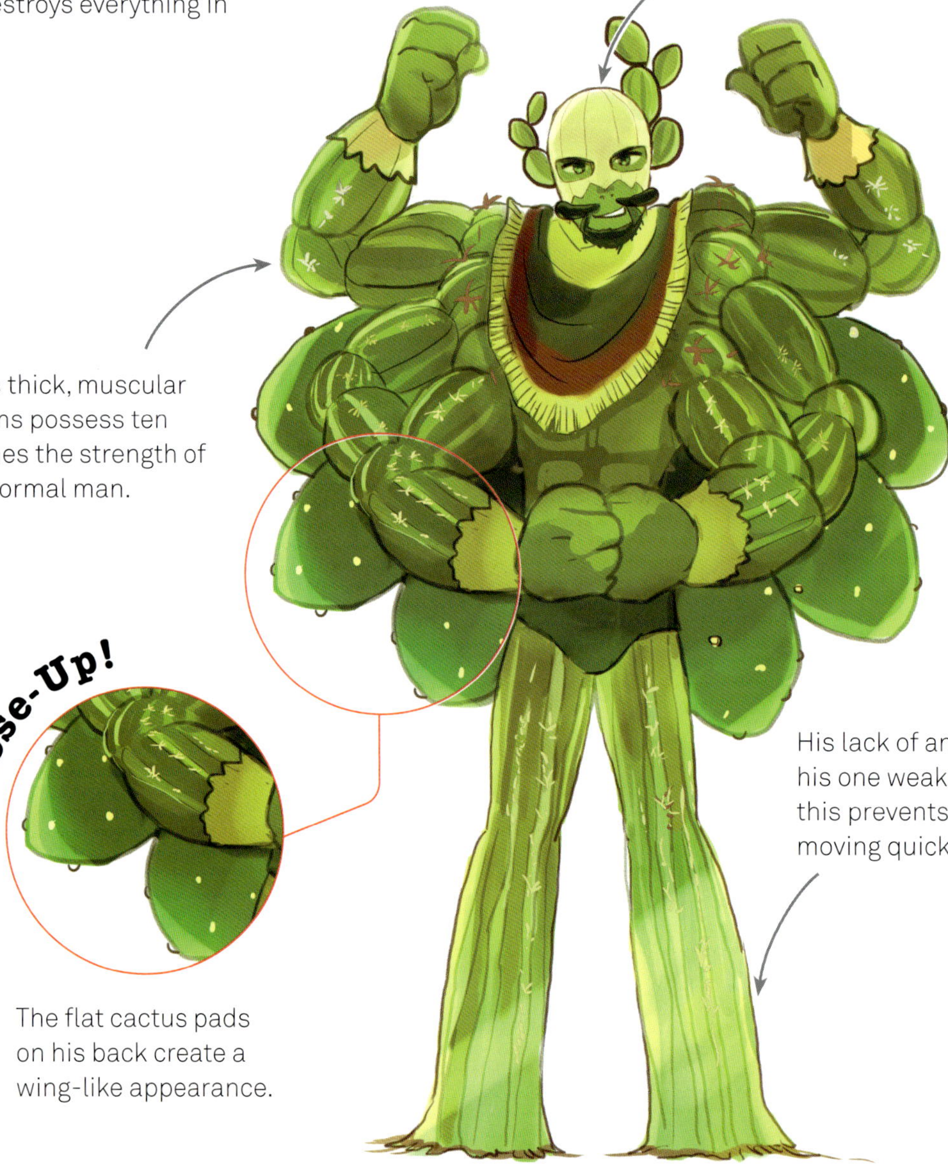

His eyes peek out from behind his mask.

His thick, muscular arms possess ten times the strength of a normal man.

Close-Up!

The flat cactus pads on his back create a wing-like appearance.

His lack of ankles are his one weakness—this prevents him from moving quickly.

COLOR TIP:

He is almost entirely composed of shades of yellow and green. Add some dark accents to prevent monotony.

VILLAINOUS TRAITS

1. Skilled wrestler
2. Immense strength
3. Anger management issues

◂ Back View

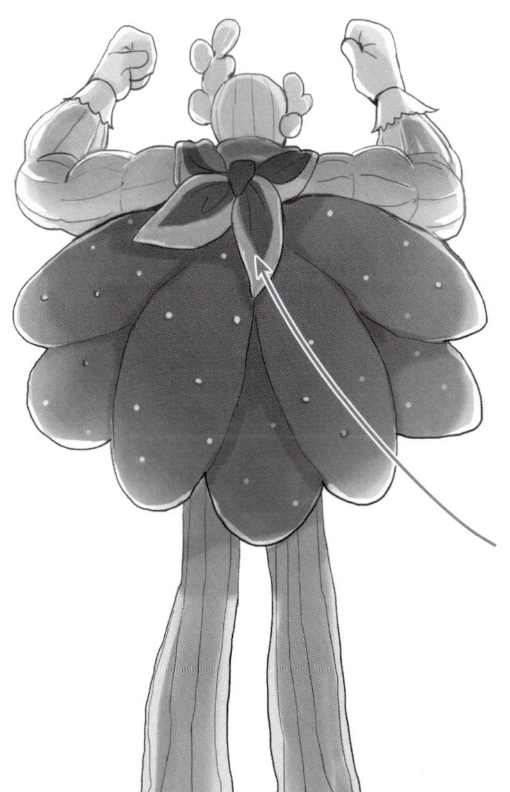

His scarf is reminiscent of a western bandana.

▾ Action View

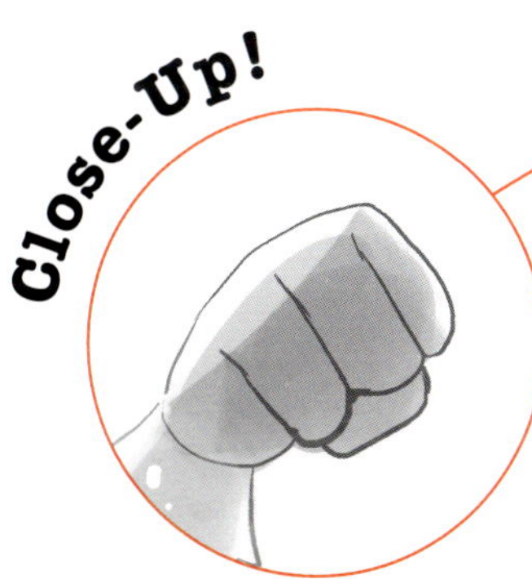

His powerful fists are a symbol of strength.

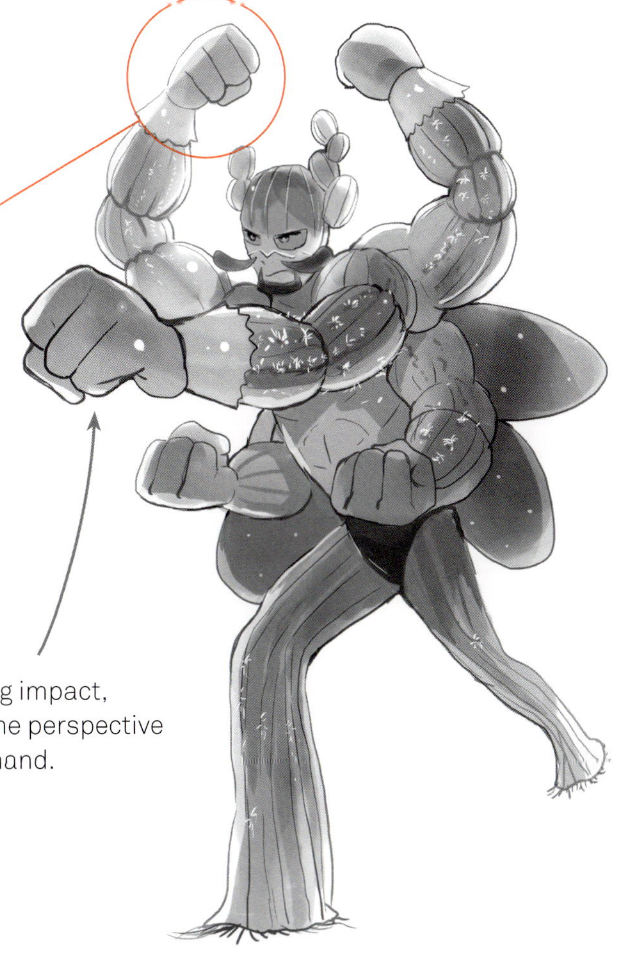

For a big impact, focus the perspective on his hand.

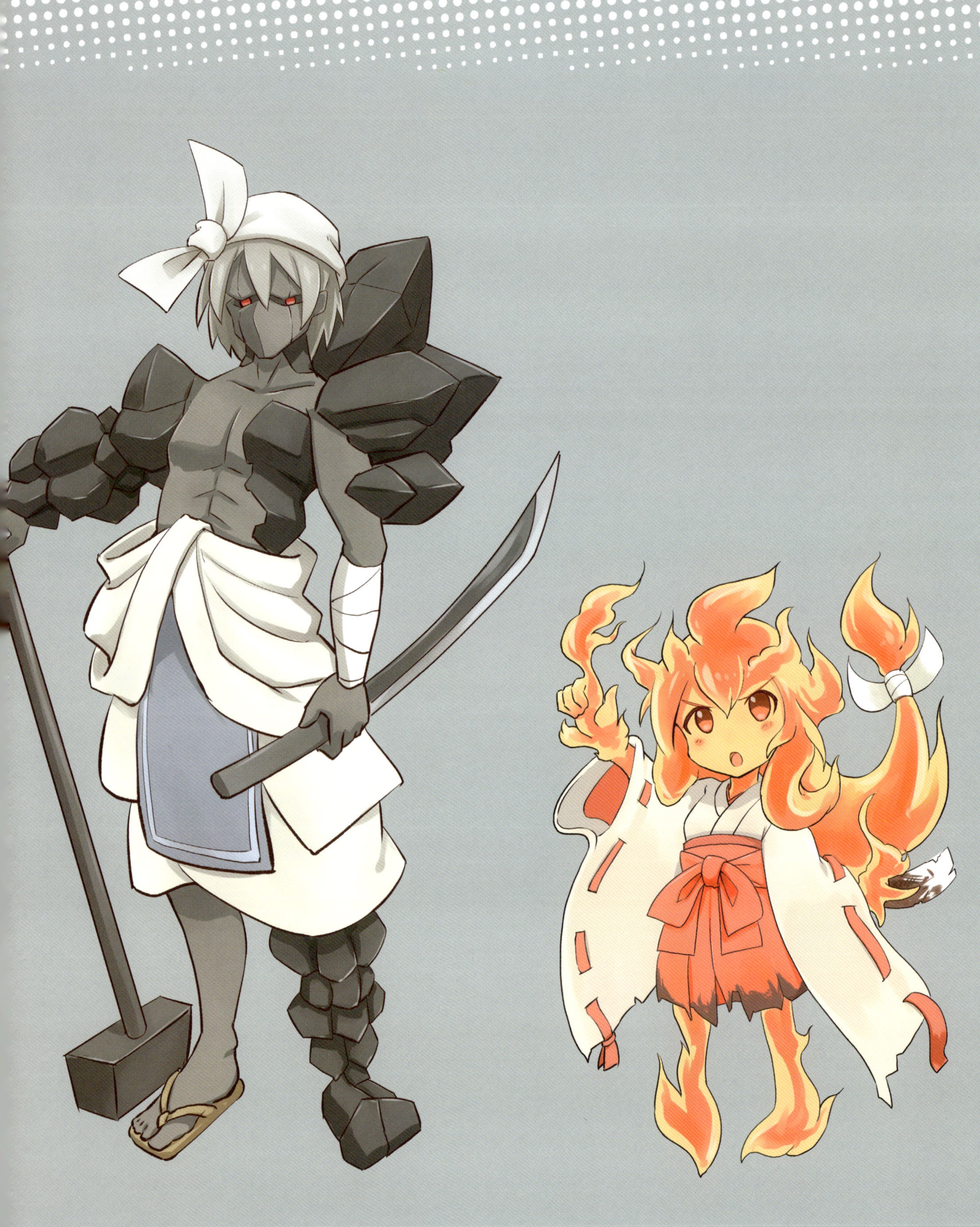

CHAPTER 5

ELEMENTS

These element-inspired villains are the most advanced characters in this book—mixing the human form with inorganic materials requires skill. Although there are many challenges to drawing these villains, there is also a lot of freedom to incorporate interesting colors, shapes and character traits.

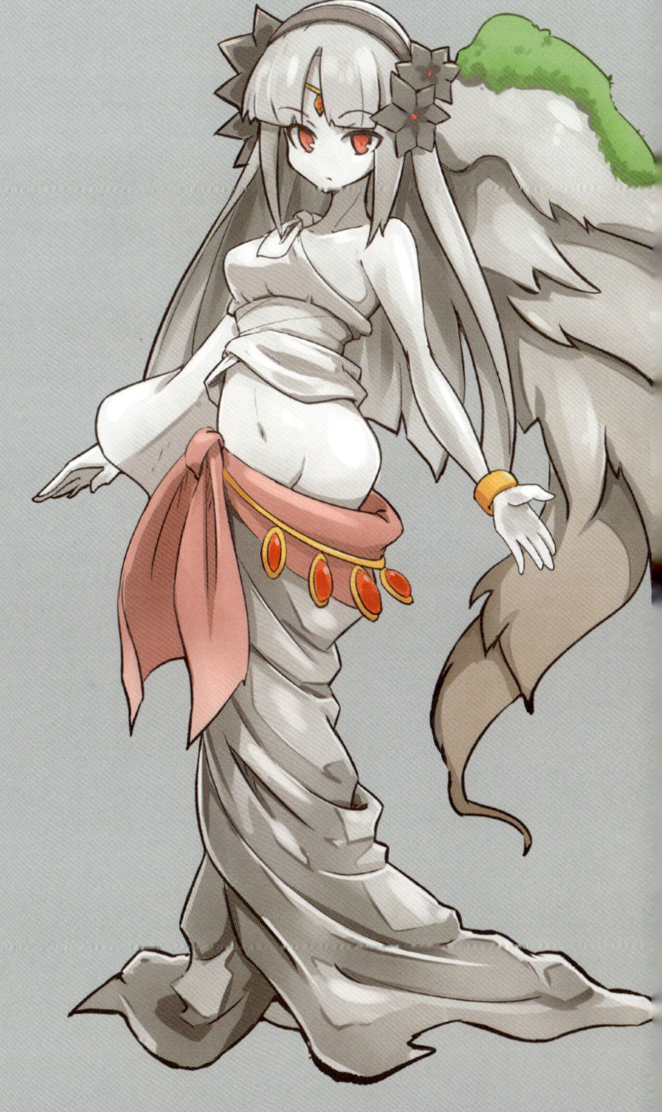

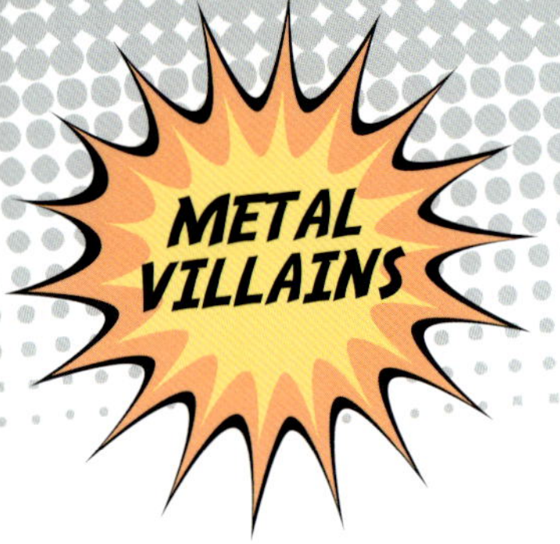

The Automaton

This chilling creature is part human, part robot. Controlled by a wind-up screw, she possesses no thoughts of her own and shows no compassion to her victims. Her weaknesses are radio waves and magnets.

▼ Front View

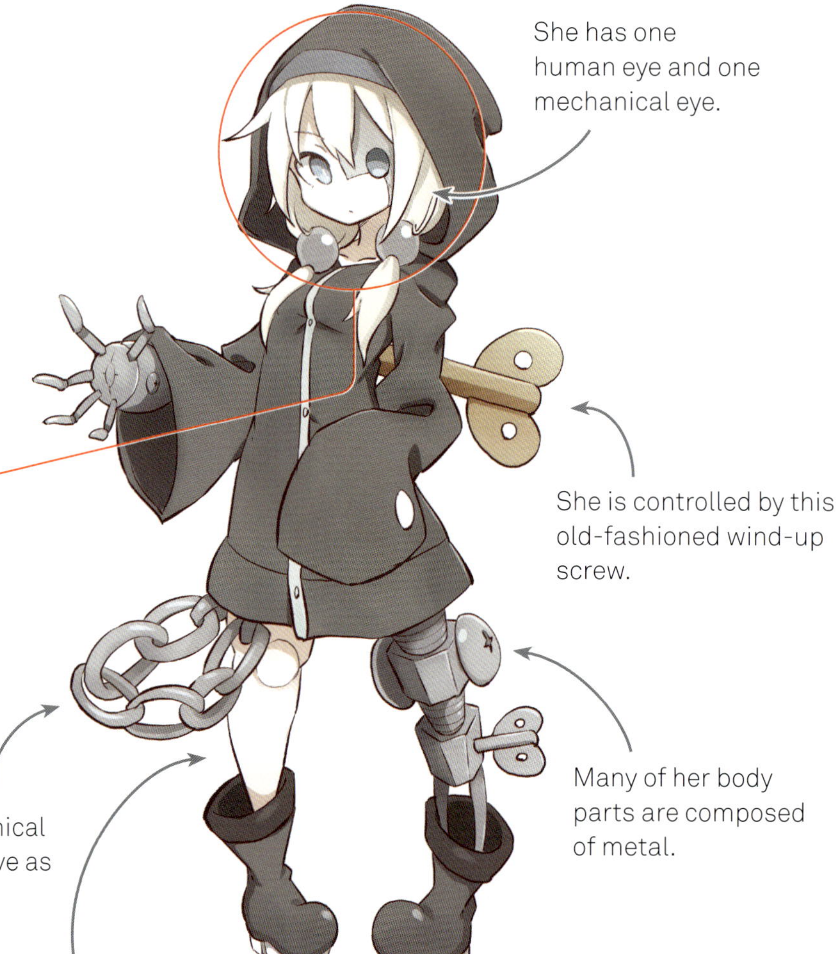

She has one human eye and one mechanical eye.

Close-Up!

Her eyes possess an eerie, haunted expression.

She is controlled by this old-fashioned wind-up screw.

Her various mechanical body parts also serve as weapons.

Many of her body parts are composed of metal.

Draw petite features for the human aspects of her body.

Color Tip:

Use shades of dark gray, but be careful to avoid saturation. Bright highlights will capture the sleek surface texture of metal.

VILLAINOUS TRAITS

1. Cannot feel pain
2. Shows no mercy to her victims
3. Electrical conductivity

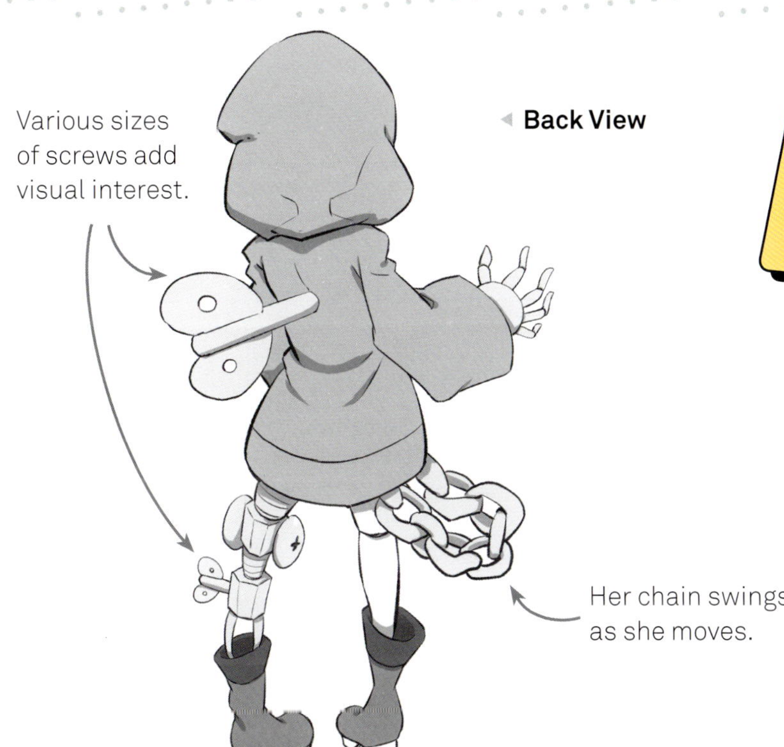

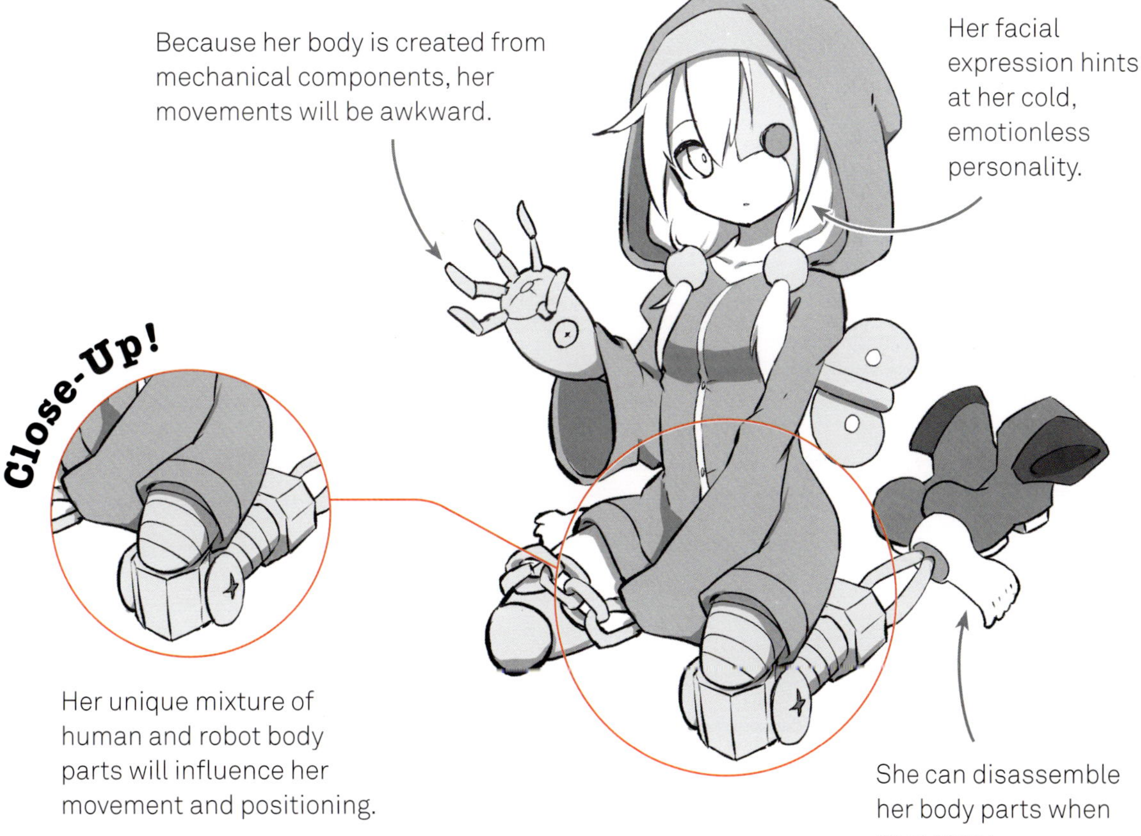

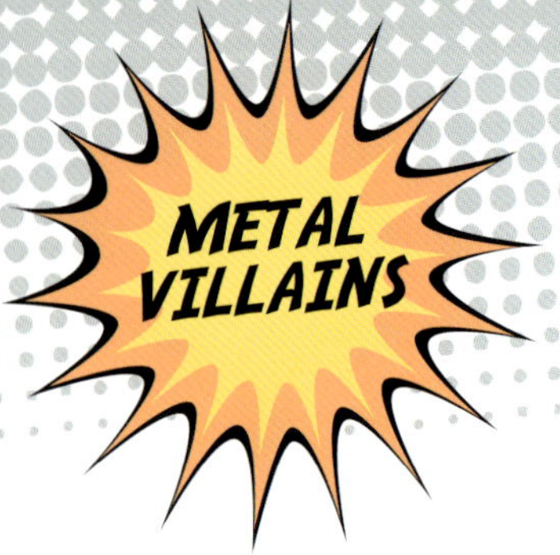

The Metallic Goddess

This mystical goddess possesses powers of elemental transmutation—anything she touches turns to metal. She is also able to hypnotize victims using her bewitching red eyes. She loves listening to heavy metal music and eating greasy junk food.

▾ **Front View**

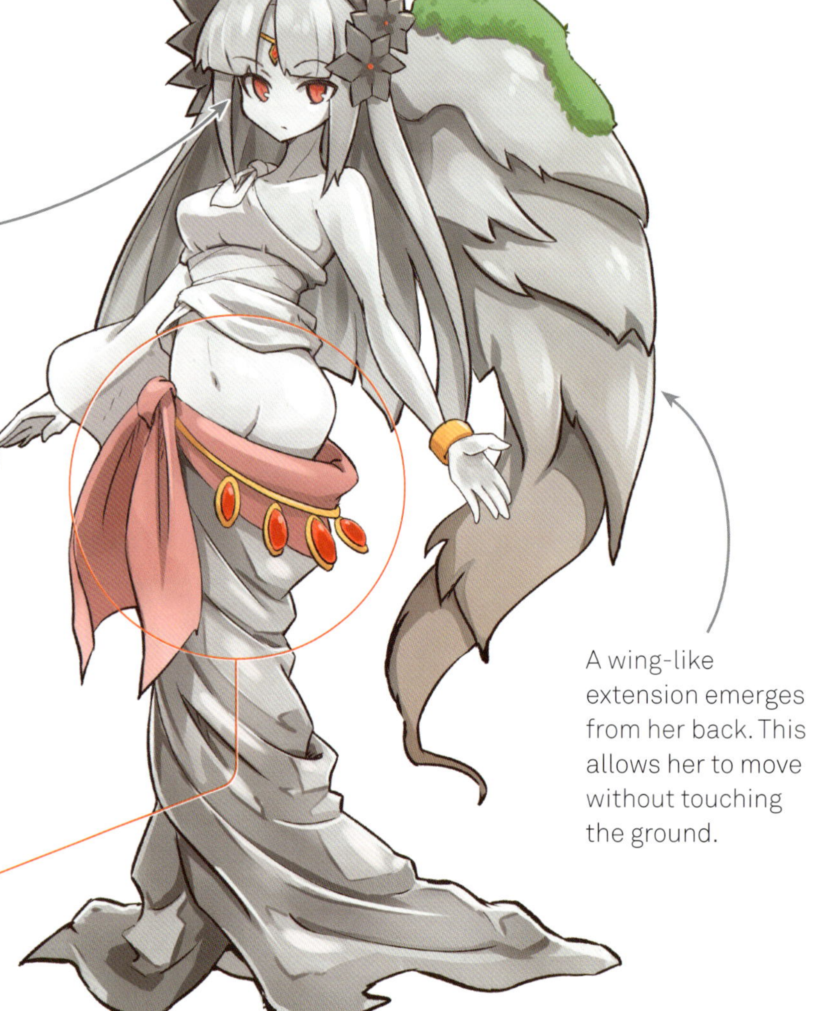

Red eyes give her an evil look.

Her skin is a light shade of metallic gray.

A wing-like extension emerges from her back. This allows her to move without touching the ground.

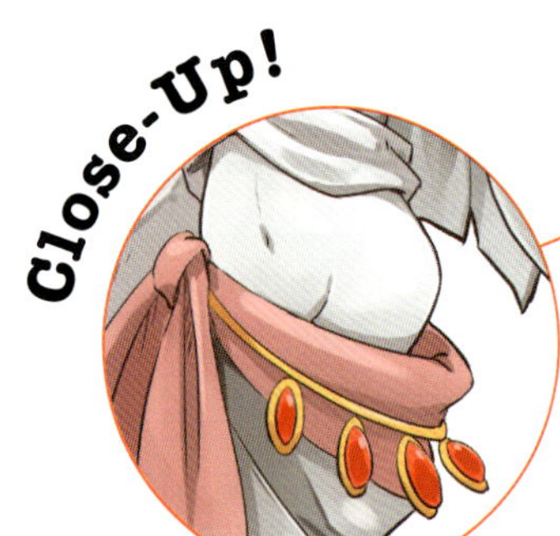

Add feminine details like soft fabric and pretty jewelry.

COLOR TIP:

Use gradated metallic gray for her entire body, then embellish with pink and red accessories.

VILLAINOUS TRAITS

1. Hypnotizing eyes
2. Immortality
3. Elemental transmutation

▶ Back View

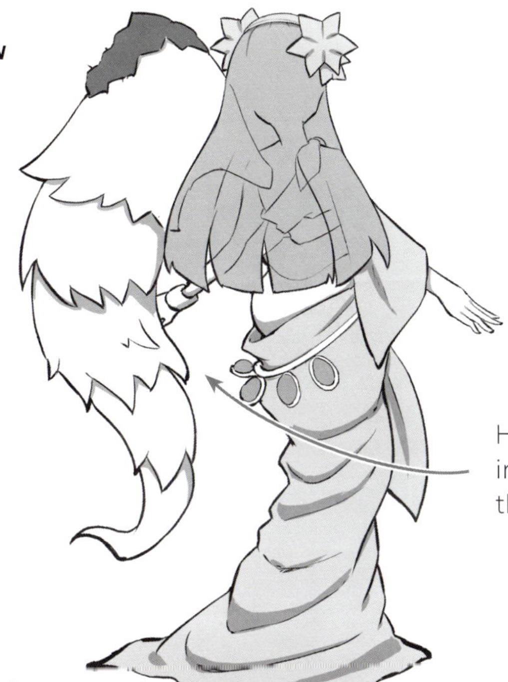

Her distinct wing makes her instantly recognizable from this angle.

Close-Up!

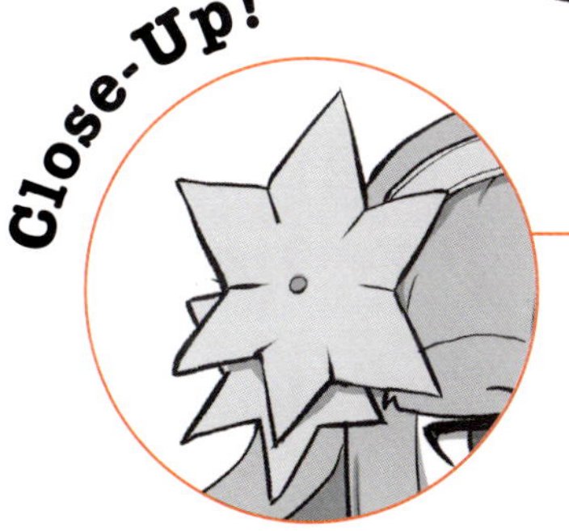

Her pinwheel-shaped hair accessories are made from hard metal, so use sharp lines.

▼ Action View

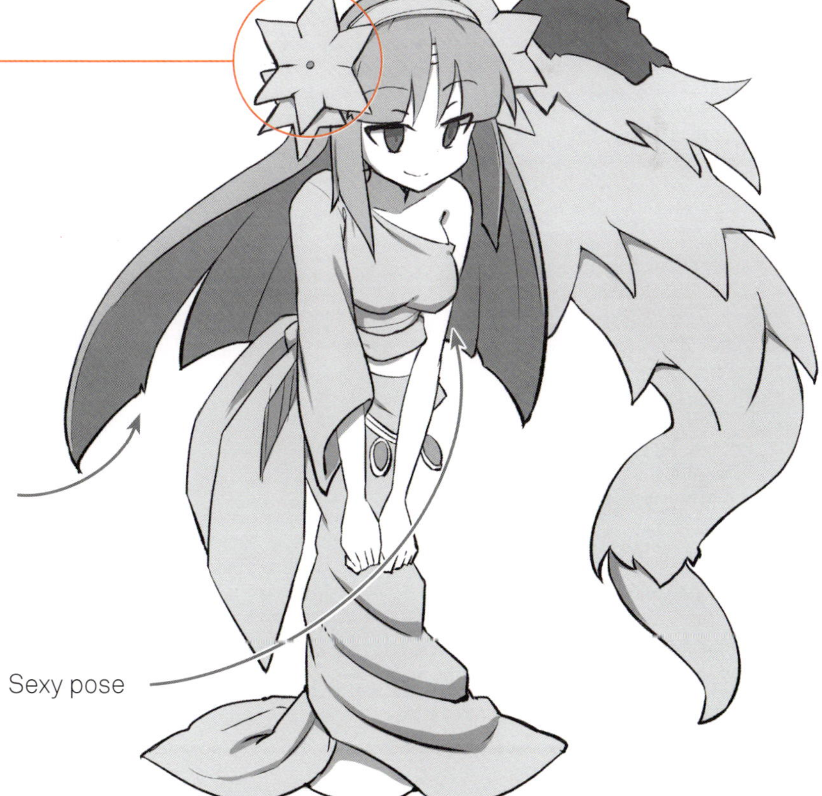

Imagine her moving in a slow, sinuous manner.

Sexy pose

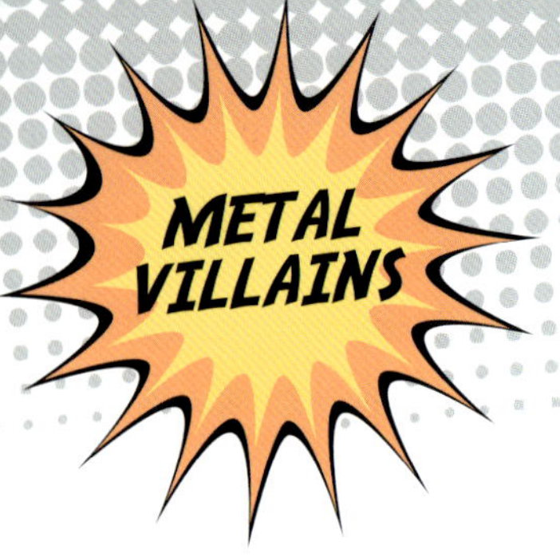

THE MELTING MERCENARY

Conceived as part of an evil experiment, this character was designed to be a professional soldier. His arms and legs can liquefy, allowing him to trap victims in toxic goo. One of his arms features a multidirectional machine gun that shoots thousands of bullets per minute. As a mercenary, he never attacks without permission and obeys the commands of his superiors.

▼ **Front View**

Long hair has a humanizing effect.

Hide the majority of his face behind a mask.

His weaponized hand and masked face give him a futuristic soldier look.

Extremely muscular arms and legs

Use wavy lines to capture the shape of the dripping liquid.

Close-Up!

Draw emotionless eyes to suggest a cold, detached personality.

He can transform the shape of his arms and legs.

COLOR TIP:

Due to his metallic nature, he is composed entirely of gray. Make sure to use different shades of gray, as well as black and white accents, for visual interest.

VILLAINOUS TRAITS

1. Liquefaction
2. Machine gun hand
3. Extremely strong and obedient

▼ Back View

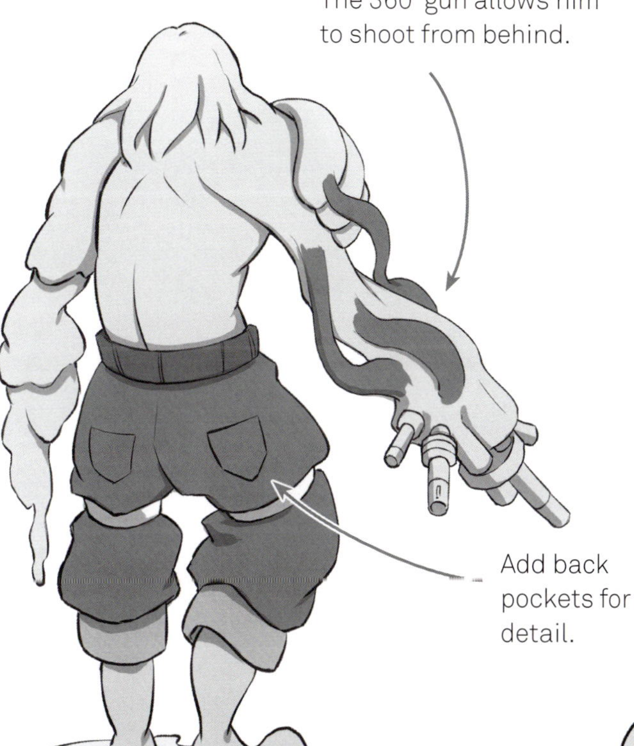

▼ Action View

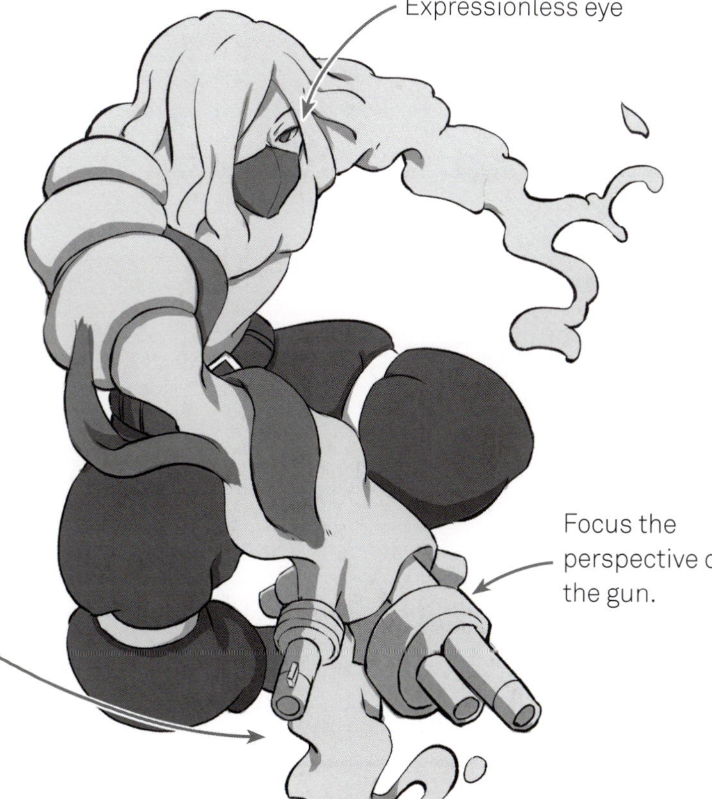

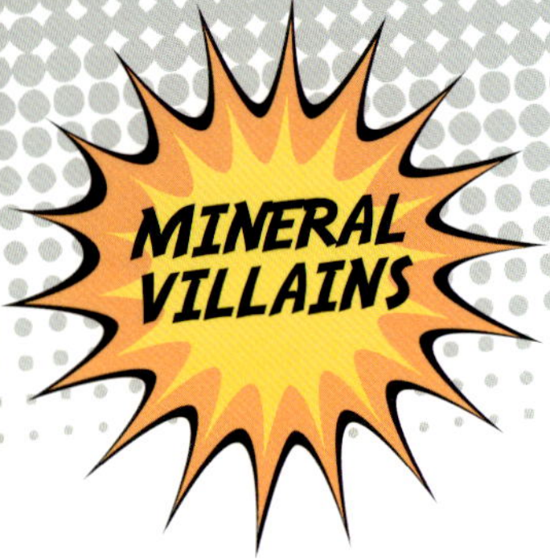

The Crystal Elf

This elfin character draws her magical powers from the crystalline growths that cover her body. Just like minerals, she flourishes in small, dark spaces, so you can usually find her lurking in caves and mines.

▼ **Front View**

The geometric crystal shape works well for a decorative hairstyle.

Her crystals are the source of her magical powers.

Crystals and other minerals grow on her body.

Close-Up!

Use sharp, angular lines to capture the hard, glassy texture of the crystals.

COLOR TIP:

Use subtle browns, yellows and grays for her body and clothes in order to make the colorful crystals stand out.

VILLAINOUS TRAITS

1. Sharp pick axe
2. Magic crystals
3. Crystals also have healing powers, making her nearly immortal

Back View

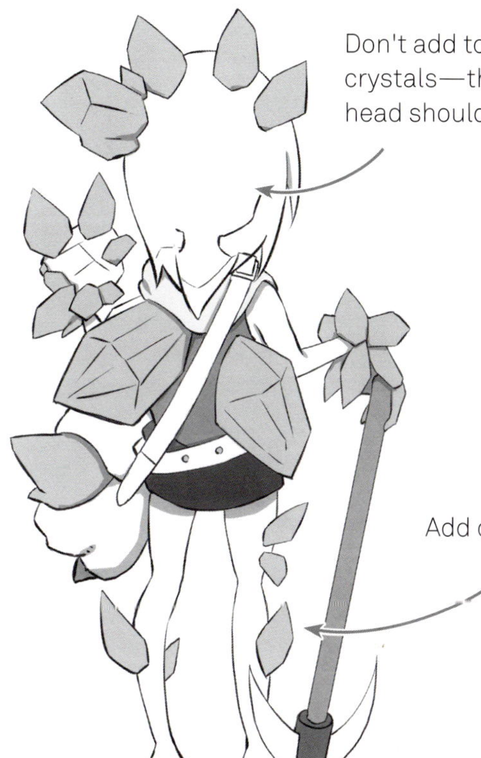

Don't add too many crystals—the shape of the head should still be visible.

Add crystals to her legs as well.

Action View

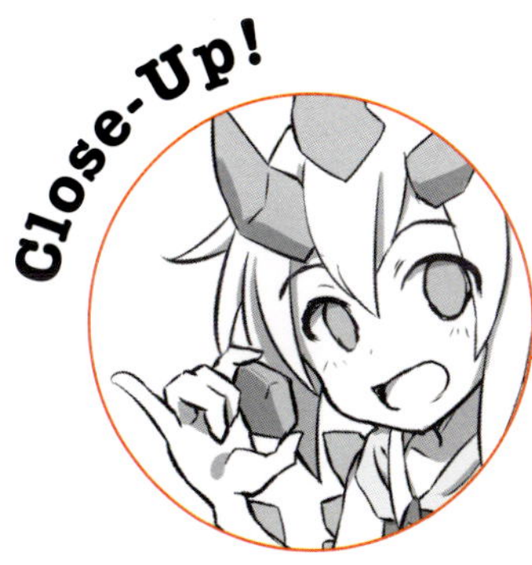

This pose and facial expression suggest an impish, mischievous personality.

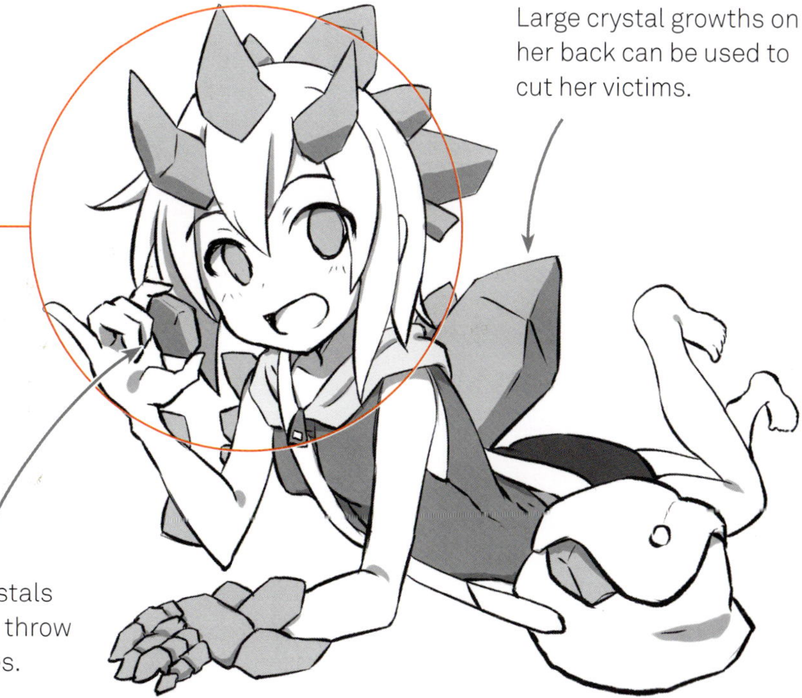

Large crystal growths on her back can be used to cut her victims.

She can detach crystals from her body, then throw them at her enemies.

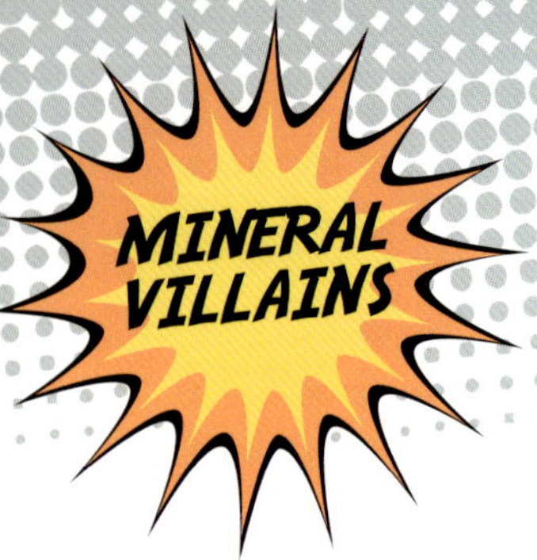

The Ice Empress

This beautiful and elegant lady is considered to be an ice queen for two reasons: her sizeable gemstones and her cold heart. Her skin is embedded with powerful jewels that she uses for gravitational, solar and molecular manipulation.

▼ **Front View**

Her traditional Chinese dress represents beauty and elegance.

Her skin is embedded with rare and powerful gemstones.

Use white highlights to capture the shiny, translucent nature of gemstones.

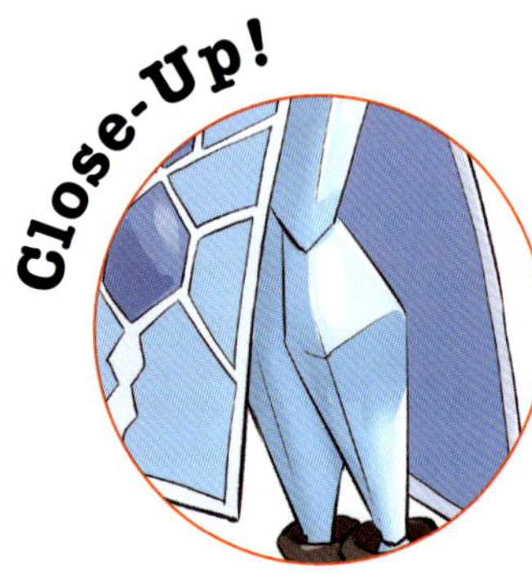

Use faceted, gemstone-inspired shapes for her arms and legs.

Color Tip:

Using a cool blue color scheme for her body and clothing will really make her green eyes pop.

VILLAINOUS TRAITS

1. Coldhearted and manipulative
2. Powerful gemstones
3. Vain

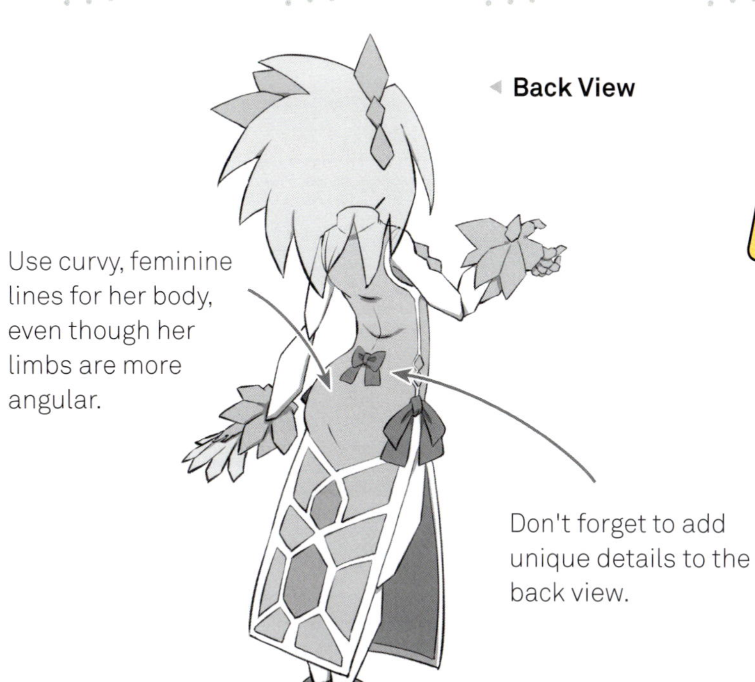

Action View

Close-Up!

Position her body in an authoritarian stance—as an empress, she often commands others.

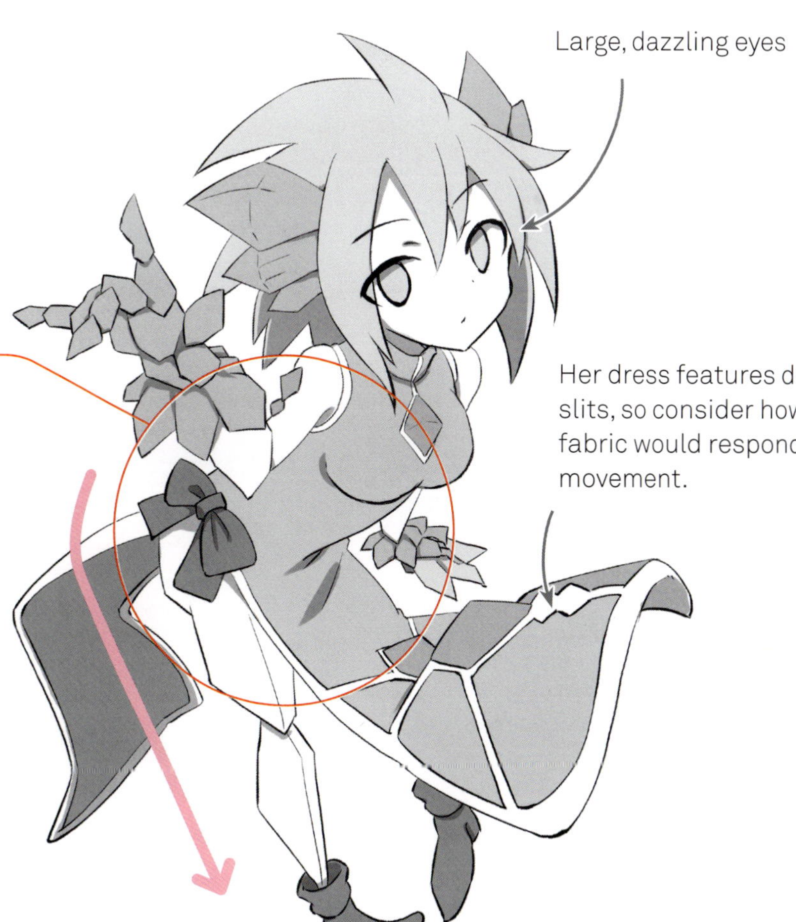

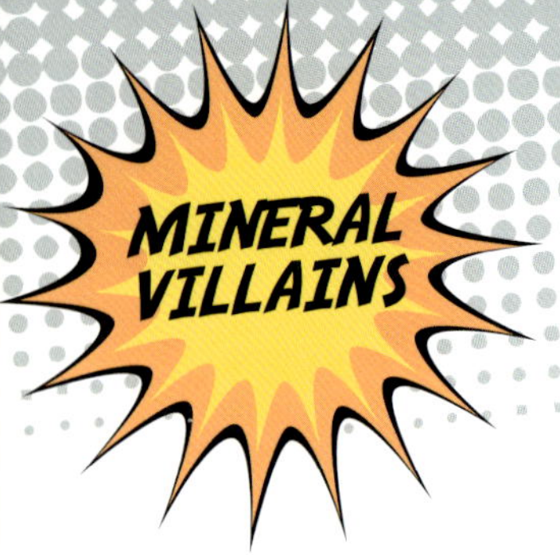

THE BLADEMAKER

As a swordsmith, this character is respected for manufacturing the highest quality weaponry. Ancient craftsmanship and combat secrets have been bestowed upon him from his elders.

▼ **Front View**

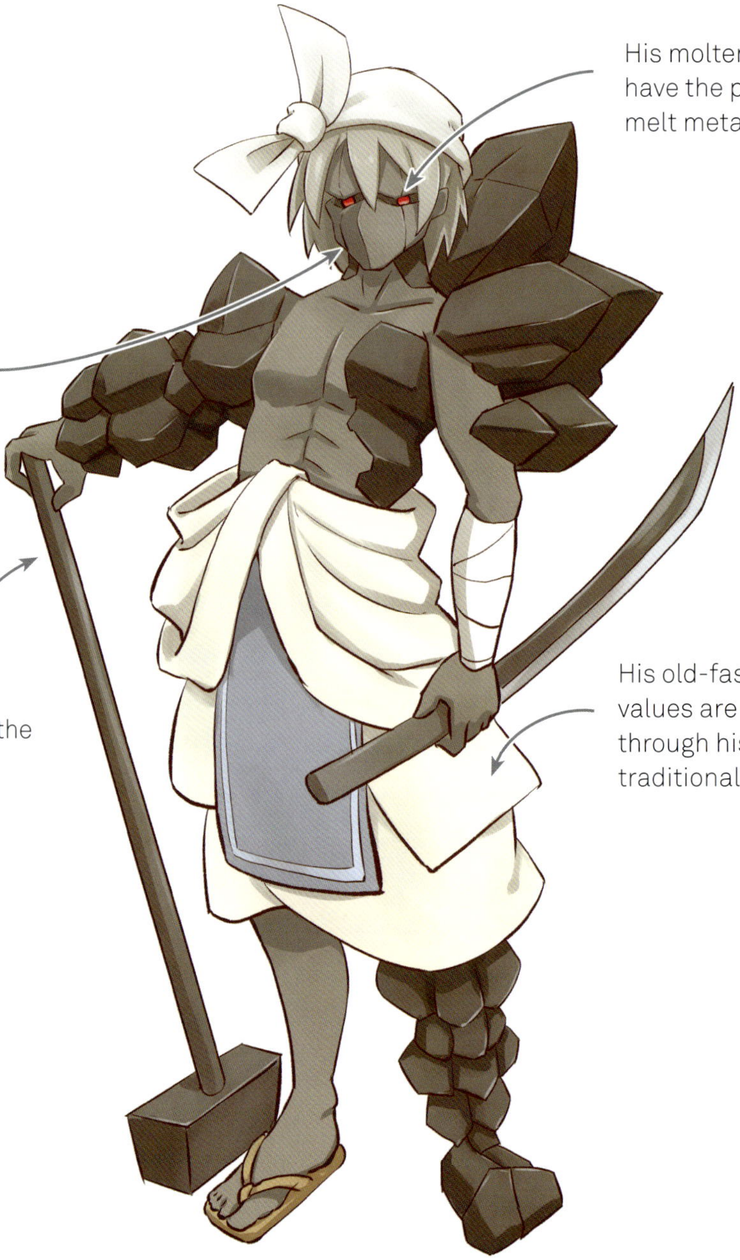

His molten red eyes have the power to melt metal.

The lack of a mouth creates a menacing look.

The massive scale of the weapons contributes to his intimidating impression.

His old-fashioned values are reflected through his traditional clothing.

COLOR TIP:

Use monochromatic shades of gray inspired by coal and graphite, then add pops of red and blue for contrast.

VILLAINOUS TRAITS

1. Talented swordsmith
2. Eyes that can melt metal
3. Magnetic manipulation

▸ **Back View**

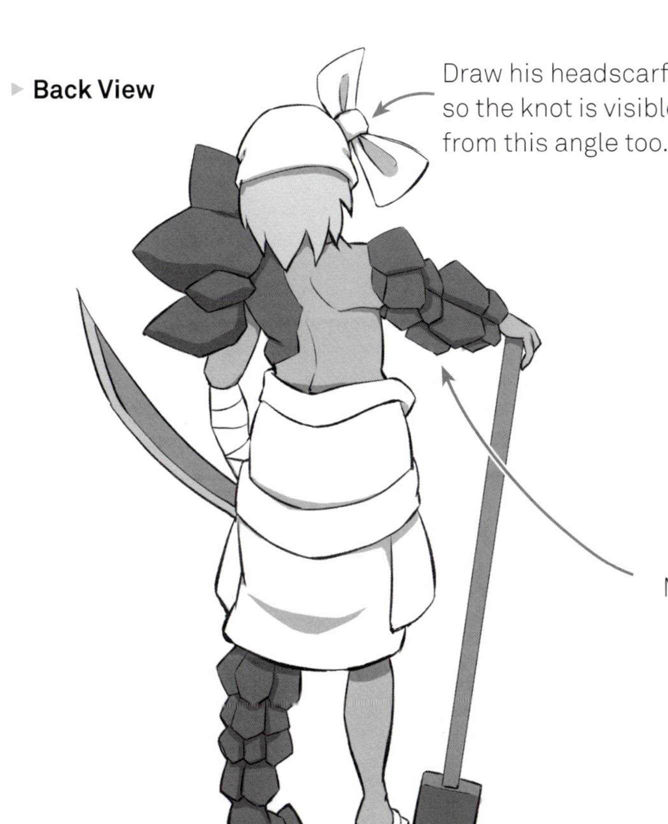

Draw his headscarf so the knot is visible from this angle too.

Masculine body language

▾ **Action View**

Close-Up!

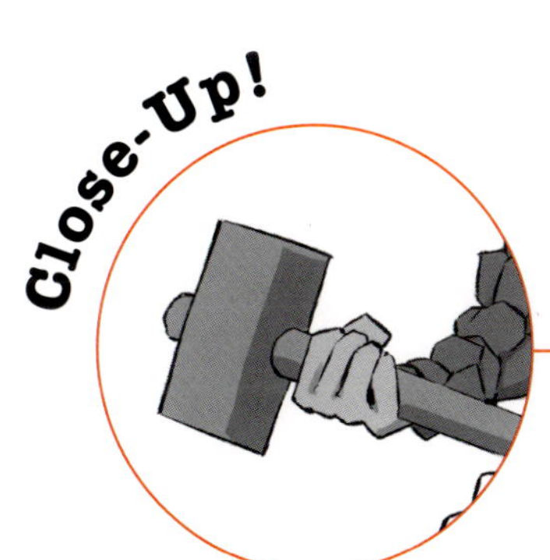

The manner in which he grasps the hammer highlights his strength and comfort around weaponry.

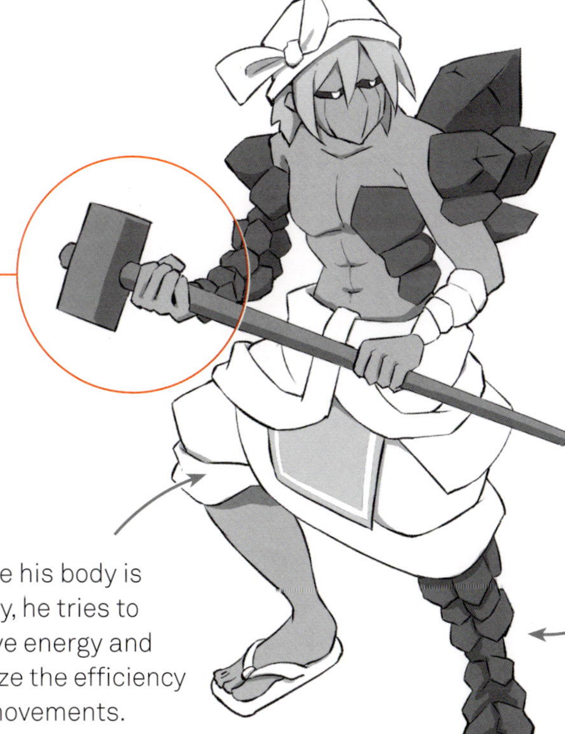

Because his body is so heavy, he tries to conserve energy and maximize the efficiency of his movements.

His leg is composed of heavy minerals, so consider the effect it will have on his movement.

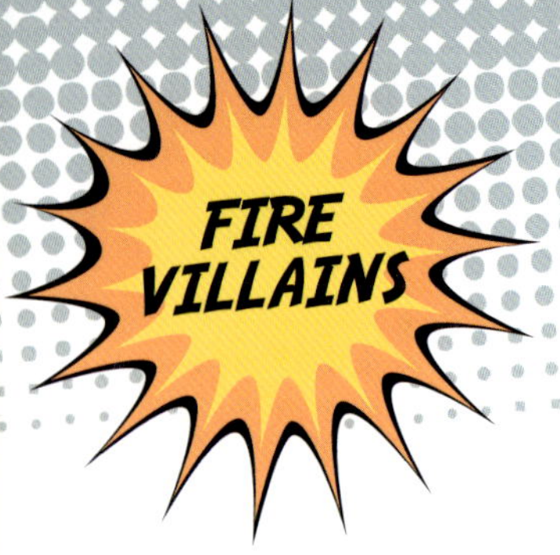

The Little Flame Thrower

This young and energetic villain has a fiery disposition with the hair to match. Because she's not always in control of her emotions, she occasionally throws flames accidentally. She hates water but is a big fan of BBQ.

▼ **Front View**

Incorporate the flames into her hairstyle.

Intense flames match her angry facial expression.

Traditional Japanese clothing

The hemline of her clothing is scorched.

COLOR TIP:

Red, orange and yellow are the natural color choices for this character.

VILLAINOUS TRAITS

1. Bad temper
2. Flame throwing capabilities
3. Can jump and fly easily

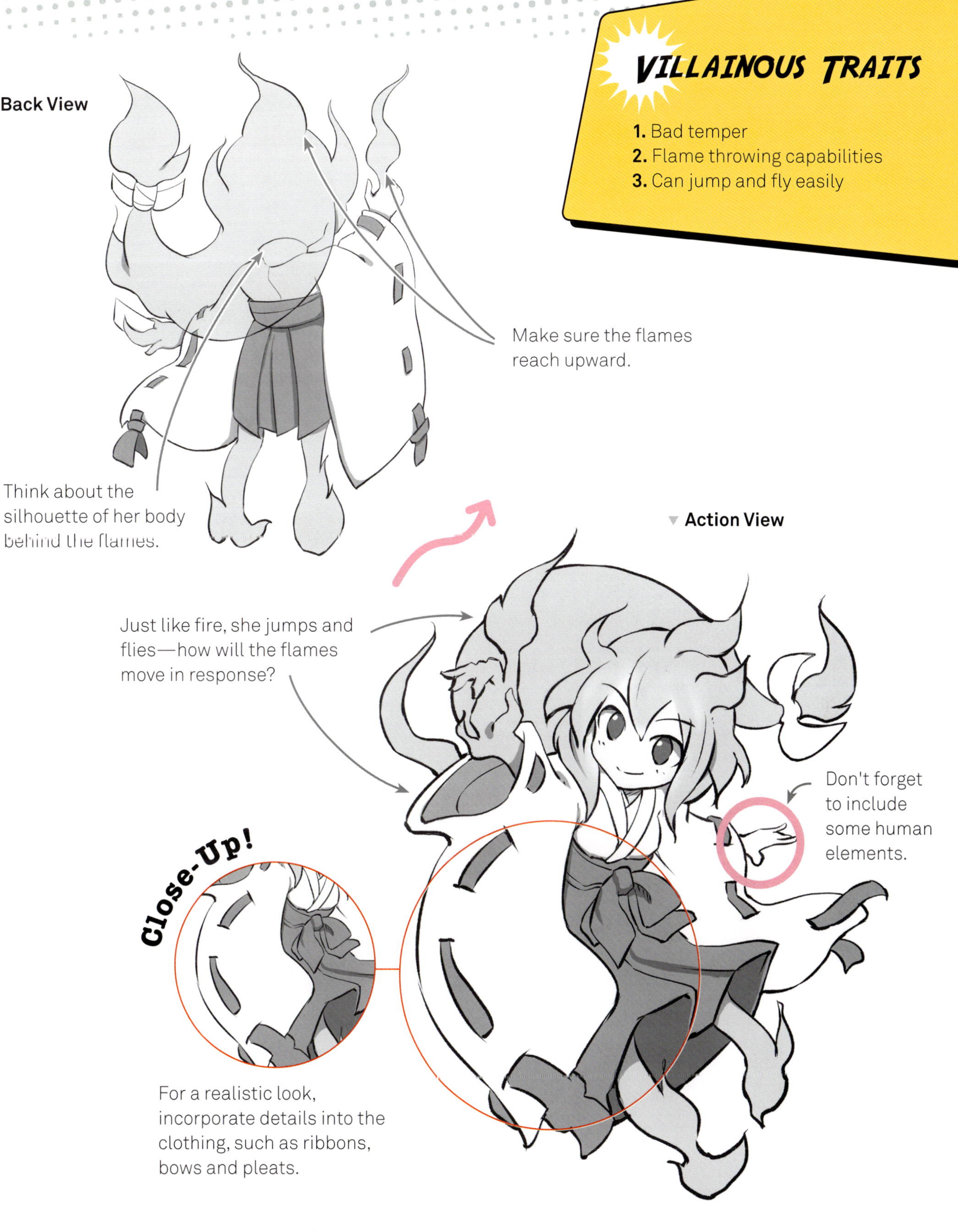

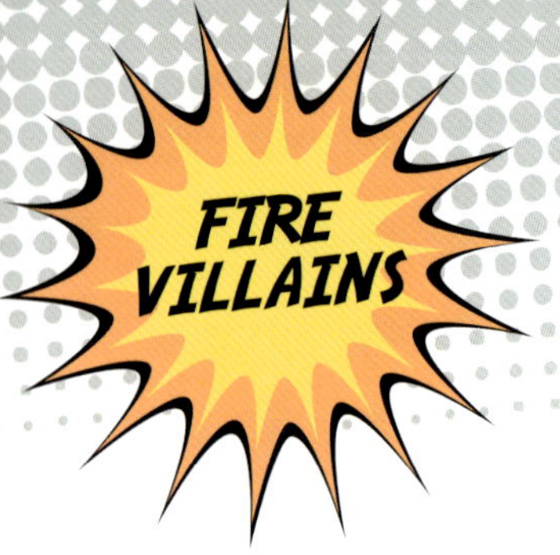

The Smoky Sprite

In contrast to the wild, flame-inspired juvenile character, this woman is all refinement and class. She quietly floats around, sneaking up on her victims and hypnotizing them into a trance.

▼ **Front View**

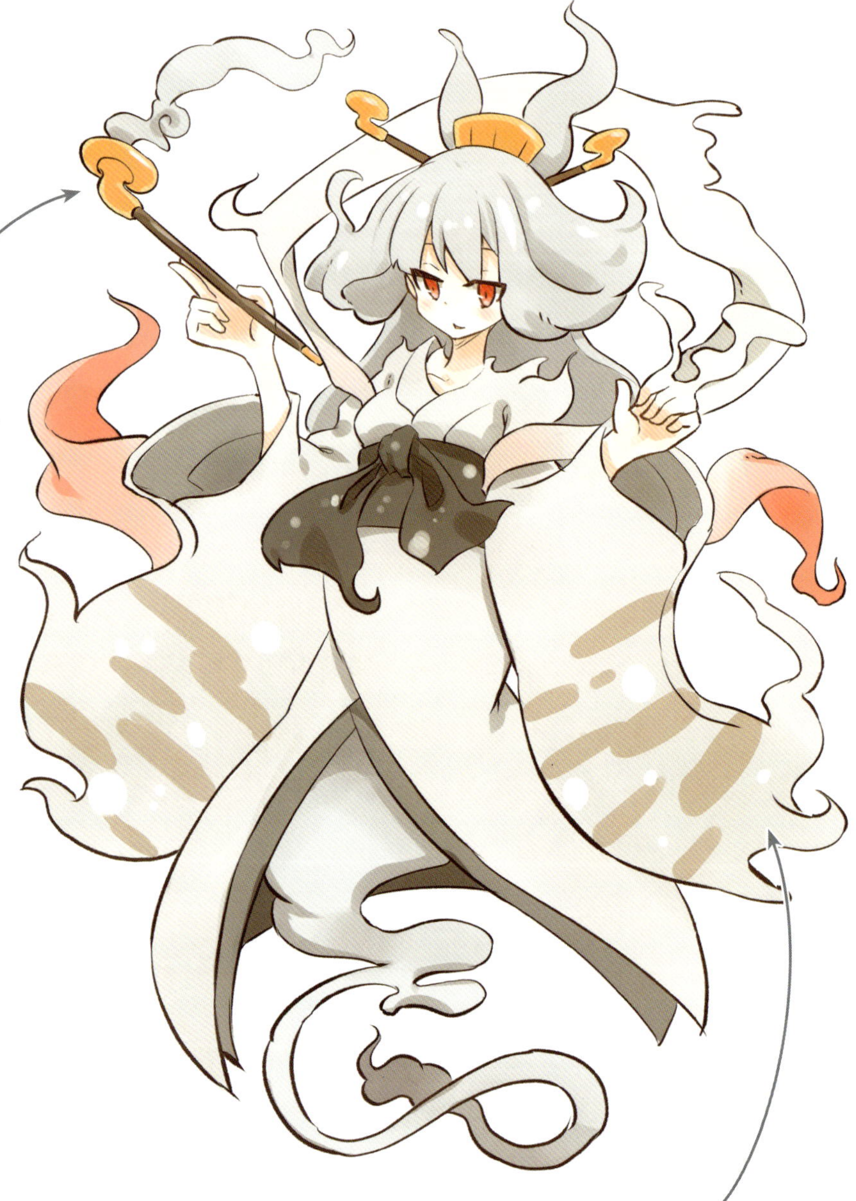

The smoke from her pipe can lull victims into a hypnotic trance.

The shape of her shoulders and sleeves is inspired by puffs of smoke.

Color Tip:

Use pale gray for the base, then add black, pink and yellow accents. When adding these colors, opt for less saturated hues to emphasize the ethereal nature of this character.

VILLAINOUS TRAITS

1. Invisibility
2. Lulls victims into a trance with her smoke
3. Shapeshifting capabilities

▶ **Back View**

Her billowing sleeves are a significant part of this drawing, so make sure to capture their flowing shape.

▼ **Action View**

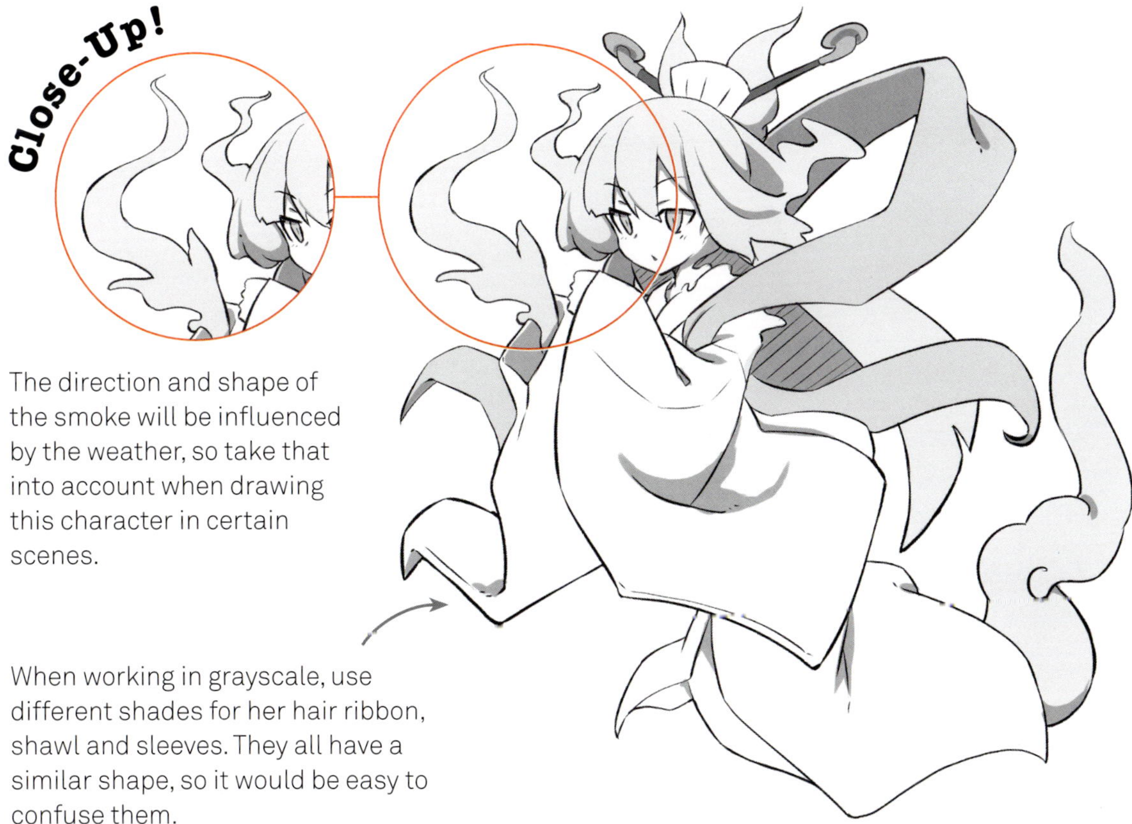

The direction and shape of the smoke will be influenced by the weather, so take that into account when drawing this character in certain scenes.

When working in grayscale, use different shades for her hair ribbon, shawl and sleeves. They all have a similar shape, so it would be easy to confuse them.

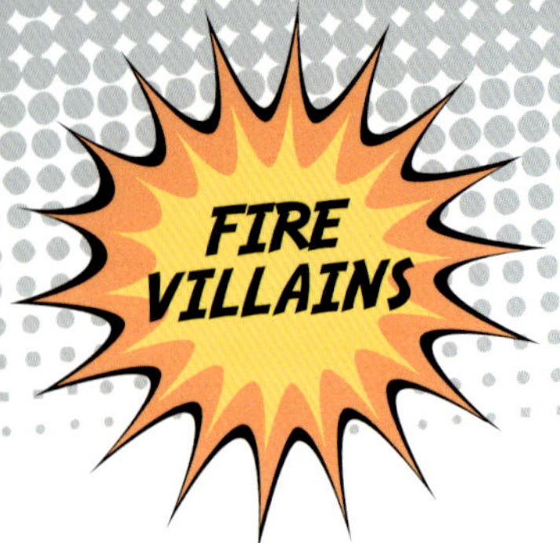

The Smoldering Spirit

This steampunk-style character is highly dangerous. He uses an enchanted lighter to manipulate the oxygen levels within a room in order to weaken his victim's resistance. His pipe emits powerful smoke rings, plus he can vaporize and disappear at a moment's notice.

▼ **Front View**

His pipe is large in proportion to his face. The pipe is one of his greatest assets, so you want to make it stand out.

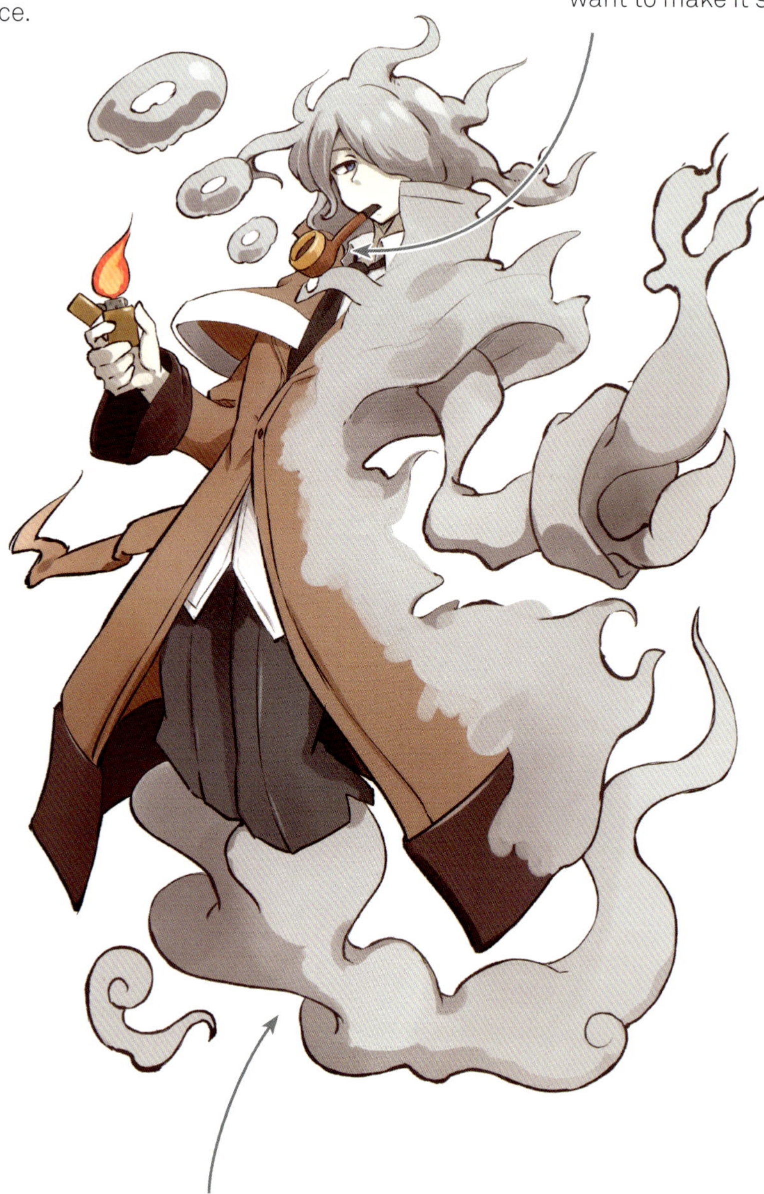

COLOR TIP:

Use quiet, neutral colors for his body and clothing. Eyes will be drawn to the red and yellow of the flame.

Half of his body appears to be vaporizing into smoke.

▸ **Back View**

Use soft, curved lines for the smoke and more severe, angular lines for the body.

VILLAINOUS TRAITS

1. Vaporization
2. Pipe traps victims in a ring of smoke
3. Lighter can manipulate oxygen levels

Draw little wisps of smoke dancing around his body.

▾ **Action View**

Use fluid, curved lines to capture the transitory nature of smoke.

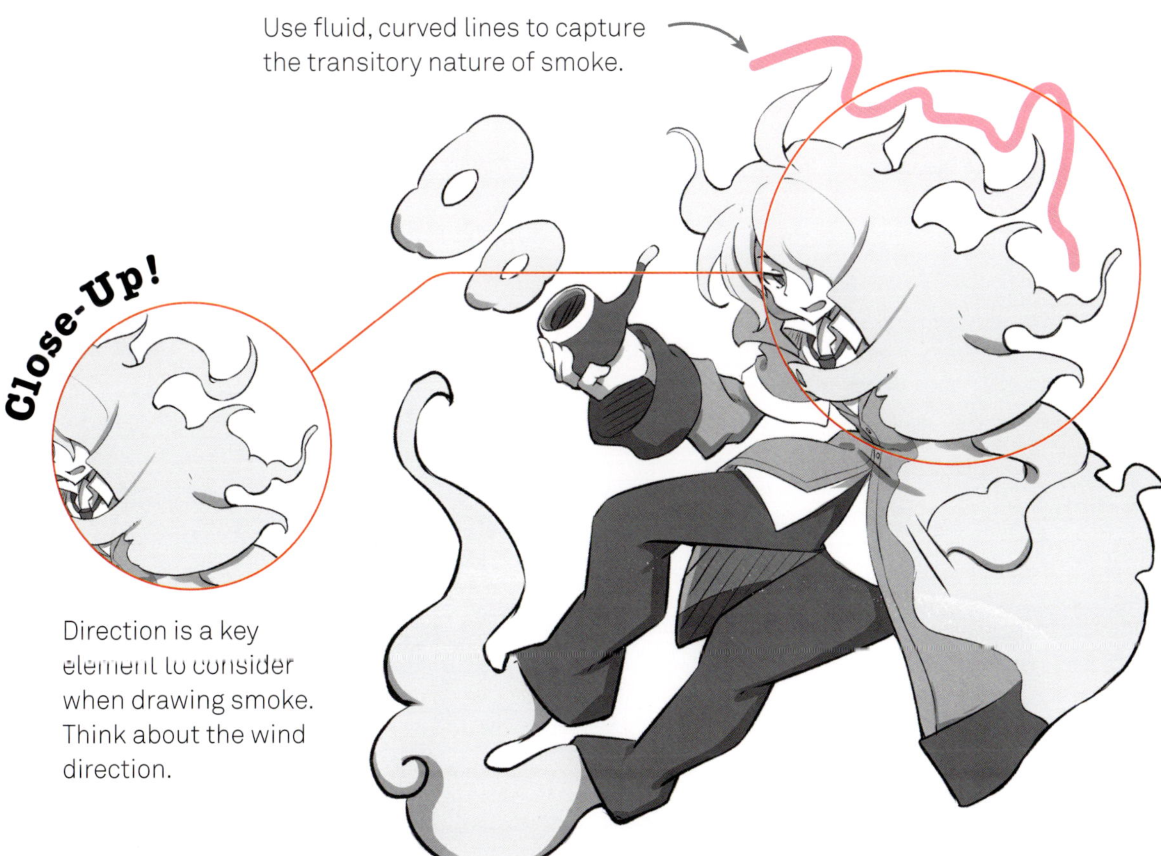

Direction is a key element to consider when drawing smoke. Think about the wind direction.

THE RISE OF VILLAINS

Once a niche genre, manga villains are growing more popular.

In recent years, there's been an explosion in the popularity of villains within manga. There's also been an exponential increase in the amount of manga, anime and movies featuring non-human characters, so it was only a matter of time before these two genres merged.

One of the earliest examples of this trend involves a series of stories featuring a centaur as the main character. These stories garnered attention due to their masterful balance of fantasy and reality.

After that, romance stories featuring female hybrid characters, like Harpies, grew popular. Recently, a number of stories about mermaids have been published in quick succession.

The popularity of villainous manga characters only appears to be increasing, so it's safe to say that there's no end to this trend in sight.

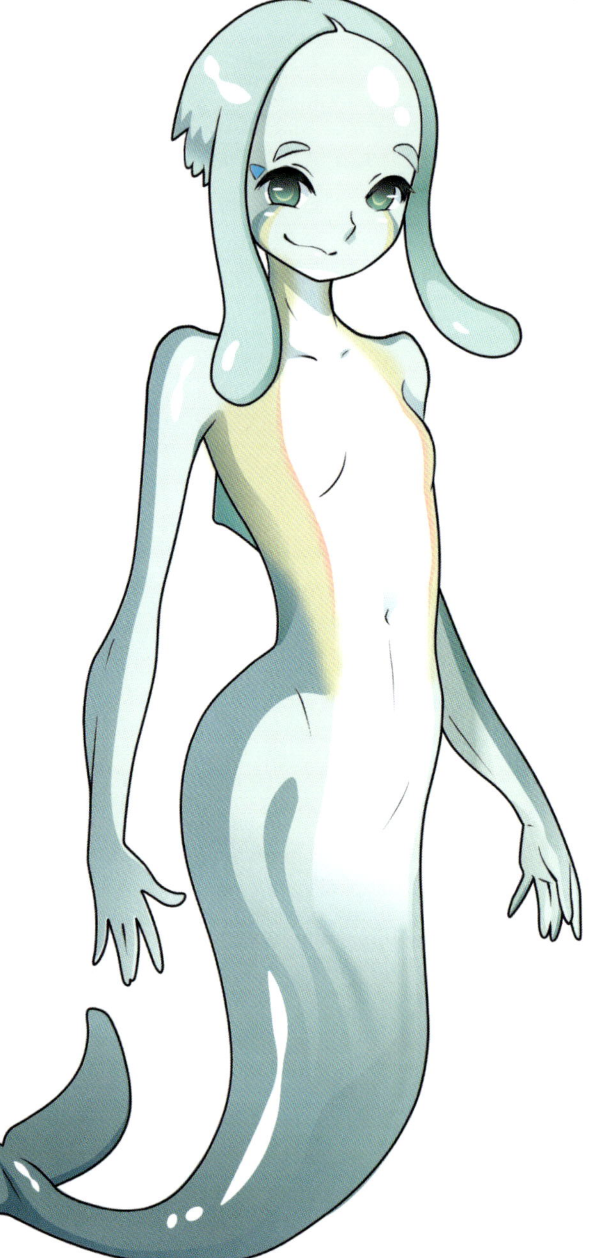

ABOUT THE ILLUSTRATORS

Several artists collaborated in order to produce this book.

Azami Togeshiro CHAPTER 1

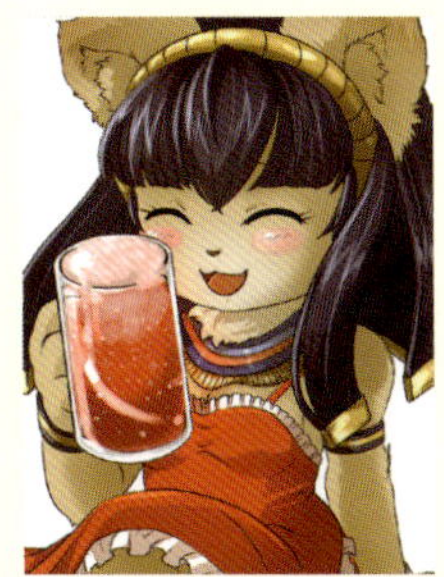

Azami Togeshiro loves to draw animals, especially dragons. Her favorite characters to draw are female villains.

Takami Fujiwara CHAPTER 2

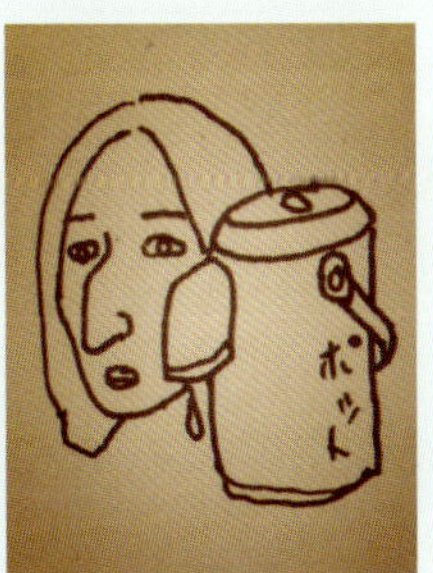

Takami Fujiwara was born in Tokyo in 1989. She studied oil painting in college and now works as an illustrator, filmmaker and designer. Her favorite characters to draw for this book were the jellyfish and crab villains.

Kurohimekiryu 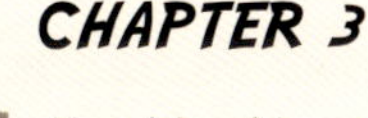 CHAPTER 3

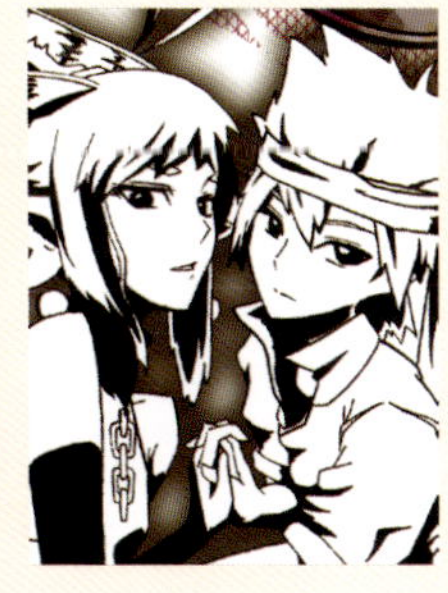

Kurohimekiryu is a former game designer who now works as a freelance artist.

pon-marsh 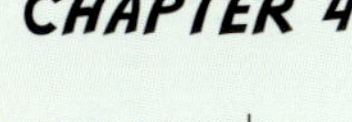 CHAPTER 4

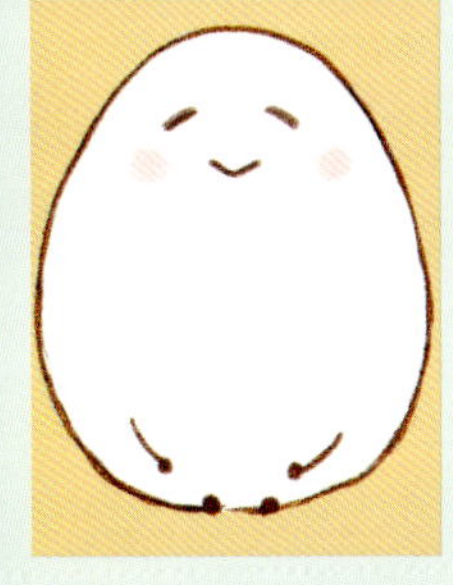

pon-marsh mostly works as an illustrator for children's books.

Senhappyaku CHAPTER 5

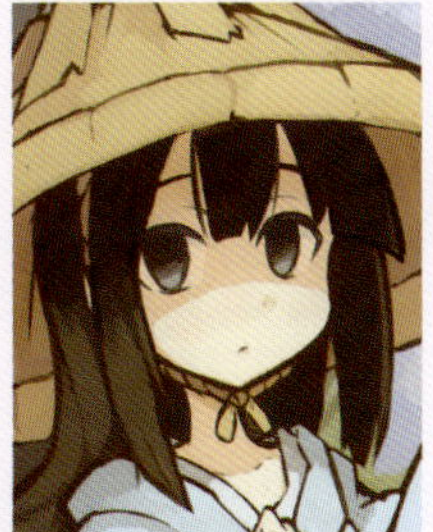

Senhappyaku has worked as a freelance illustrator since 2015 and specializes in characters who wear traditional Japanese clothing.